P9-AGA-006

The Complete Guide to
NORTHERN CALIFORNIA GARDENING

The Complete Guide to Northern California Gardening

Maureen Gilmer

TAYLOR PUBLISHING COMPANY
DALLAS, TEXAS

Published by
Taylor Publishing Company
1550 West Mockingbird Lane
Dallas, Texas 75235

Designed by David Timmons

Library of Congress Cataloging-in-Publication Data

Gilmer, Maureen.
The complete guide to northern California gardening / Maureen Gilmer.
p. cm.
Includes index.
ISBN 0-87833-842-X
1. Gardening—California, Northern. I. Title.
SB453.2.C3G53 1994
635' .09794—dc20 93-33779
CIP

Printed in the United States of America
10 9 8 7 6 5 4 3 2 1

To Jim, *mi vida.*

CONTENTS

Preface

My father was born where the California sycamores grow, and he would carry a love of these majestic gnarled trees throughout his long life. This *Platanus racemosa* is a native that inhabits the dry stream canyons throughout the state. Strangely, a single species demanded all his attention, as if the trees were an intrinsic part of his being. I vividly remember the annual rites, as we would lie in the tall spring grass watching his strange communion with the land and its native trees. Over time the bare-root saplings became his other children, silently vying with us for the honey of his love.

He planted his sycamores all around our house. Often we would find him tieing up the branches to encourage them to grow more unevenly, explaining that in the wild they would be browsed by deer and torn by the wind. He waged a perpetual war against gophers and bark borers that threatened these other children. He would peel away the loosened bark to show us the destructive white grub at the end of its tunnel. As if it were my own skinned knee, he carefully cleaned the wound, dressing it as gingerly as a surgeon.

Over the years, the trees grew and my father's hair gradually silvered. Where once we rode our bicycles by a tiny sapling, we later waxed our cars under its protective shade. Other homes would struggle in the valley heat while ours was wonderfully cool under the canopy of massive leaves.

Although he no longer lives in that old family home, my father will never really lose his babies, for they remain as deeply in his heart as their roots stretch into the fertile valley soil. I know the memory of his trees has compelled me to plant my own children, and they stand in landscapes I've designed throughout California. My father's relationship with the California land and its trees has left me with a special magic. It is a priceless inheritance that we all may share by simply planting a tree and helping it to grow.

FACING PAGE: UNIQUE WOODWORK ARBOR WITH PASSION VINE, POTTED PLANTS, AND GARDEN PERENNIALS.

Introduction

Northern California is an almost mystical place unlike anywhere else in North America. Here we may experience a complete range of climates and land forms, each with its own unique native plant community. From the highest elevations of the Sierra Nevada Mountains to the spectacular cliffs above the Pacific Ocean, this Eden on the coast provides the ultimate climate for gardening.

Since most people aren't experienced gardeners, this book is designed to provide the most important information and make it easy to find. All the plants profiled are suitable for beginners and readily available in north state nurseries. I believe that if the plant isn't readily available from commercial sources it isn't worth talking about, as it would only create confusion for readers.

Gardening is a process which requires patience and diligence if plants are to grow and thrive. The satisfaction of watching a tiny seed grow into a brilliantly blooming plant is second only to that of raising a child. Many feel that the compulsion to plant trees reveals a subconscious desire for immortality, or perhaps a need to leave something noteworthy behind after we are gone.

A backyard oasis of green and growing things can help to offset the loss of the natural environment, and provide a soothing alternative to the bleakness of urban sprawl. As we become increasingly distanced from our agrarian roots, the need to return to the soil grows stronger. Rather than resist the urge, why not begin today, and use this book to help transform your yard into more than a landscape? Let it be a personal garden which reflects your love of California and the beautiful plants which grow so well here.

FACING PAGE: WEATHERED DOORWAY WITH SLICED REDWOOD BURL PAVING AND A PORTION OF AN OLD PICKET FENCE.

The Basics for Beginners

A simple definition of gardening is the process of giving plants enough light, water, oxygen, and soil fertility to survive. Making plants thrive and bloom in top form can be difficult and it's easy for beginners to become discouraged. That's why this entire chapter is devoted to the essential basics of gardening.

Northern California's Climate

The hard statistics of climate maps are general, and not always reflective of what is really happening in a garden. Part of the gardening

FACING PAGE: EMPIRE MINE STATE HISTORIC PARK, GRASS VALLEY, NEVADA COUNTY. ABOVE: *DELPHINIUM AJACIS (JACK BODGER)*

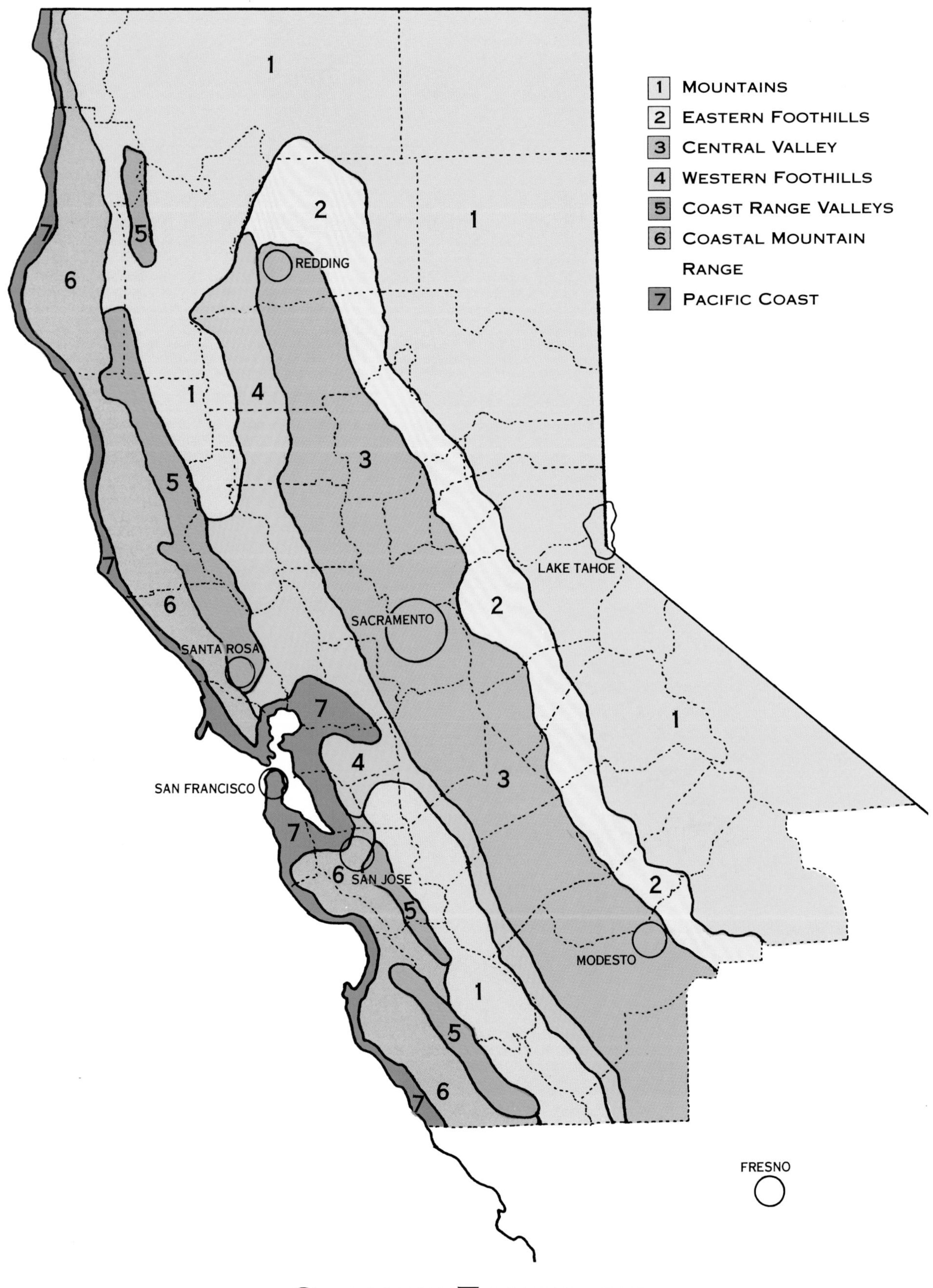

Climate Zones of Northern California

experience is close observation of what's happening within your outdoor space and how that influences how plants grow.

CLIMATE ZONES

Northern California can be broken down into seven basic climate zones. These lie in north-south bands shaped by the coastline and our inland mountain ranges. The group of actual conditions at an individual site within a zone is called its microclimate. It is unwise to take climate zones as law, because they are just guidelines to help you better understand the overview of climate patterns.

Zone 1 Mountains

Elevations above 2,500 feet—Sierra Nevada Mountains, Cascade Range, and Salmon Mountains.

This zone will experience winter temperatures lower than any other part of the state. Heavy snow and deep ground freezes are not uncommon. The growing season can be as short as three months in the high country, but it becomes proportionately longer as the elevations drop. For this arid region, garden plants must be both cold hardy and drought tolerant. Soils are very thin, rocky, acidic, and of low fertility. Locals begin plants indoors or in greenhouses to extend the growing season enough for vegetables to ripen.

Zone 2 Eastern Foothills

Elevations below 2,500 feet—West-facing foothills of the Sierra Nevada and other northern ranges.

The entire western slope of the Sierras drains through these foothill canyons. But many homesites which cannot draw off of surface resources are limited to water pumped from domestic wells. Well production can vary from 1 gallon per minute up to about 60 gallons per minute, which illustrates how important drought-tolerant gardens are to this area. Native vegetation is made up of some of California's most beautiful native flowering trees and shrubs. Rainfall is heavier on these slopes than in the valley below. Higher elevations may experience light snows and shallow soil freezing. All sites should expect occasional frosts ranging as low as 10°F to 25°F.

Late spring frosts can be expected until May. Soils vary considerably from very deep, consistent clay to rocky ridge tops. All are acidic and of marginal fertility. They can be improved with additional organic matter and phosphorus supplements to make nutrients more available to garden plants.

Zone 3 Central Valley

Sacramento Valley, northern San Joaquin Valley.

Within this central valley zone are some of the finest agricultural soils in California. Most are very deep and fertile, with pockets of dense clay that may inhibit drainage. Underground hardpan layers occur in various

PRIVATE GARDEN ALONG THE SLOPES OF DEER CREEK IN NEVADA CITY, NEVADA COUNTY.

EMPIRE MINE STATE HISTORIC PARK, GRASS VALLEY, NEVADA COUNTY.

MOUNTAIN SEASONS INN, BROWNSVILLE, YUBA COUNTY.

MOUNTAIN SEASONS INN, BROWNSVILLE, YUBA COUNTY.

WHEATLAND ALMOND ORCHARDS.

WINSHIP HOME, YUBA CITY, SUTTER COUNTY.

locations ranging in depth from 12 inches to 30 feet. Groundwater is plentiful, with domestic wells supplying outlying homesites. Most suburban and urban areas are serviced by municipal systems.

Winter produces severe tule fog which may be very dense and linger for extended periods. Delta breezes cool the Sacramento and Stockton areas during the summer. Greatest extremes of heat and cold will be primarily to the north and south of Sacramento, beyond the coastal delta influence. Winter lows rarely drop below 20°F except in the north end of the valley where there is snowfall and occasional dips to 15°F. Summer highs may reach well over 100°F and hover there for weeks at a time. Hot north winds cause excessive drying in late spring, summer, and fall.

Zone 4 Western Foothills

Foothills on the west side of the Sacramento Valley from Redding southward past the Sacramento Delta.

These foothill areas all have a hot dry climate similar to that of the Sierra foothills. Rocky soil and steep grades can be found mingled with deeper soil, grassy hills and oak woodlands. Openings in the foothills such as the Altamont Pass can be noticeably cooler in the summer because of persistent winds and greater coastal influence. Some areas may experience occasional dense coastal fog.

Winter low temperatures vary, but the average is about 15°F to 20°F. The tops of many ridges will be warmer than the low pockets during winter because of increased solar exposure and rising warm air movement. Foothills north of San Francisco experience very intense summer heat with highs easily exceeding 100°F. Occasional snows may blanket the hills to elevations as low as 1,000 feet.

Zone 5 Coast Range Valleys

Sheltered valleys between western foothills and coastal ranges.

The numerous vineyards in these sheltered valleys attest to their ideal conditions for gardening. Soils are typically fertile and deep. Surrounding foothills provide winter protection from wind and hard frosts. Summer heat is reduced by coastal influences that sometimes travel over the foothills. There is a noticeable change in temperature from the cool coast to these much hotter coast range valleys over the distance of only a mile or so. The prevailing winds that persist on the coast are blocked by the surrounding foothills. Rainfall averages up to about 25 inches per year, but drought conditions do occur and supplemental watering is important. Winter temperatures rarely drop below 20°F.

Zone 6 Coastal Mountain Range

First range of hills on the coast.

Some of the most beautiful redwood forests lie in

this range of hills, which are kept moist by coastal fog and humidity. Most locations experience persistent winds except where windbreaks are in place, or when gardens are protected by dense forest. Summer temperatures are mild and average about 80°F. Light winter frosts do occur, but temperatures are nearly as mild as on the coast. Annual rainfall can be as high as 55 inches, although a long, dry summer makes supplemental watering necessary. In drought years rainfall totals may be much lower. Soils are often acidic, heavy clays which benefit from the addition of organic matter and phosphorus.

Zone 7 Pacific Coast

Narrow strip of coast that widens at the San Francisco Bay Area.

The coastal climate can be both a benefit and a liability. Plants requiring high temperatures may not flower or fruit in such cool summers. But perennial gardens grow lush and beautiful in the moist, clear air. Cool-season vegetables and leaf crops may be grown all year around. The growing season is very long, with only an occasional frost. Soils vary considerably from sand to deep clay and may contain high levels of salt when very close to the water. Strong winds persist throughout the summer and increase with winter storms. Shelter from windbreaks, buildings, or walls is essential to successfully grow most garden plants.

Microclimates and Their Impact on Climate Zones

Microclimates may vary drastically within a single climate zone, and even from one part of a garden to the other. Consciousness of your garden's microclimate comes gradually, and your attention to detail creates a very important intimacy with the land. Without this level of understanding, gardening becomes just a series of random activities.

• ***Temperature*** You must know the low winter temperatures of your area in order to select plants which won't be damaged by the cold. But within a single zone there can be warm or cold pockets which you must discover by walking the garden on frosty mornings. Cold spots show more white frost than the warmer areas, and this indicates what parts of the garden are the coldest.

Philo Inn, Philo, Mendocino County

• ***Solar Exposure*** The location where the sun rises and sets is always changing. A part of the garden shaded in the early spring may become very hot as the sun shifts into summer. Make a study of where the sun rises and sets at the beginning of each month or season. The changes will be most visible during the solstices and equinoxes, which will be noted in any farmer's almanac. Mark the points with a nearby fixed object like a building, power pole, or tree to serve as a record. By the time an entire year is completed, you will have a much deeper understanding of how variations in solar exposure relate to the seasonal changes in the garden.

Bald Mountain Nursery, Yuba County.

Coastal grasslands and redwood forest with sheep fencing, Mendocino County.

FORT BRAGG BOTANICAL GARDENS, MENDOCINO COUNTY.

MENDOCINO HOTEL

• *Wind* Wind can heat or cool, and dry out soil and foliage. Plants are contorted by the dry, burning effect of winds along the coastline. Central valley residents rely on the Sacramento River Delta winds to cool off summer temperatures, but occasional hot, dry inland winds can also come from the north. At higher mountain elevations, storm winds can rip trees to shreds. Gardeners must observe how wind occurs within the garden and attempt to either enhance or reduce its effects.

• *Humidity* During the winter months, ground fog rises from the damp, warm soils inland. Nicknamed "tule fog," it can linger for many days to drastically lower the daytime temperatures by denying sunlight. Coastal fogs can be persistent, but they tend to ebb and flow on a daily basis so that afternoons may be sunny with fog returning during the night. These conditions foster mildew and fungus diseases, which become difficult to control if there is insufficient air movement within the microclimate.

• *Heat radiation* Planters next to south- and west-facing building walls can be subjected to much hotter conditions than normal. Plants and lawn near paving may be burned as the surface absorbs and radiates a tremendous amount of heat. Walls and paving can combine to create a miniature heat island effect, where only the most rugged plants survive. During the winter, this factor can help to reduce frost damage as solar heat absorbed during the day is released at night.

• *Topography* At night, cool air settles in valleys or at the bases of hills to displace warmer air rising to higher elevations. This is a very subtle change that can be experienced if you spend time in the garden during the early morning or late evening. Hilltop residents describe this air movement as an "eerie warm breeze" with no definable source. When selecting plants that are marginally frost hardy in your zone, beware of unexpected low-land frost pockets.

• *Site features* Coastal gardens have a milder climate than those inland because of the warming effect of the Pacific Ocean. During summer, large bodies of water absorb and retain heat from the sun and lower temperatures around them. As winter approaches, this condition reverses itself and solar energy is released to warm the air. This occurs to a greater or lesser degree in lakes, ponds, rivers, streams, marshes, and wetlands.

Microclimates can also be cooled in summer by the evaporation of water. During the last few decades, Sacramento Valley farmers have begun to cultivate rice on a large scale. This summertime water-intensive farming causes large scale evaporation, increased humidity, and lower temperatures near the fields.

UNDERSTANDING CALIFORNIA'S SOILS

Most people have little control over the quality of their soil because extensive grading or filling can alter topsoil or eliminate it entirely. Within a single garden, it's not unusual to find deposits of radically different soil types. These changes can be difficult to detect, especially when they occur in layers beneath the surface of the soil.

Soils are evaluated in three ways: by structure, pH, and fertility. Each of these factors contributes to plant health in a different way. The most important factor is the amount of organic matter present, which is converted to humus by soil microorganisms.

SOIL STRUCTURE

All soils are composed of structural particles identified by size as either sand, silt or clay. The relative percentages of particles in your soil determine how it will behave.

Sand

Sandy soils have low fertility and fast drainage. This makes it difficult to keep enough moisture and fertilizer in the plant's root zone. Digging and cultivating is easy and is the best soil for growing root vegetable crops and bulbs. To improve sandy soil, add finely textured humus to bind the soil particles, absorb moisture, and retain nutrients.

Silt

Soils with large concentrations of silt are usually found in flood plains or areas built upon materials dredged from waterways. Dry silt can be powdery and difficult to wet thoroughly. It is generally of moderate to low fertility and also benefits from the addition of organic humus.

Clay

Clay soil is highly fertile, holds tremendous amounts of water, and is slow to drain. Wet clay expands, but when dry it contracts and cracking is evidence of how much area was once displaced by water. Heavy clays are difficult to cultivate, especially when dry. Foot traffic or digging and cultivation of wet clay can result in serious compaction. Most of these difficulties can be helped by working large quantities of humus and sand into the soil to hold clay particles apart.

NORTHERN CALIFORNIA TIP

The Sacramento Valley is a prime rice-growing region. The crop must be processed to remove the fibrous hull from each grain. Rice hulls are a very inexpensive, lightweight, and finely textured soil amendment that's hard to beat. To obtain rice hulls, contact any rice growers cooperative or U.C. Farm Advisor's office for a source near you. You may be able to get the hulls free of charge as long as you handle the loading and transportation.

TESTING FOR SOIL STRUCTURE

If you're not sure about the structure of your soil, you can try this simple home test using an empty quart jar. Fill the jar 2/3 full of water. Take a sample of soil representative of your entire site and add it to the jar until full. Seal it tightly and shake well, until all the soil is dissolved in the water. Then set the jar where it can be checked without being disturbed. Sand particles are largest and settle out in about two minutes. You can mark the jar at this point with a grease pencil or a piece of tape. After three hours, the silt will have settled out on top of the sand. Mark this point as well. Clay particles are so much smaller than either sand or silt that they can take up to forty-eight hours to completely settle. Once all the particles have settled, you can determine your soil type by the relative percentages.

Soil Type by Percentages

	Clay Soil	Silty Loam	Sandy Soil
Sand	0 to 45%	23 to 52%	85 to 100%
Silt	0 to 40%	28 to 50%	0 to 15%
Clay	40 to 100%	7 to 27%	0 to 10%

SOIL pH—THE YIN AND YANG

The term pH refers to the degree of acidity or alkalinity of a soil, and this influences the availability of nutrients. Soil pH is gauged on a scale ranging from 3.0, the most acid, to 10.0, which is extremely alkaline. The ideal garden soil, considered neutral, registers about 7.0 on this scale. There are many parts of northern California with soils that are either too acid or too alkaline, but most are neutral enough for most plants.

Acid Soils

The soil beneath forests of pine, redwoods, and oaks are made acidic by the decomposing leaf litter. Leaves release acidity as they decompose, which lowers the pH of surrounding soil. Many plants such as rhododendron and ferns are adapted to living in acid soils beneath these trees. Soils can be made more acidic by using leaves from oaks and conifers as mulches and soil amendments. Acidity can be reduced by adding lime.

Acid soils also suffer from nutrient deficiency. It's not an absence of nutrients, but a chemical reaction unique to acid conditions which locks up nutrient molecules. To counteract this problem, add fertilizer high in phosphorus, particularly during the planting process. This fertilizer "unlocks" nutrients, promotes root development, and makes plants in acidic soils grow more vigorously.

Alkaline Soils

Alkaline soils are a growing problem in northern California as a result of agricultural irrigation on slow draining clays. A high concentration of salt on the surface of the soil is indicated by a white crust called "summer snow." Alkalinity can also build up gradually in any garden soil if the water supply contains dissolved salts. This

COMMON GARDEN QUESTIONS

"There are so many fertilizers for sale with different formulas and prices. How do I know which one is the most economical?"

All fertilizer containers are labeled with the percentages of N-P-K and the total weight of the material. You can shop fertilizers the same way you would products in the supermarket by comparing price, quantity, and nutrient percentages. For example: if a 5-pound bag of 12-12-12 costs the same as a 5-pound bag of 8-10-6, the best value is the 12-12-12. The key is to find the highest percentage of nutrients per pound of product for the lowest price.

causes acid-loving plants to gradually decline, turn yellow, and finally die if salt levels reach critical proportions.

Salt can also be found in soils at the coastline. If the soil structure is sandy, the salt can be leached away with repeated applications of neutral-pH fresh water. But salt is also carried in the air, and the salinity can be gradually replaced over time.

Mineral salts from lime can leach out of concrete or mortar and into the surrounding soil. It is not uncommon to find highly alkaline pockets on newly constructed homesites. Often the only sure way to solve extreme soil alkalinity is to excavate planting areas and replace the soil.

SOIL FERTILITY

Soil fertility is based on the availability of three basic nutrients: nitrogen, phosphorus, and potassium. All fertilizers contain one or more of these nutrients, and their percentages are indicated by three numbers on the label. The first number shows the nitrogen content, the second the phosphorus content and the third is potassium. They are abbreviated N-P-K, with the K representing potassium. Soils must also contain small amounts of other micronutrients and trace elements essential to plant life.

• ***Nitrogen*** Promotes leaf and stem development. Main ingredient in lawn formulas. Overdose prevents flower and fruit production. Common source: manures.

• ***Phosphorus*** Essential to development of roots, fruit, and flowers. Unlocks acidic soil nutrients. Common source: bonemeal.

• ***Potassium*** Responsible for active growth, aids nitrogen and phosphorus. Common source: lime, wood stove ashes.

Testing Your Soil Fertility

Most soils contain enough fertility to support plants. But it's helpful to know if your soil is deficient in a particular area because this tells you what kind of fertilizer to use. You can buy a do-it-yourself soil testing kit, available at most garden centers, which are very accurate and tell you the levels of N-P-K present in your soil. Some kits also gauge soil pH, and it's a good idea to test if you suspect an alkalinity problem.

IMPROVING SOIL STRUCTURE

A well-drained, fertile soil is an ideal growing medium and the key to successful gardening. Very few soils are perfect to begin with. Most require continual improvement by adding amendments and fertilizers. Amendments used to alter soil structure don't necessarily increase fertility. In some cases they can actually reduce it. Fertilizers directly increase nutrient levels, but don't always have the ability to improve structure. Materials that fulfill both roles are the most favored by gardeners.

Soil Amendments

Amendments for improving structural qualities of soils are divided into fresh organic matter and humus. Woody materials like sawdust are needed to lighten heavy clay soils and improve drainage. Slow-to-decompose redwood and cedar shavings have the best long-term effect on clay soils. However, as they break down the cellulose into humus they require nitrogen, which is then robbed from the surrounding soil. To prevent a nitrogen deficiency, you must always compensate for additions of fresh woody organic matter by adding a sprinkling of nitrogen fertilizer.

Sand and silty soils have far less microbe activity, which means humus worked into the soil remains there much longer than in fertile, active clays. Humus, such as compost or well-rotted manure is important in binding soil particles together and increasing water-holding ability.

Most gardeners underestimate how much material it takes to improve the soil over even a small area. Buying amendments by the bag is expensive and inconvenient for larger projects. Fortunately, most parts of northern California have industries involving timber, livestock, and farming, and all generate high-quality organic matter for soil improvement. Consider your best material one which originates close to home, is inexpensive to buy or free, is dry, and is lightweight.

• ***Wood chips*** Wood chips or shavings can be purchased by the bag at garden centers, but only buy those labeled "nitrolized" or be prepared to add extra nitrogen. Obtaining wood byproducts directly from a lumber mill is the most economical. Another good source for free chips is from tree trimming companies which will deliver a truckload free of charge rather than pay landfill fees. Beware of using overly large wood chips, or those from poison oak, black walnut, and eucalyptus trees.

• *Compost* Compost is a form of humus made up of the remains of partially decomposed plant materials. It can be purchased ready for use in plastic bags or made at home in a bin. To create compost you must allow the heap to process for many months before it is suitable for use. Compost is one of the best all-purpose amendments because it loosens the soil and provides nutrients at the same time. It is most valuable for improving sandy soil because of its fine texture and high water holding capacity.

• *Leaf mold* This is a second cousin to compost that isn't as high in nutrients, but makes an excellent soil amendment. More importantly, it decomposes much faster than compost and is ready to use in just a few months. Rather than lament that huge pile of leaves each fall, turn it into a valuable resource by creating a leaf corral of wire field fencing. Leaf corrals from 3 to 4 feet deep and 5 to 7 feet wide are easiest to work with. Only put dry leaves into the corral and discard any sticks, pine cones, or other hard materials. Compact the leaves in layers with a scattering of fertilizer and garden soil to speed up the process. In about six months you'll be able to remove the wire corral and take advantage of a terrific soil amendment.

• *Animal manures* Manure improves soil structure better when combined with livestock bedding such as shavings, straw, or sand. Manures should be aged to prevent burning plants, and even then still contain a large amount of weed seeds. You can buy bagged, seed-free steer manure from home improvement centers.

IMPROVING SOIL FERTILITY

Fertilizer is food for plants that replaces or adds nutrients to the soil. It can be derived from either chemical or organic sources. Chemical fertilizers are quick-acting, but they also move out of the root zone just as fast. Organic fertilizers are less potent and slower to become effective, but remain in the soil longer and may improve structure as well.

Chemical Fertilizers

Chemical fertilizers are widely available and very easy to use. Some are formulated for specific uses, although most gardens need only an all-purpose balanced fertilizer for trees, shrubs, and bedding plants. Lawns require a different formula with high levels of nitrogen. You'll be fertilizing the lawn more frequently than other plants, and buying in quantity really makes sense. Shop around for a brand of lawn fertilizer that is the most economical, based on its nitrogen percentages and weight.

• *Dry granules* Granulated fertilizers are scattered onto lawns or into cultivated garden soil where they dissolve and are carried downward to the root zone by watering. They must be diluted with water immediately after application to prevent burning plant leaves or roots. This easy-to-use form is the most widely used fertilizer on the market today.

• *Systemics* Systemics contain ordinary fertilizer as well as a weed killer or insecticide. As roots take up the fertilizer, the insecticide travels throughout the plant to increase its pest resistance. Weed killers in systemic fertilizers are toxic to selected plants and should be used with care in order to prevent accidental poisoning.

• *Liquid concentrate or water soluble crystals* Liquid concentrate or soluble crystal fertilizers are mixed with water and then applied in solution directly into the soil. These are less likely to burn, and are especially helpful in heavy soils where drainage prevents granules from dissolving properly.

• *Tablets and spikes* Fertilizer can be compressed into hard shapes that dissolve very slowly when placed in the soil. They are convenient to use but are far more expensive than granular fertilizers. Fertilizer spikes are most effective for trees where they are pushed deeply into the soil around the dripline. Big blue fertilizer "starter tablets" are carried by most garden centers. Starters are placed in the planting hole to give new plants a head start.

Organic Fertilizers

A fertilizer is considered organic if it is derived from natural animal, vegetable, or mineral matter. Some organic fertilizers such as animal manures have the ability to improve both soil fertility and structure. They also contain important micronutrients and trace elements. These act to stimulate microorganism activity and contribute to a plant's natural ability to resist pests and disease. Vegetable and fruit gardeners prefer to use organics to keep their produce chemical-free.

• *Manure* This is the oldest fertilizer known to man, and the best ones come from cows, poultry, swine, sheep, and even bats! Manures are loaded with micronutrients and trace elements which are very helpful to prob-

COMMON LANDSCAPING MISTAKES

Some unscrupulous plant sellers stock plants during the summer months that aren't frost hardy. This isn't much of a problem with inexpensive bedding plants. But when expensive and showy plants like blooming bougainvillea vines are displayed, most people can't resist them. They pay a high price, take it home and plant it. With the first winter frost their beautiful evergreen vine defoliates, and as winter progresses it dies. This places the burden of proof on the consumer, which illustrates an important reason why you should know the botanical name of any plant you buy. With that name you can find out its temperature tolerances before you invest your money.

INSTALLING WEED BARRIER LANDSCAPE FABRIC. (*REEMAY COMPANY*)

lem soils with low fertility. Nitrogen levels in manure range from 2 to 8 percent maximum.

• ***Bloodmeal*** Bloodmeal is an old-time source of slow-release nitrogen. It's a powdered byproduct of packing houses and contains about 14 percent nitrogen, which is unusually potent for an organic source. It works well when scattered around the bases of acid-loving plants, and may also discourage browsing deer and rabbits.

• ***Bonemeal*** Also a byproduct from packing houses, bonemeal is a good source of organic phosphorus with calcium and other trace elements. It can be very quick acting and provides 3 percent nitrogen and 15 percent phosphorus. Used to promote root development, it is preferred by avid bulb enthusiasts over any other product. It can be mixed into the bottom of planting holes for trees and shrubs to unlock nutrients in acid soils.

• ***Fish emulsion*** Fish emulsion has been in use for a long time, and many gardeners value it as one of the few organic fertilizers sold in solution. Recent studies proved that the kelp extracts in fish emulsion actually contain a growth hormone which stimulates cell division. Fish emulsion is easy to use and rarely burns, making it popular with organic vegetable gardeners as well as cats. It's mixed with water and applied to the soil around plants.

THE VALUABLE MULCHES

Mulches are essential to successful gardening in northern California. A mulch is any material spread upon the surface of the ground to conserve soil moisture, discourage weeds, and regulate soil temperature. When mulch is placed over bare soil it acts as a one-way barrier that allows water to enter the soil, but prevents its escape through evaporation. This dense layer denies light to sprouting weeds, and those which do germinate in the mulch can be pulled out easily. Inland, where summers are hot and dry, mulches help to shade the root zones of small plants and keep them cooler.

Organic Mulches

Mulches derived from organic matter will eventually break down into humus and become part of the soil. Just about any kind of organic matter can be used for a mulch as long as it can be spread out into a thick layer. Mulches can be both aesthetic and practical. Landscapers use ground bark to cover up disturbed soil just after planting because of its uniform size and coloring. Vegetable gardeners are less finicky, and mulch with anything that's available. Buying mulch by the bag is very expensive because an effective layer should be at least 2 inches thick, preferably more. But low-budget gardeners have discovered unusual sources of materials, such as straw, that are inexpensive and plentiful.

Inorganic Mulches

Mulches of natural or colored gravel can be used to cover large areas of soil, but gravel alone is not able to completely eliminate weed growth. Black plastic sheeting denies oxygen from the soil causing it to "sour." A new geotextile that still blocks light but allows for water and oxygen movement is called "weed barrier fabric." This fabric is widely used today, and although more expensive than the plastic, it holds up much better.

OBTAINING PLANTS

Healthy, attractive plants begin with quality nursery stock. Selecting the right plant takes into consideration exposure, soil type, frost tolerance, disease resistance, and water requirements. In order to save time and money you must learn a plant's name, what form to purchase, when to plant and how to put it in the ground.

HOW PLANTS ARE NAMED

Learning plant names isn't as difficult as you think. Each plant has a Latin botanical name, and some have a common name as well. Using common names because the Latin terms sound intimidating can create confusion, because many plants may share the same common name.

Each botanical name consists of a genus and species, something like our first and last names in reverse. The genus indicates the general group to which a plant belongs. The species is like a first name, which identifies that plant within the genus. Occasionally a third name will follow which applies to new cultivars and hybrids of an existing plant. This name is usually capitalized within single quotation marks.

The beauty of plant nomenclature is that the names are often symbolic and suggest something about the plant itself. Sometimes the Latin name tells us the plant looks like another unrelated plant. **Platanus acerifolia**, the London plane tree, was given its species name because it has maple-shaped leaves. "*Acer*" is the genus for maple and "*folia*" means leaves. An example of a cultivar name is the weeping Japanese cherry, ***Prunus subhirtella* 'Pendula.'** This flowering cherry is unique because it has "pendulous," or weeping, branches.

After hearing these names often enough, you'll find they suddenly become part of your vocabulary. Although you may recognize the name when written, pronunciation is a different matter. It's a good idea to consult the experts at a garden center to help you say the names properly. Knowing the common name too helps when speaking with less plant-minded people.

WHERE AND HOW TO BUY LANDSCAPE PLANTS

The retail gardening industry in California is experiencing a gradual change. The intimate neighborhood nursery has evolved into a more diversified garden center. Plants are purchased from large-scale growers rather than being propagated on the premises. In this process, personal service often decreases as the variety of products increases. The consumer is forced to be more selective and knowledgeable when buying plants, and knowing where to buy can also contribute to more successful gardening.

URBAN BEDDING PLANT SELLER.

WHERE TO BUY GARDEN PLANTS

All plants in table are sold in containers except where indicated.
G. Center=Garden Center, Nursery
H. I. Store=Home Improvement Store

Plant	G. Center	H.I. Store	Supermarket	Mail Order
Trees	good	poor	poor	fair
Shrubs	good	fair	poor	poor
Groundcover	good	poor	poor	poor
Bedding Plants	good	good	fair	fair
Bare-Root	good	fair	poor	good
Seed	good	fair	poor	good
Selection	good	poor	poor	good
Special Order	yes	no	no	yes
Service	good	fair	poor	fair
Price	high	low	moderate	high

How to buy

Buying plants is like going to the produce department for fruit. You select the largest, most unblemished apple of the lot. It doesn't make sense to pay the same price for a damaged apple as you would a perfect one. This same concept applies to buying plants. A plant in poor form at the store will rarely grow into a healthy adult.

• *Container grown trees and shrubs.* Plants are sold in pots sized: 1, 2, 5, and 15 gallon. Pricing is based on the size of the pot, not necessarily the species of plant, although there are a few exceptions. Very large specimen trees are sold in wood containers called boxes, with the smallest measuring about 24 inches square. This is a great way to obtain instant trees for a new landscape, but be prepared to pay dearly for them. Since boxed trees are very heavy, it's not a good idea to plant them yourself. Protect your investment and consult a professional to do the planting so there are no mistakes, which could jeopardize the health of the tree. Even more important is the potential of injuring yourself or a bystander. The container sizes increase to 36 inches, 48 inches, and all the way up to giant boxes, which are widely available throughout northern California.

• *Container-grown bedding plants and groundcovers* Bedding plants are grown from seed each year in disposable plastic containers called six-packs. Each hold six plants, and containers vary in size and price. Bedding plants may also be sold in 4-inch pots which each contain one very large plant in full bloom.

Groundcover plants are grown from rooted cuttings in flats. A flat is a shallow tray that contains around 50 to 72 small plants, and is much more economical than buying them in individual containers. Many groundcovers with carpetlike growth habits will completely fill a flat, and the mass must be cut up like a sheet cake to divide into plantable units.

• *Checking plant health* A good plant should be well shaped and free of broken branches, scars, bruises, or dried leaves. The bark should be clean and healthy, without gouges from rough handling. Check the roots by turning the container upside down while supporting the rootball with your hand, and tap the edge on a hard surface. This should force the rootball out just enough to reveal the rooting conditions. A good plant has lots of dark soil in the pot and a few roots. Avoid those with a dense, yellow mass of roots, or with roots coming out the drain holes. Coiling or visible surface roots also indicate an unhealthy, pot-bound plant.

Shake the plant to see if any white flies come out of the foliage. These and other insects attack weaker, poorly growing plants that have lost some of their natural disease resistance. Be sure to inspect the back sides of the leaves because many damaging insects hide there. You should never introduce any new plant into your garden if there are signs of pests or disease.

• *Bare root trees and shrubs* Bare-root stock is field-grown, then dug up while dormant and shipped to garden centers. Bare-root trees are less expensive because they are lighter and easier to ship. Trees and shrubs purchased from mail order catalogs are typically deciduous bare-root stock. This is the most economical way to purchase deciduous plants.

Bare-root plants are heeled into sawdust or sand at the nursery to keep roots moist while on sale. Sort through them and choose those with the greater proportion of fibrous roots. Avoid any with dry, damaged, or crushed roots. Look for gouges in the bark or broken branches. When buying roses, plants should have at least three fat canes (branches) for better form. After purchasing all bare-root plants, make sure the roots remain moist while in transit. Either plant them immediately after purchase, or heel each plant into loose moistened garden soil until you have time to plant them properly.

• *Balled and burlapped* We don't see plants sold this way too often in California, but occasionally you'll find field grown conifers and Japanese maples with their rootball bound in burlap. These plants go into the ground as is, and the burlap eventually rots away. While they are on sale, the garden center must keep the rootball thoroughly wet, and it should feel solid and firm. A loose or cracked rootball indicates it may have dried out or roots have been damaged. Dried or shedding foliage is also a bad sign. Look for damage to the trunk resulting from field digging and avoid those with any open wounds.

GUIDELINES FOR SUCCESSFUL TRANSPLANTING

When plants are moved from containers or growing fields into your landscape they are being transplanted. The only real planting you do is from seed. Plants are shocked by transplanting no matter how carefully they are placed in the ground. The best way to reduce shock is to keep the rootball intact, transplant at the proper time of year, and make sure plants are well tended afterwards.

The northern California climate allows us to plant container-grown stock nearly all year around except in the high country subjected to soil freezing. The worst planting time is in the heat of the summer when plants lose water faster than their disturbed roots can replace it. Bare-root and balled-and-burlapped stock must be planted in winters while dormant. You'll know when the best planting times are by what's on display at garden centers.

Most woody trees, shrubs, and vines in northern California are transplanted from container-grown stock. Specifics on how to plant are detailed later in the chapters on individual types of plants. How well you follow these guidelines has a lot to do with the plant's later overall vigor. During the warm months, planting in the evening insures the maximum number of hours for adjustment before the hot sun rises. Some people like to dig the holes in the morning, then plant in the cool of the evening.

It is very important that the plant is placed at the exact same depth in the soil as it was in the pot or growing field. This point is indicated on the trunk or stem by a change in color. If planted too low, crown rot may result. Crown rot destroys the bark in a ring which cuts off the vital movement of water and nutrients from the roots to the rest of the plant. This occurs most often with most woody trees, shrubs and vines, although there are exceptions. It is frequently the result of loose soil settling beneath the rootball after planting is completed.

Never pull a bedding plant out of the container by its stem or branches. Be ready to hold the rootball firmly with your hand because bedding plant soil mixes tend to be sandy and don't hold together well. Do not squeeze the stem or crush it because plants are very tender at this stage.

Planting Bare-Root Stock

Bare-root plants are vulnerable. If the roots dry out, even for just an hour, they may be severely handicapped or die. If you can't plant right away, dig a shallow hole, place the roots inside with the plant lying down. Then cover all the roots with a thick mound of moist soil. If the weather is cool, they can remain there safely for a week or more.

A few hours before you plant, place the roots of bare root stock in a bucket of water and let them soak until you're ready. When you've got all the tools and materials ready, inspect the trunk and roots of the first plant closely. Cut off any crushed, broken or damaged roots, then place it back into the water. Dig your planting hole large enough to contain the roots without bending. Then improve the excavated soil by mixing in fertilizer and humus.

Look at the plant again and note the crotch at the bottom of the trunk where the roots split off. You should also see a discoloring on the trunk that marks the soil line in the field where it was grown. You must make sure this level is maintained in the new planting hole to prevent crown rot. Use the improved soil to make a firm cone at the bottom of the planting hole. The soil cone should be tall enough so the plant can be placed on top of it with the roots spread out and still remain at the proper planting level. Tightly pack the soil cone to reduce settling later on.

Gently spread the roots apart and place the plant on top of the cone of soil. Try not to leave air space between the top of the cone and the crotch of the roots. Set the plant, then gently fill the hole with soil. Be careful as you pack it down so the cone isn't damaged and the plant stays in place. Add fertilizer tablets: 3 per tree, 2 per shrub or vine. When the hole is filled, pack the soil and construct a watering basin. Water in thoroughly, but since the plant is dormant, it may not need much more water for awhile. Since you're planting in winter, beware of rainy weather which can cause roots to rot in slow-draining soils.

OLD REDDING

CHAPTER TWO

DESIGNING WITH PLANTS

A poorly designed landscape can be just as expensive to build as a well-planned one. Time and money spent on efficient design is the key to obtaining the best value for each construction dollar you spend. Hastily planned landscapes result in the wasting of space, a commodity few California homeowners can afford to sacrifice. Plants make up the living part of a landscape, the perishable commodity which can be costly to replace. Details frequently ignored at the planning stage can result in eroded slopes, dangerous steps, and undrained, soggy soil.

FACING PAGE: A STONE COTTAGE ENTRY WITH MAGENTA PINK HYBRID LUPINE. ABOVE: A NEAR PERFECT PLANTING OF OLD ROSES AND COLORFUL PERENNIALS FOR THIS VICTORIAN HOUSE.

DOCUMENT AND ORGANIZE

High-quality landscape design is the result of a step-by-step process that addresses all aspects of the site in an orderly way. This process requires considerable thought on your part and cannot be rushed. Often the solutions to design problems occur to us in our most relaxed moments, when the brain's creative ability is at its highest level. Good design also demands that you, as the user, understand exactly what your personal needs are. Designs cannot be created in a vacuum of information, and the better your needs are defined, the more accurate the final outcome will be.

DOCUMENTING YOUR SITE

Before any designing can take place, you must fully document the site by creating a base map. The base map contains anything within the property lines which will remain or become an integral part of the new design. Accuracy is important because errors in measurements at this stage can create huge problems later on. To draw a base map you'll need the following items:

- 24-inch x 36-inch sheet of 1/8-inch gridded drafting vellum. (Vellum erases better than plain paper. Buy 2 extras.)
- Masking or drafting tape.
- 1/8-inch=1 foot drafting scale or ruler.
- Soft pencils (HB or #2) and a BIG eraser.
- 45-degree plastic triangle.
- Plastic circle template.
- Carpenter's measuring tape.

How to Measure Your House and Lot

The bulk of the information on the base map must be measured in the field, then later drawn to scale on the vellum sheet. You'll be citing the house within property lines, identifying windows, doors, gates, existing trees and shrubs, existing paving and utilities. The easiest way to begin is to sketch out (not to scale) the house on a plain sheet of paper showing all windows and doors, then surround it with the property lines. Within these lines draw all the other existing items as accurately as you can.

Use the carpenter's tape to start measuring, and assign a single dimension to each piece of building wall or window or fence, and so forth. Show measurements in feet and inches like 5 feet 7 inches, and if less than 4 feet they can be shown strictly in inches. You can locate trees by taking two separate measurements off two known points like a fence or building corner. Use three points to set the house within the property lines. The final result will be a wrinkled, dirty field drawing which contains most of the information you'll need to draw a base map.

Drawing the Base Map

The base map should be drawn on the sheet of drafting vellum at a scale of 1/8-inch=1 foot. You can expect most corners to be at 90 degrees, which is helpful in aligning the plan with the grid lines on the paper. First identify north on your field drawing, then draw the property lines on your paper with north pointing toward the top of the page. Next, draw building walls with a heavy, thick line, but use a much thinner one for windows. Doors are shown as blank openings in the walls. Draw in all the existing features like slabs, walks, wood decking, trees, shrubs, and the limits of planters to remain. When the plan is completed you can go back into the yard to pick up remaining items like utility meters, hose bibs, sprinkler valves, and outdoor electrical sockets. Add your name, the scale, and show which direction is north by a heavy black arrow, especially if north isn't at the top of the sheet.

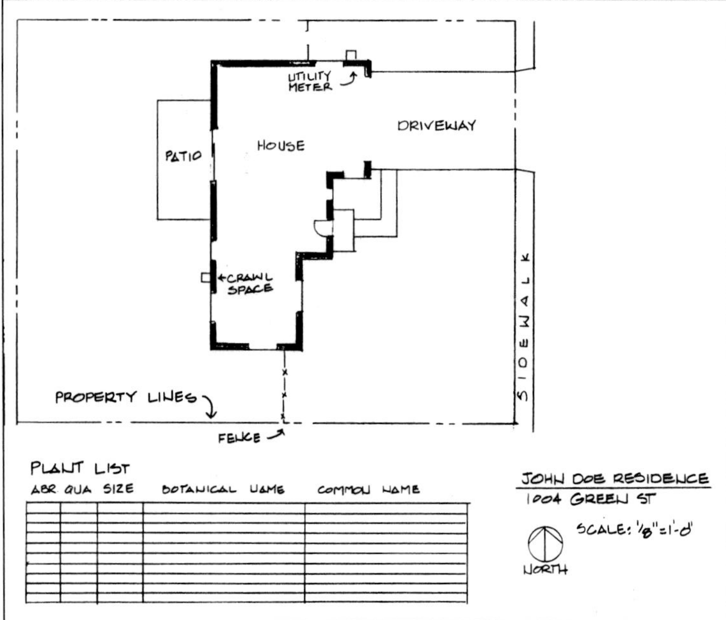

DRAWING OF A TYPICAL RESIDENTIAL BASE MAP, SHOWING HOUSE WITH DOORS AND WINDOWS, PROPERTY LINES, PAVING, AND OTHER EXISTING FEATURES. THE BLANK PLANT LIST SHOWS HOW TO ORGANIZE THE INFORMATION WITH ABBREVIATION OF THE PLANT NAME, THE QUANTITY OF EACH PLANT ON THE PLAN, THE PURCHASE SIZE, BOTANICAL NAME, AND COMMON NAME.

EVALUATING ALL SITE INFLUENCES

Man has the unique ability to change his environment, and knowing the factors which influence the microclimate of your site dictate how to improve it. Cataloging gives you a much better understanding of what's going on.

• *Solar exposure* How the sun reaches different parts of the site will have a bearing on how you plant. The south and west sides of the house will be warmer in both winter and summer. The eastern side is more moderate, while north may be in shade except during the long days of the summer solstice. The sun rises and sets at a different point during the summer than it does in the winter. If you live in the warm coastal or central valleys, knowing where to plant trees can help you create a significant cooling effect on the house and nearby outdoor spaces.

• *Wind* Homes all along the coast must contend with persistent winds, which grow progressively colder to the north. If not blocked, outdoor living spaces will be chilly and plants will suffer. It's important to know the actual angle of this wind as it reaches your homesite in order to properly locate and size windbreaks. Homesites inland, around the Sacramento Delta area, rely on the cooling marine breezes during the hot summers. Plants should be arranged to channel, rather than block this type of wind.

• *Views* We can't always improve bad views outside our property lines, but we can try to block them with screen trees, fences, or outbuildings. Some of the most common offending views include power poles and lines, multistory buildings, neighbors' homes, streets, and parking lots. Those who value privacy will be concerned about how much of their landscape can be "viewed" by others. There can also be bad views within the property lines, like utility areas, which must be screened on a smaller scale. Homes on view lots require special care so that plantings do not block the view but frame and enhance it.

• *Noise* People who live in cities know how much noise can be created by streets or freeways. Homes on hills can have noise problems as sound travels upwards. Noise can be buffered and absorbed with plants, or camouflaged with the sound of water from a garden fountain.

• *Vulnerability to fire* Rural or suburban homesites adjacent to undeveloped areas will be the most vulnerable to fire. These areas should be well defined in order to allow sufficient space for buffer zones to be irrigated and planted with low fuel volume species.

SOLVING PROBLEMS WITH PLANTS

Designing is really the act of solving problems. A good design deals with the most difficult and essential parts of the plan first. As you drew your base map and identified site influences, you probably became aware of problem areas. Here are a few examples of common problems and how they can be solved.

• *Maximizing the passive solar landscape* Identify where you require shading from southern or western sun. Deciduous trees are perfect solutions, as they allow more sun into the garden during winter and leaf out conveniently before the heat of summer. This is very important in the central valley where ground fog can linger for weeks in winter making sunshine precious. During the blistering inland summers, shade from tree canopies becomes the best way to reduce home air conditioning bills. If you live in a cool place like San Francisco and want to maximize all the solar radiation you can, keep trees away from the east, south, and west side of outdoor living spaces.

A young tree may require five to eight years before its canopy becomes large enough to cast a sizeable shadow. If the budget allows, you can purchase larger, boxed trees and have them planted where shade is needed. Another solution would be to construct a shade arbor sized to create sufficient usable square footage beneath its protective cover.

• *Blocking or enhancing the breeze* You can block wind on a large scale with rows or clusters of evergreen trees. These should be chosen and arranged in proportion with the homesite. Smaller windbreaks of hedges can be created within the garden or where blocking the view is undesireable. Constructed windbreaks include fences, masonry walls, and carefully sited outbuildings. For more information on windbreak trees and plants, refer to the section "Coastline Gardens" in chapter 11.

• *Visual screening* Hedges and fences are the best way to screen views within the site. They function the same way walls and partitions do inside a house. Sometimes a semitransparent fence of lattice panels, for example, screens well and still allows light through. This factor makes fences appear much softer and gives the illusion of greater space.

COMMON LANDSCAPING MISTAKES

Slopes should be designed with great care to prevent mud slides, and also to insure plants are able to grow on the surface. The steepest plantable slope should be no greater than 2:1. This ratio means every foot of rise requires two horizontal feet. The maximum slope for lawns is 3:1, but much less is preferable. If water runs off too fast, it cannot be absorbed into the soil for evenly green turf.

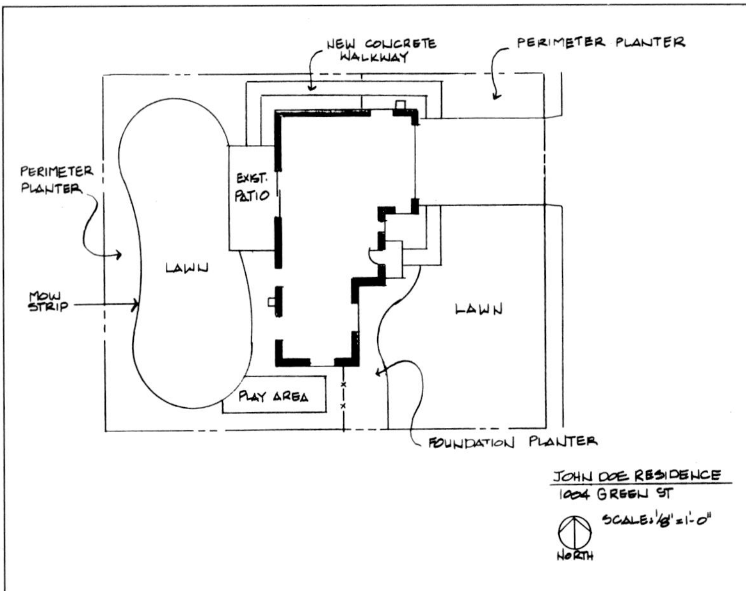

Drawing of base map with additions of paving and planting areas. Areas of lawn, perimeter, and foundation plantings have been defined with mow strips. Paving is limited to new walkway on north side of the house. A play area on the south side is located out of the way of the main yard.

In urban areas, especially San Francisco, multistory buildings invade privacy from windows above. This can be mitigated by planting trees which don't grow very tall, but have broad, flat foliage canopies. The sacrifice here is sunlight in favor of privacy. Another possibility is a small, carefully placed shade structure to support vines that can be trained to allow plenty of sunlight through while obscuring the view from above.

• ***Slopes and grade changes*** If you are considering any grade changes which result in steep slopes or require retaining walls, it's best to hire an experienced professional. Grading design solutions for many may be very expensive to build, and improper construction may result in bodily injury, slope failure, and tremendous liability for the homeowner.

• ***Buffer zones*** A buffer zone serves as a transition from the landscape to an adjacent use. This concept is behind creation of fire protection belts. They serve to separate the homesite from wild areas which may be subject to wildfire. Homes on top of hills are at greater risk of fire because the flames travel up the slope with the wind. This zone should be planted according to the section "Planting For Fire Protection" in chapter 11.

IDENTIFY MAJOR PLANTING FEATURES

• ***Water gardens*** Fish ponds and water gardens should be designed with simple shapes, which are easier to clean and help to keep the body of water at a more consistent temperature. Choose a place clear of overhanging trees, as leaf litter quickly reduces water quality. The pond should receive at least six hours of daylight in order to support water lilies and other aquatic plants.

• ***Kitchen garden*** Vegetable gardens may lie fallow during the off season, and should be screened off from outdoor living spaces. A southern or western exposure is important. To decide how large to make the plot, sketch out a miniature floor plan of a fully planted garden, and don't forget to designate space for a compost pile. Make sure your gates are wide enough to fit a wheelbarrow through comfortably.

Kitchen gardens in raised beds can be easier to care for. Each raised bed should be worked out on the plan with about 3 feet clear on all sides for access. If you want fruit trees and are pressed for space, allow a narrow strip for dwarf trees along the north edge of your kitchen garden.

• ***Rose garden*** Roses are sun lovers, and should not be shaded in the morning or the plants may suffer from mildew and other fungus diseases. Afternoon sun inland can be potent, and roses will benefit from some shade late in the day. Place rose gardens out in the open and away from solid fences, walls, and buildings that restrict air movement.

• ***Lawn*** Irrigation is a major factor in how lawns are designed. Complete coverage is essential to an evenly green lawn. Sprinkler heads throw water in patterns ranging from 90 degrees to 360 degrees, with a radius of about 8 feet or more. Lawns designed with areas narrower than 8 feet can result in incomplete coverage, soggy, or over-

NORTHERN CALIFORNIA TIP:

Concrete mow strips separate lawn from planting areas. The cost of concrete is minimal, but strips are expensive because of the labor required to build the forms. Since you must pay for the labor anyway, why not widen the strip from the standard 8 inches to 12 inches or even 18 inches so it also functions as a convenient walkway around the lawn? There will be only a small charge for the additional concrete.

THIS PAVING LOOKS LIKE STONE, BUT IS ACTUALLY CONCRETE TINTED BLACK AND IMPRINTED WITH THE PATTERN. THIS METHOD CAN BE USED TO SIMULATE OTHER MORE EXPENSIVE PAVING MATERIALS SUCH AS TILE OR FLAGSTONE.

THIS DRIVEWAY IS CONSTRUCTED OF POURED CONCRETE WITH AN EXPOSED AGGREGATE FINISH. THE STRIPS IN BETWEEN EACH SQUARE WILL BE SET IN BRICK FOR ACCENT AND TO BREAK UP SUCH A LARGE EXPANSE OF PAVING.

dry patches of grass. Whenever possible, shape the lawn with very gradual curves or corners no less than 90 degrees.

OTHER PLACES FOR PLANTS

When you look at planting areas, pay attention to sprinkler pattern, just as you did for the lawn. There are two types of sprinkler heads used for shrubs: strip sprays and standard sprays. A standard spray has a minimum radius of about 3 feet and heads are placed on *both* sides of the planter for even coverage. This means that planters narrower than 3 feet won't work with most sprinkler heads.

Although they are difficult to adjust, strip sprays were invented to irrigate narrow, problem areas. The heads are placed in single file down the center of the planter with the supply line directly beneath them underground. This presents an obstacle to planting and limits root ball depth.

• ***Vine pockets*** Vine pockets are small openings in pavement at the base of a post or column that allow the vines to grow up and onto an arbor. Vine pockets should be at least 18 inches square, but preferably larger, to accommodate a 5-gallon sized rootball. Vines planted in pockets have very little soil surface and require frequent, but slow, deep waterings. Bubbler heads make the best sprinklers for vine pockets because they do not spray.

• ***Foundation planting*** This kind of planting covers up unattractive features around a house, such as exposed footings, crawl holes, air vents, utility meters, exposed plumbing, and clean-outs. The reason you drew windows and utilities on your site plan is to help you design foundation plantings that won't interfere with visibility. Make planters at least 4 feet wide to provide adequate space for larger shrubs and trees. If a tree is to be part of the foundation planting, the planter area may be a few feet wider still, to place the roots and canopy safely away from walls, roofs, and footings.

• ***Perimeter plantings*** Planters laid out along perimeters soften the rigid shape of a lot and provide background for other features. Lawn growing right up to the base of a fence makes mowing and edging more difficult. Sprinkler overspray discolors natural wood fencing, and these planters help hide the stains. Perimeter plantings can also be located around raised decks, beside steps, and along walkways.

• ***Herbs*** If you aren't planning a kitchen garden but still would like some culinary herbs, they should have their own planting space. Designate a planter close to the kitchen door where they are conveniently handy. Sometimes an unused sideyard or planters near utility areas are the best choice.

EXTERIOR DECORATING

The enhancement of outdoor space using plants can be considered "exterior decorating." In this part of the process you will be creating a working planting plan.

THE HARDSCAPE

Hardscape is a term which refers to any constructed part of a landscape. Typical hardscape items are paving,

A PORTION OF A PATIO PAVED WITH MODULAR CONCRETE UNITS CALLED INTERLOCKING PAVERS, WHICH ARE AVAILABLE IN A VARIETY OF SHAPES AND COLORS. PLACED ON A BED OF SAND, THEY FIT TIGHTLY TOGETHER WITH THE CONCRETE BAND AROUND THE OUTSIDE TO KEEP THEM IN PLACE.

A PATIO WITH TERRA COTTA TILES SET UPON A CONCRETE SLAB. USE ONLY HIGH QUALITY TILES OUTDOORS BECAUSE MANY MADE IN MEXICO ARE POORLY FIRED. CHEAP TILE WEARS AWAY AND CHIPS VERY EASILY, EVEN IF COATED WITH A SEALER.

water features, fences, walls, and structures. The cost of these items can be manipulated by the type of materials you choose. For example, if you have 200 square feet of patio, it can be built for much less in plain concrete than brick.

To help determine what kind of construction costs you're looking at, you must measure the units on the plan and multiply them out. For example, if you have 15 feet of walkway that's 3 feet wide, the total (L x W) is 45 square feet. If your contractor is charging $2 per square foot, then you can roughly estimate the cost as $90. For walls and fences, your cost should be in linear feet instead of square feet. Topsoil to fill raised planters and other bulk materials are priced by cubic feet or cubic yards. With these fixed pricing units, you can contact other contractors and compare their prices to find the best value.

Paving

Paving is the most common constructed element in a landscape. You can think of it as you would floor coverings in the house, and it is priced in a similar way. Poured concrete, brick, precast pavers and wood decking are the most common surfaces found in California landscapes.

•*Concrete* Optional surface textures include broom finish, salt finish, and exposed aggregate. Concrete can also be tinted with dyes to reduce glare and simulate more expensive materials. The tint can be either mixed with the cement in the truck or seeded onto to the surface just after the concrete sets up. Concrete can also be bordered or broken up with brick ribbons, but this is far more costly, as masons are involved.

•*Brick* Brick can be laid over the top of existing concrete or new slabs. A less expensive alternative is to set the brick onto a base of leveled, compacted sand without mortar joints.

•*Wood decking* Decks can be constructed of either redwood or Douglas fir treated with wood preservative. Decks are difficult to build where conditions limit the amount of clearance underneath for posts, beams, and joists. Environmental restrictions on logging are making lumber an increasingly expensive material, and decks may not be cost effective in the future.

Walls and Fences

Landscape walls can serve many purposes. They may act as freestanding barriers, retaining walls, or very low, wide seat-walls. Based on the designated height, material, and foundation, a wall can be priced out on a linear foot basis.

Fences also serve to define and separate outdoor spaces. They need not be total barriers, and are often a purely visual means of creating a certain character in the landscape.

The poured concrete wall of this raised planter was designed to be 18 inches tall by 16 inches wide. These dimensions allow it to double as a seatwall. The concrete was sealed and then painted white.

The same wall while still formed up and filled with concrete. Curved walls are more expensive because of the labor required to build these intricate forms.

A low planter wall constructed with a concrete block core. On the outside river cobble has been used as a veneer, and the top cap is terra cotta tiles with a brick border.

A simple rustic gate gives this walled garden a very attractive, yet casual entry.

DRY STONE WALLS ARE INEXPENSVIE TO BUILD IF A SUPPLY OF STONE CAN BE FOUND NEARBY, AS SHIPPING CHARGES ON SUCH HEAVY MATERIALS ARE COSTLY. HOMES IN THE FOOTHILL AND MOUNTAIN REGION OFTEN HAVE AN ABUNDANCE OF STONE AVAILABLE, MAKING THIS TYPE OF WALL A REALITY FOR GARDEN BUILDERS ON A BUDGET. BUILT WITHOUT MORTAR, THIS WALL MUST BE THICKER THAN OTHER TYPES OF WALLS TO HOLD TOGETHER.

ALTHOUGH NOT TECHNICALLY A FENCE, THIS HEDGE ALSO FUNCTIONS AS A VISUAL SCREEN. THE GATE ITSELF IS HUNG ON A POST CONCEALED WITHIN THE FOLIAGE OF THE HEDGE.

A PICKET FENCE NEED NOT BE OVERLY ORNATE TO PROVIDE A VICTORIAN OR COUNTRY CHARACTER. THIS ONE IS PERFECTLY DESIGNED WITH A SCALE AND SIZE IN KEEPING WITH THE NINETEENTH-CENTURY HOUSE BEHIND.

Decorative fences should respond to both the materials and architectural character of the house. This fence is perfectly matched with the lines and appearance of the garage.

Rather than dispose of your prunings, they can be woven into a wattle fence such as this one. They can also be woven through a wire field fence to make it more solid and attractive.

This rustic fence was modeled after the redwood sheep fences of the North Coast, and soon it will become patterned with lichens and moss. Its unusual character comes from the uneven lengths and widths of the pickets. For new fences, split cedar is more readily available and less expensive than redwood.

A gazebo may be completely open or enclosed, such as this one that can double as an office, studio, or even a guest house.

THIS STRUCTURE WAS DESIGNED TO PROVIDE A SHADED OUTDOOR DINING AREA THAT WASN'T TOO DARK. PAINTING THE LATTICE WHITE HELPED TO INCREASE AVAILABLE LIGHT WITHOUT SACRIFICING SHADE. EVENTUALLY JASMINE VINES WILL WEAVE THEMSELVES THROUGH THE LATTICE TO PERFUME THIS SPACE WITH ITS FLOWERS.

THIS RUSTIC WOODWORK CREATES A PERFECT ENTRY FOR THE BUILDING AND ALSO SUPPORTS A THRIVING PASSIONVINE. WOOD NEED NOT BE STAINED DARK, BUT SHOULD BE LEFT TO WEATHER TO ITS NATURAL PATINA.

Structures

Structures in landscapes include storage sheds, shade arbors, patio covers, and gazebos. Design and height should conform to local building codes, and placement must be within the designated property line setbacks. If the structure is to have a solid roof, you may be required to obtain a building permit.

THE PLANTING PLAN

Creating a planting plan can be difficult and frustrating if you can't identify plants. It's worth the expense to take your space plan to a landscape designer who will help you select and arrange the plants. Plants are perishable, and can be very expensive to replace if not properly selected. But avid gardeners will find planting design the most personally satisfying of all the garden-making tasks.

HOW TO DRAW A PLANTING PLAN

The planting plan will be your complete guide to plant location, name, purchase size, and quantity. This becomes your chief means of telling a plant seller or landscape contractor how to estimate the cost of your project. It also helps you manipulate plant sizes and prices to fit your budget.

To draw a planting plan you'll need the scale and a circle template. A large piece of tracing paper can also be helpful. Each plant should be drawn on the plan as a circle. The size of the circle is dictated by the scale of the plan and the diameter of the plant at maturity. For example, to draw a 3-foot diameter plant at 1/8-inch-equals 1-foot scale, use a 3/8-inch diameter circle. Your template may not have a circle large enough for big trees, so you'll have to indicate the trunk with a solid black circle and freehand sketch the limits of the canopy.

The circles of each plant may touch other circles, but should not overlap or they will be too crowded. Place a letter or number inside each circle to indicate the plant name. Then key the letter or number into a master plant list on a separate piece of paper.

Annual plants aren't included in this part of the process because they are temporary. You can leave spaces for them in between permanent plants. If you get too busy to plant them, you won't leave a giant, unplanted area in the garden.

Factors for Plant Selection

The goal of designing with plants is simple: Choose the right plant for the right place. The plants profiled in other chapters of this book are chosen for both their availability and overall success in northern California. Professional designers know that even though a certain plant may be just right for the garden, if it isn't available from suppliers a substitution must be made. A common dilemma of this industry is that the demand is often far

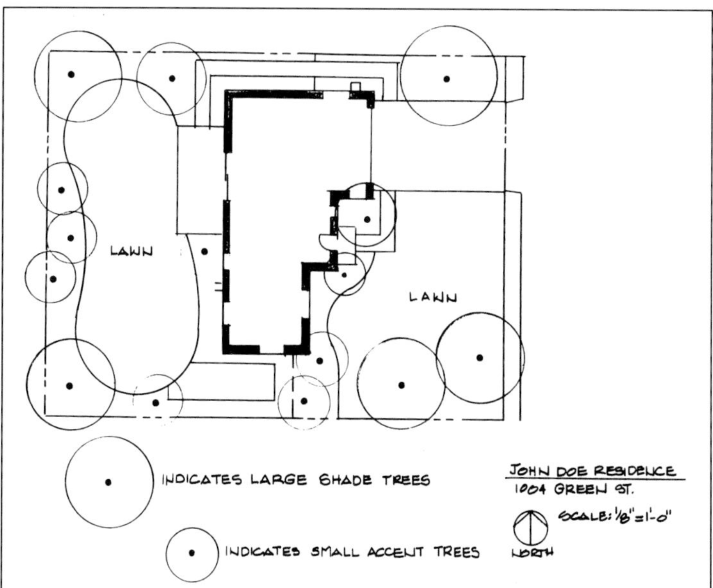

Drawing showing additions of trees to planting areas. The size of the circles indicates larger shade trees and smaller accent trees. The first plants to locate on the drawing are trees, because they will influence the site exposure. Plants around and beneath them will be forced to adapt to increasing shade.

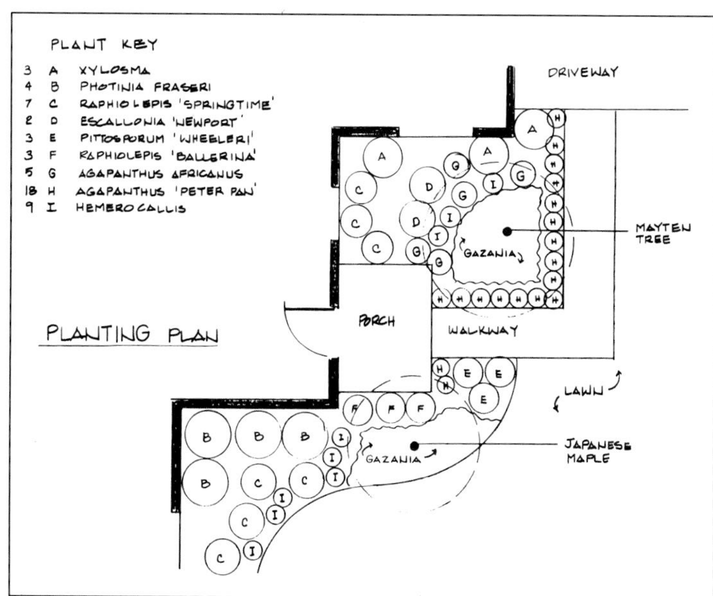

Drawing of a portion of the previous plan showing a close-up of how plants are laid out. Planters with trees, shrubs, perennials, and groundcovers are shown using an alphabetical code system. In the upper left-hand corner is a key showing what plant name goes with each letter. The gazania groundcover is shown as a zone, and the approximate square footage is used to determine how many gazania plants are required to fill the space at the designated spacing. On the larger base plan this information would be plugged into the empty plant list.

broader than the supply.

• ***Climate*** If a plant won't tolerate the low winter temperatures in your climate zone it will die. Refer to chapter 1 for more on northern California's climate zones, and also take a look at chapter 12 for the varying degrees of frost sensitivity. Just because you find a plant for sale locally doesn't mean it is frost tolerant in your area.

• ***Exposure*** The plants you select *must* be suited to the specific exposure of the designated area. This is the first step in narrowing down the choices of what you can and cannot plant. Plants for southern and western exposures must tolerate full sun and reflected heat. Planters on the north side of buildings may rarely see full sun, and only shade plants will survive there. Eastern exposures are more variable with direct morning sun and afternoon shade.

• ***Size at maturity*** Don't be fooled by the neat little plant in a pot at the nursery because it may grow into a gigantic monster. You must evaluate plants by their size *at maturity* which includes both the diameter and height. Plants too large for the space provided create a tremendous amount of maintenance, and their encroachment may stunt and overwhelm other plants nearby. To assist with selection, the plant profiles in other chapters of this book include the approximate height and diameter of each plant for you to work with.

COMMON LANDSCAPING MISTAKES

Using many different types of trees in your landscape plan is insurance that if disease strikes one species, the garden won't be devastated. Some people become focused on a single type of tree for their landscape, and this makes it highly vulnerable. It's safer to select a mixture of conifers, broadleaf evergreens, and deciduous trees for a well-rounded planting plan.

• ***Rooting characteristics*** This factor is most important with trees because their roots can cause tremendous damage. All trees seek water, and in the process they can heave paving, crack building foundations, and invade sewer lines. Before selecting any tree for your plan, take note of the rooting characteristics and make sure it is located away from utilities and paving. In chapter 3, you'll find each tree species evaluated according to its rooting type along with a discussion of root control devices.

A 7-STEP PLANTING PROGRAM

Step 1. Locate the Trees

Trees are the dominant plants in your landscape. Their locations influence how plants will be used in the areas around them. Draw the exact location of each tree with a blackened circle about 1/8-inch in diameter. Lightly sketch in the limits of the canopy above or leave it out entirely if the drawing becomes too confusing. Trees can be used as individual specimens, in casual groves of three or five, or as windrows.

Things to remember about trees: Litter, rooting, longevity, growth rate, fall color, spring flowers.

Step 2. Arrange the Shrubs

Shrubs will be the backbone of your landscape and should be placed with care. All plants appear more natural when arranged in odd numbered groups of three or five, or as single specimens. The color mass of flowering shrubs can be made much bolder by planting in masses. Pay attention to the height of each plant, placing the taller ones behind the shorter species. Don't place any shrubs within 3 feet of the trunk of a tree to avoid competition. Try to mix evergreens in with deciduous shrubs so that when they lose their leaves, the planting is still balanced.

Things to remember about shrubs: Varigated or bronze leaves, spring flowers, size, berries or fruit, thorns, bees, water requirements, drainage.

Step 3. Perennials

Perennials also include ferns, ornamental grasses, some bulbs, and exotics. They are used as permanent filler plants to provide interest, color, and variety in between and in front of shrub masses. You can arrange perennials in different ways. Plant them in a row as a border along walkways or lawns. Create a sea of low-growing foliage, and use plants with unusual leaf shapes such as blades or fronds.

Things to remember about perennials: Frost tolerance, length of bloom, aromatic foliage, bees, hummingbirds, flower color.

Step 4. Vines

Vines must have a surface or structure to climb on or they become groundcovers. A single vine may be capable of covering a large area, and over-planting may result in an enormous, tangled mass. Use vines to break up long fence lines, increase shade beneath arbors, and to frame gates and doorways. They are excellent for covering ugly sheds or discolored, broken fences.

Things to remember about vines: Invasiveness, pruning, method of clinging, fragrance, growth rate, fall color.

Step 5. Groundcovers

Groundcovers make great fillers in between shrubs and perennials. If large areas are to be devoted to groundcover, use a few different types in individual masses so that if one doesn't grow well, the others can fill in. You can show creeping shrubs the same as you would other shrubs, with a circle for each plant. Spreading plants are set out with close spacings, and may be indicated by simply cross hatching the area where they will grow. The number of plants needed from flats can be estimated by calculating the square footage of the area using the table in chapter 5.

Things to remember about groundcovers: Creeping shrubs, spreading plants, weed control, degree of slope, longevity, woodiness.

Step 6. Tally the plants

Once all the plants are shown on your plan, each should be identified by a letter or number. Take your working plant list and print it legibly on the plan. If there isn't enough space, you can use a separate sheet of paper. Then count how many of each plant you have and add the total to the list.

Step 7. Size the plants

California landscapers usually plant trees from 15-gallon containers. Shrubs and vines are 5 gallon, and perennials either 1 gallon or 4-inch pot. Designate the size of each plant so the landscape contractor or nursery can prepare an accurate estimate.

Your plant list should be organized this way:

Abr.	Qua.	Size	Botanical Name	Common Name
a	3	5 gal.	*Photonia fraseri*	Toyon
b	7	1 gal.	*Hemerocallis*	Daylily
c	1	15 gal.	*Liquidambar styraciflua*	Sweet gum

When the plant list is completed, you can calculate a rough figure of what the plants will cost by multiplying the total number of plants by the retail price of the container size. In the example above, you need three 5-gallon *Photinia fraseri* shrubs. If the cost is $25 per 5-gallon plant, you can figure a total price of these shrubs to be $75. If the price exceeds your budget, you can change the 5-gallon plants to 1-gallon, or the 15-gallon tree to 5-gallon without diluting the design. You'll just have to wait a bit longer for the plants to mature.

WORKING WITH SPRINKLER IRRIGATION

If you are planning to include a sprinkler system in your project, it should be designed and installed by professionals. With water in short supply, a professionally designed sprinkler system insures you are getting state-of-the-art equipment. No one can afford to waste water with an inefficient design and sloppy installation. With so many new irrigation products on the market, it takes an expert to know what's best for your individual project.

Most landscape contractors design and install sprinkler systems of all kinds. If you choose to do the installation yourself, or have it estimated by a number of different installers, then consult a professional irrigation designer. You'll have to pay for the plan, but it's worth the money. Most systems installed today are either drip systems or standard low-flow spray systems.

CHAPTER THREE

A Tree for Every Need

Trees planted around homes are one of California's most important resources. They should be thought of as more than just a landscape plant, because tree canopies can modify microclimates, reduce air pollution, cut down ultraviolet light and reduce noise. Mature trees on residential lots can mean a significant increase in property value, not to mention their contribution to lowering utility bills.

FACING PAGE: CREATIVE GARDENER JIM THOMPSON DESIGNED AND CONSTRUCTED THIS GATEWAY TO BECOME PART OF THIS MASSIVE CYPRESS TREE. THE TREE IS A REMNANT OF A NORTH COAST WINDBREAK. ABOVE: MATCHED ROWS OF SWEET GUM TREES IN FULL COLOR LINE THIS DRIVEWAY.

WHY WE PLANT TREES

• ***Shade*** In hot inland areas, planting trees for shade makes a landscape useable in the summer. The old neighborhoods beneath elms in downtown Sacramento have just as much pavement as new subdivisions, but are noticeably cooler just because of the shade. A tree's depth of foliage works better than any other sheltering device because it absorbs five to seven times more light and heat. Trees have the unique ability to modify the air quality around them, filtering out pollution as they "breathe." A good candidate for a shade tree must have a broad, umbrella-shaped canopy.

• ***Screen*** Trees are one of the best ways to create privacy, especially when the landscape is adjacent to multistoried buildings. Screening can be created by a windrow effect along property lines, or with broad headed trees that create a protective ceiling of foliage. The best screening trees are tall, narrow evergreens that can be planted close together for maximum density. Trees are also useful in blocking views of highways, industrial or commercial sites, and other unsightly areas visible from the home.

• ***Windbreak*** Persistent winds are a problem in coastal areas. The contorted, wind shaped trees of the northern California coastline illustrate how serious damage can be. A windbreak may be a windrow, or a single row of trees. Trees selected for dense windbreaks must be spaced 3 to 4 feet apart. Old plantings of eucalyptus and cypress reveal how important this factor is in the longevity, growth rate, and overall effectiveness in blocking wind.

• ***Visual quality*** All homes look better when framed with the soft foliage of large trees. Trees help to visually separate houses, which is important in higher density subdivisions where homes are very similar. Trees also provide a single landscape plant that can become an enormous asset to a homesite, especially when it is illuminated by landscape lighting, and when in bloom or turning colors in the fall.

TALL, NARROW TREES PLANTED CLOSE TOGETHER SCREEN OFF VIEWS AND BLOCK WIND.

CONSIDERATIONS IN SELECTING TREES

Some factors to consider when selecting a tree may be purely visual while others relate to growth characteristics. Make an informed choice because you will have to live with that tree for a long time.

• ***Deciduous or evergreen*** Don't automatically rule out deciduous trees because of messy fall leaf drop. In northern California, deciduous trees are the perfect choice for reducing energy bills in both summer and winter. We experience tule and coastal fogs, which can linger for weeks on end. The ground under evergreen trees becomes overly moist and cold, growing little more than a crop of moss. Deciduous trees are leafless in winter, and allow the weak sun to warm building walls and outdoor living spaces. It is always a good idea to plant a mix of trees, with a few evergreens to provide some greenery during the winter.

• ***Root systems*** Everyone wants trees that grow fast, but this characteristic is usually supported by a very aggressive root system. You'll find this most often with riparian (wetland) trees such as willow, poplar, and alder. Some drought tolerant trees can be just as aggressive in their search for a limited water supply. In small city lots, planting a tree with invasive root systems can heave pavement, and crack masonry and building foundations as it seeks out water. Roots can also invade water lines, septic tanks, leach fields, and sewer lines.

• ***Shape or form*** The shape or form of a tree is its silhouette at maturity, which dictates how it functions in

TREE ROOT DAMAGE TO ADJACENT PAVING. (*REEMAY, INC.*)

a landscape. Form will tell you whether a tree will fit in the space provided. Do not rely on how a young container-grown tree looks at the garden center because it may change form a number of times before it matures.

• ***Litter*** Trees cause litter as a result of flowering, producing seed, and during seasonal leaf drop. Litter is a problem around swimming pools, outdoor living spaces, and driveways. Take extra care to consider the stains caused by berries and the birds that eat them, especially near cars and light-colored paving. Large seed pods can become a hazard to foot traffic. Tree litter isn't as much of a problem on turf areas because it can be cleaned up as the lawn is mowed.

• ***Local climate*** Northern California's diversity of climate makes selecting trees a bit tricky. Too much cold and some trees will suffer from frost burn. Too much heat and they will wither each summer. The safest way to tell is by studying the tree you're considering in your community. If there are older trees of that variety growing successfully, then you can assume it is a suitable choice. If there are a few young trees of similar age, they may be replacements from losses due to periodic hard freezes or droughts which have killed off the older specimens. When you can't find any examples of that tree growing locally, you can bet there is a problem.

• ***Longevity*** This factor is sometimes difficult to judge because it will vary with climatic differences. It seems that the fastest growing trees burn out the quickest. Lombardy poplars are notorious for short life spans, along with willows and black locusts. Slow-growing hardwoods are the longest lived, but they may take your entire lifetime to mature.

• ***Leaf size*** Deciduous or evergreen, large thick leaves are easiest to remove from a swimming pool with a skimmer net, while large soft leaves disintegrate on the bottom. Trees with compound leaves like California pepper or honeylocust fall apart almost immediately. Pine needles are nearly impossible to collect, and most species shed constantly.

• ***Growth rate*** Most people are naturally impatient, and this keeps fast growing trees in demand, particularly in new subdivisions. But the trade-off for fast growth is often invasive rooting, short life span, and overwhelming size. The fruitless mulberry, once thought the perfect solution to landscaping California's postwar suburbs is now considered a liability with its rank growth, but in small gardens and courtyards, slow growth is essential for the tree to remain in scale with the space.

• ***Height and diameter at maturity*** The small tree you buy at a garden center may turn into a monster if you don't know how big it will be as an adult. Trees are measured by their overall height and the diameter of the foliage canopy. Small trees are needed beneath power lines or other utilities to prevent conflict. Knowing the expected diameter will help to determine the amount of shading a tree will provide. On large homesites, dimensions are essential when selecting trees massive enough to be in scale with the land around them.

• ***Special features*** Once a tree has passed this rigorous list of practical considerations, the final selection can be made by the special features it offers. These endearing qualities are what gives life to a landscape, with fiery autumn foliage or snowstorms of white spring blossoms. Unusual bark, colorful berries, and strange growth habits each offer a unique character to the landscape.

HOW TO BUY TREES

If you buy a tree from a reputable source, you can be assured it will be quality stock. It's worth the few extra dollars to protect such a long-term investment.

WHAT SIZE TO BUY?

Trees in California are available in containers all year around, and also as dormant bare-root stock during the winter months. Trees are priced and sold according to

NORTHERN CALIFORNIA TIP

Many trees known for their colorful leaf change in the fall do not perform well in warmer parts of northern California. The most vibrant color is a result of a warm dry summer and early autumn rains with nights cooler than 45°F. We don't often have these low temperatures in valley and coastal locations, and each fall has slightly different conditions, making the leaf color vary from year to year. Among the most unreliable species are maples and eastern type oaks.

their container sizes, either 1, 5, or 15 gallon, regardless of what kind they are. The 1-gallon trees are cost effective for quantities needed for windbreaks. The 5-gallons are usually limited to eucalyptus and other fast-growing species. Trees in 15-gallon containers have strong trunks and well-developed branching structures. Taller trees are easier to stake, and less likely to be stepped on.

Specimen trees are sold in wooden box containers, the smallest measuring 24 inches square. Boxes graduate up to 36 inches, then 48 inches and onwards up to giant specimens over 100 inches square. Boxed trees are expensive, heavy, and require special equipment to move and plant them. It's best to have a landscape contractor purchase and plant your specimen tree, because if it dies from improper handling or poor quality stock, the contractor is obliged to replace it.

Deciduous trees are sold at garden centers from late December through the end of February as bare roots. These trees have been field grown, then dug up while dormant and sold with no soil attached to the roots. This makes them much easier and lighter to ship, and the savings is passed on to you.

WHERE TO BUY TREES

The best place to buy landscape trees is from a nursery or garden center. This is a reliable source for plants, and prices are fairly standard. Garden centers doing brisk business will have a rapid turnover in trees, which keeps most of the stock fresh from the growers. If the tree dies after you plant it, many garden centers will assume the loss and give you a replacement.

Pick Out a Good Tree

Trees are an expensive investment in time and money, and like any other product it's important to get your money's worth. Take the time to sort through and inspect every individual. Look for three things when hunting for a quality tree:

RULE OF GREEN THUMB

Eucalyptus is one of the most popular landscape trees in California. A study was conducted to find out which size is the most economical using 5-, 15-, and 24-inch boxes. When planted at the same time, the 5 caught up with the 15, and the 15 eventually overtook the 24-inch box. Studies have shown that this also applies to other species of landscape trees. Although smaller trees don't have such an immediate impact, in the long run they usually out-grow the much larger container trees.

NORTHERN CALIFORNIA TIP

Because fall coloring of deciduous trees is unreliable, it is best to buy them in containers. There is considerable variation within a single species, and to obtain the best individual it must be seen while in fall color. This is impossible to do with bare root trees or when container grown trees are dormant and without their leaves. The best way is to visit a garden center or nursery in the fall to see the true coloring of container-grown trees. If one seems to have more color than the others, buy it and feel confident you are making a good decision.

• ***Shape*** The tree should have a uniform shape and even distribution of foliage in proportion with its height and diameter of the trunk.

• ***Health*** The trunk and branches should have bark that is free of wounds or gouges. There should be no broken or missing branches.

• ***Roots*** Container tree roots should have plenty of room to grow, and must not circle around on the surface of the soil or poke out through the drainage holes.

Bare-root trees are sold from December through February. Never buy a bare-root tree without a tag labeled with its variety because even experts have problems telling them apart at this age. Select bare-root trees that have the greatest number of thin, fibrous roots which have not dried out, nor been broken or crushed . If you can't plant your bare-root trees right away, heel their roots into a moist pile of leaves, sawdust, sand, or soil and keep them evenly wet.

PLANTING A TREE

Even the most perfect tree can be ruined if planted incorrectly. You'll only have to do it once, and extra care makes sure it becomes a healthy, vigorous adult.

PRE-PLANTING TREE CARE

Trees are living things that should be properly handled at all times to reduce the trauma of a change in environment. If the foliage head sticks out a window or the trunk, wrap it in burlap, a tarp, or any other protective material before you drive away. Wind can tatter foliage and rapidly pull moisture out of the leaves. Careless transportation may snap tender twigs, larger branches or even the trunk.

When you get home, immediately unload your tree

and set it in a well-drained, shady location. Check the soil moisture, and if it feels dry, fill the container with fresh water to cool it off and help ease the adjustment. Plants in containers have restricted root systems that can dry out quickly in warm weather. If more than a few days pass before planting, it will need to be watered every day.

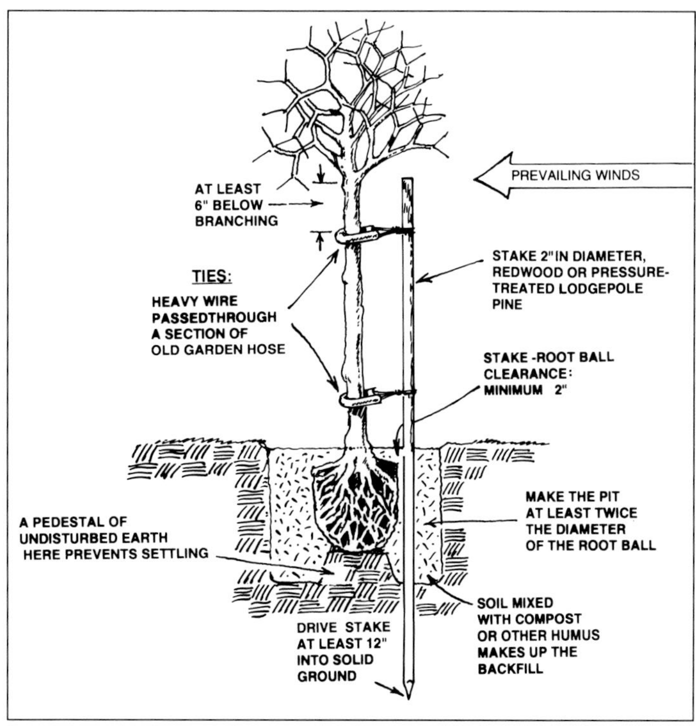

Consider Root Control Devices

Even the most well-behaved trees hunt for moisture trapped beneath paving or on the surface of lawns. Relatively inexpensive root barriers are well worth the cost and effort to install, and make it possible to plant trees in tight conditions. They must be put into the hole when the tree is first planted.

One model acts as a physical barrier and is made of rigid, heavy plastic that comes in two pieces which fit around the root ball. This shell prevents surface rooting; proper installation requires gravel packing on the outside to move water straight down to where roots are encouraged to grow.

Another product is not as well tested over time but has been accepted by some cities and counties. It consists of flexible plastic sheets that are impregnated with long-lasting, slow-release nodules of herbicide. When roots come in contact with the sheeting, the herbicide kills the tiny root hairs and halts growth, forcing the plant to move downward in the soil.

Five Golden State Steps for Successful Tree Planting

1. Dig the right hole.
Planting holes for container grown trees should be twice the diameter of the rootball. The bottom of the hole should be dome-shaped with a flat, high center, but lower around the edges so water drains away from the rootball. The dome must be undisturbed soil, high enough to set the tree at the same level it was in the container.

2. Placing the tree.
Gently remove the tree from its container and hold the rootball together tightly. Place the tree carefully in the hole. Turn it around until the best side is facing front. Now is the time to install root control barriers and pound support stakes into the undisturbed soil at the bottom of the hole.

3. Backfill the hole.
Gradually backfill the hole using the excavated soil enriched with compost and a few tablespoons of phosphate fertilizer. Replace the soil in layers, using the end of the shovel handle to pack it down as you fill. When the hole is halfway full, evenly space big blue fertilizer tablets around the hole, 1 inch away from the rootball. Use 5 per 15-gallon tree and 3 per 5-gallon tree. Fill in the rest of the hole and pack the soil down with your foot. Recheck the base of the trunk to make sure it hasn't settled below the proper level.

4. Create a basin and water generously.
When the hole is full, use the remaining soil to make a watering basin around the trunk and fill it with water. If settling of the soil around the *outside edge* of the rootball occurs, add more compost to bring the grade up to normal.

RULE OF GREEN THUMB

Many trees die within the first month after planting from crown rot, a disease caused by planting woody trees and shrubs lower than the soil level in the container. It also occurs when extra soil is mounded up around the trunk. This condition rots a ring around the base of the trunk to cut off delivery of nutrients and water to the foliage above. When a plant is set too high and the rootball is partially exposed, roots can harden off into trunk. But the trunk cannot become a root if covered with soil, and the bark rots when denied exposure to air. It's best to leave the soil beneath the rootball in the undisturbed flat topped dome to prevent unexpected settling.

NORTHERN CALIFORNIA TIP

Sunscald is one of the most common killers of young trees in Northern California. New trees have very young branching structures and foliage heads too small to properly shade their trunks. West- and south-facing sides will discolor and then blister, creating easy entry for damaging insects and diseases. In commercial orchards farmers paint young trees with white latex tree paint. For a more attractive and nearly invisible choice for landscape trees, the trunks can be wrapped in special tree tape or brown burlap.

5. Tie the tree to support stakes.
Tie each tree to its stake(s) in two points, one near the top of the tree and one much lower. You can nail the wrapping to the stake, but keep it loose around the tree to prevent girdling. In hot inland climates prevent sunscald with paint or tree wrap until the tree develops sufficient canopy to shade the bark.

AFTER-PLANTING TREE CARE

Keeping newly planted container trees evenly moist is essential, particularly during the hot summer months. Trees planted in lawns are vulnerable without a watering basin. The lawn sprinklers will not provide enough water to support the tree. To make sure your new lawn tree gets enough water, saturate the entire rootball once a week. To do this, place the end of a garden hose at the base of the trunk, then turn on the water to a trickle and leave it on overnight. Do this more frequently in hot weather until the tree is more established.

Mini-sumps to Move Water in Dense Soils

Trees grow incredibly fast once their roots reach the water table. But young trees root only on the surface due to shallow applications of water from sprinkler systems in heavy soils. To encourage tree roots to bypass this surface condition you can dig miniature sumps which help to speed water to deeper levels in the soil.

Dig sumps with a post hole digger or power auger either while the tree is being planted or in the first few years of growth. The hole should be as deep as possible, and large enough to contain a length of 4-inch perforated plastic drain pipe, which keeps the hole open. After digging, drop the pipe into the hole and then fill the center with gravel. When water is applied to the surface of the soil either by hand or sprinklers, it should drain into the sump and fill it up. The water filters into the soil gradually to draw roots downward.

Supporting Newly Planted Trees

Staking young trees is important where seasonal winds are strong or when planting from containers sized 15 gallons and larger. Stakes provide support, but in order to develop a stronger trunk, trees should be able to move a little with the wind. Long-lasting tree stakes should be either pressure-treated lodgepole pine or foundation grade redwood 2x2s. Stakes function better when pounded deeply into undisturbed soil at the bottom of the planting hole, and not through the rootball.

Trees may be supported with one stake placed on the upwind side of the rootball, but if conditions are severe a second stake may be required on the opposite side. Tie the tree to each stake in two places using soft rubber tree ties or wire protected by a piece of garden hose. The legs of discarded pantyhose are excellent for tying trees because the material is strong, flexible, and soft. After the first year, gradually loosen the ties and eventually remove them, one at a time over a few months to help the tree grow stronger.

When specimen trees are either very large or have multiple trunks, guy wires are the best means of support. Guy wires are made of heavy wire or cable with one end anchored to a stake in the ground and the other end attached to one of the main branches or trunks. Make sure you use a piece of hose on the branch end of the wire to avoid damaging the bark. Most trees require three guy wires, but in some situations more may be necessary. Sometimes a turnbuckle on each wire will help to keep it tight as the tree grows and shifts. Be careful when installing guy wires near paving or in lawns because they can be hard to see and present a hazard to foot traffic.

PRUNING TREES

There is always confusion over when and how to prune trees. Except for fruiting varieties, most require very little pruning at all. The chief problem is created when species such as fruitless mulberries and London plane trees have been "dead headed" by tree pruning companies. This severe pruning insures the tree company must return every year or two to cut back all the resulting rank growth. All trees, if carefully shaped when young require no additional pruning at all, except perhaps a mild thinning to allow more sunlight through the canopy.

THE BASICS OF MAINTENANCE PRUNING

Never attempt to prune a tree unless you know exactly why you are doing it. Maintenance pruning is the removal of selected branches for three reasons: signs of pests or disease, broken branches, and conflicting growth

HOW *NOT* TO PRUNE YOUR TREES. ONE OF THESE TWO FRUITLESS MULBERRIES IS YOUNG AND SHOWS HOW DEAD HEADING BEGINS BEFORE THE TREE HAS A CHANCE TO DEVELOP A STRONG BRANCHING STRUCTURE. THE OLDER TREE IS BADLY SCARRED FROM REPEATED HEAVY PRUNING. BOTH TREES ARE ESPECIALLY UNATTRACTIVE DURING THE WINTER.

patterns. It is important that you inspect your trees each year for these signs and take care of them promptly.

Disease Whenever you see signs of cankers, gall, fireblight, or other diseases that affect only a part of a tree, early removal will discourage spreading to other areas. This also applies to fungus growths, ant colonies, and even mistletoe. Be sure to sterilize your pruning equipment with alcohol before moving to the next tree.

Damage Trees can develop broken branches from wind storms or snow loads. Damaged limbs can be a safety hazard, and the wound becomes an inroad for disease. Broken limbs removed by proper pruning will encourage more replacement growth and less die-back.

Conflicts Whenever branches touch each other, the constant movement of the canopy creates friction wounds. Prune out these conflicting branches so that only the largest and healthiest one remains to develop properly.

COMMON GARDEN QUESTION:

"My backyard has always been shaded by a large oak tree. It blew over in a storm last winter and now I have to replace the tree and plants it once shaded. Is there any way to obtain compensation for the loss?"

Mature trees are an important asset for any homesite, and when one is lost, there will be an impact on the property value. Many homeowner's insurance policies have allowances for trees lost this way, and the IRS also permits a casualty deduction in some cases. Report the loss immediately to your insurance company so the value of the tree can be determined before it is hauled away. It is a good idea to document your trees and landscaping with photographs. When a loss or damage does occur, there will be no question of how important the tree was to the value of your property.

Shaping Young Trees

It's much easier to shape a tree when young than to correct problems at maturity. A tree should develop an evenly shaped branching structure that is loose enough to allow the movement of light and air throughout the foliage. Overly dense trees develop weak branching patterns, greater wind resistance, and become havens for insects that hide in the confusion.

As a canopy tree matures, you may have to perform the following pruning activities:

1. Gradually phase out lower branches to provide clearance to walk beneath the canopy.
2. Remove broken or conflicting branches on an annual basis, during winter when deciduous trees are bare.
3. Remove whiplike watersprouts which grow straight up from main branches on the inside of the tree.
4. Remove suckers from the base of the trunk or rootstock. They siphon off precious moisture and nutrients from the foliage canopy.
5. For specifics on fruit tree pruning, refer to chapter 14.

All pruning should be done in winter when trees are dormant and sap levels are low. If a tree is pruned during its growing season, even the cleanest wounds will become a freeway for borers to enter the tree. One exception is removal of dead branches on deciduous trees, which stand out clearly only while the tree is in leaf. Reduce moisture loss by sealing wounds with latex paint, or pruning sealer products.

PROBLEMS WITH TREES

Each year there are new pests and diseases that afflict trees in northern California, and experts are struggling to keep ahead of the changes. The best way to avoid problems is to plant pest- and disease-resistant trees. Because many tree diseases are hard to identify, take advantage of the free services of experts at the University of California Agricultural Extension network. You can also consult with a certified arborist for a fee.

COMMON PESTS AND DISEASES OF LANDSCAPE TREES

Healthy trees have their own means of resisting pests and diseases. When trees are weakened by drought, frost, or other kinds of damage, they become easy targets for pests. The best protection for your trees is to keep them healthy by providing plenty of water and fertilizer. Refer to the appendix for more detailed information on insect pests and least-toxic controls.

Mistletoe

As much as we love it during the holidays, mistletoe is a parasite that will eventually overwhelm a tree. It is spread to new trees by birds. Disturbing mistletoe while it is fruiting can help it to spread. Go after mistletoe while it's still small and without berries by cutting off the clump, and treating the remaining stem with herbicide designated for mistletoe. If it is near the end of a branch, cut off the end about 12 inches above the infected area.

Ant Farming

Don't panic if you discover colonies of ants on your trees. The presence of ants indicates there may be other insects such as scale and aphids, which can harm plants. Ants may also originate from inside the tree where the colony is nesting in soft, decaying wood.

Borers

The larvae of these beetles cause serious damage as they tunnel beneath the bark of trees. Bark damage from sunscald or careless equipment use is the most common point of entry. The obvious signs of borer damage are patches of loose bark and tunnels underneath filled with mealy residue from the larvae. Treat borer damage as soon as it occurs by cleaning up the wound, and follow the tunnels until you find the larvae or an exit hole.

Equipment Damage

Trees growing in lawns take a terrible beating from mowers and string trimmers, which can girdle the soft bark of a youngster in seconds. Repeated bumping by lawn mowers gouges the bark and invites borers. You can buy plastic sleeves to protect the bases of your trees, or keep a collar of bare ground, about 12 inches to 30 inches from the trunk, on all sides. This keeps equipment away from the trunk and also allows water to filter directly into the root zone.

Wildlife

Deer and rabbits can severely damage trees. Both animals are more active at night and may rarely be seen. Deer chew both leaves and bark, especially during the winter when other food sources are dormant. A buck can ruin tree bark when rubbing felt from its antlers. When food is scarce, rabbits gnaw bark from tree trunks, which is often mistaken for mower damage. There are many types of materials said to discourage both rabbits and deer, but most have to be renewed on a regular basis, and effectiveness may vary with individual herds. The only sure protection is fencing.

PRESERVING NATIVE OAK TREES

All native oak trees in northern California are sensitive to disturbances in their environment. An established oak tree is most affected by changes to the soil beneath the limits of the canopy, an area called the dripline. Whenever the soil is raised, lowered, compacted,

CALIFORNIA NATIVE *QUERCUS LOBATA*, THE VALLEY OAK, IN THE DRY GRASSLANDS OF ITS NATURAL HABITAT.

A RARE EXAMPLE OF A NATIVE CALIFORNIA OAK TREE GROWING IN IRRIGATED LAWN.

watered or tilled, there will be an impact on the oak tree's health.

Builders are trying to work around native oaks, and although there may be strict guidelines for protection, the trees often die anyway. Although the area within the dripline of an oak remains untouched, development can change the way water moves on the land and sometimes this alters groundwater availability. Even oaks in livestock pastures are susceptible to soil compaction from cattle collecting in the trees' shade.

PRESERVING THE DRIPLINE

The soil within the dripline of a native oak tree is sacred ground. Do not cultivate, trench, or move equipment across it, and it's even helpful to prevent foot traffic. The natural buildup of leaves and litter provides valuable humus for the surface feeder roots. Gradual compaction of the soil over a few years may reduce the downward movement of water and food, causing serious damage.

Oaks expect water only at specific times of the year, and live off rainfall and sometimes groundwater. When this rhythm is interrupted by watering too often or in the wrong season, an incurable condition called oak root fungus (*Armillaria mellea*) may occur, which will kill the oak and other landscape plants as well. If the soil outside the dripline is kept constantly moist, this too can stimulate growth of the fungus into the drier area. To be safe, you can extend the limits of your preservation zone beyond the official dripline.

Define the dripline or preservation zone with a redwood headerboard staked into place. The soil within the board should be covered with about 2 inches of ground bark, crushed walnut shells, or other suitable organic matter that won't pack down. It must act like the natural litter to keep roots cool and retain moisture. The mulch also helps to discourage weeds, because herbicides should not be used within the dripline.

HOW TO PLANT NATIVE OAKS

If you want to plant native California oaks around your home, don't go out and buy container grown seedlings. By the time a baby oak is just 2 inches tall, it may have a deep tap root that moves quickly downward into the soil seeking moisture necessary to survive its first dry season. When oaks are container grown, the tap root is so distorted it will probably die within a year.

The most successful plantings of native oaks have been with partially germinated acorns. This places viable seed directly in the soil where it will readily sprout and root deeply. Compensate for a natural mortality rate by increasing the number of acorns you plant. Follow these three easy steps:

1. Gather fresh acorns in the fall from nearby wild trees. Soak them in water for a day and throw out any that float.
2. Put the acorns into a plastic bag and store it in the refrigerator for one month.
3. The acorns are now ready to be planted in January or February to receive the late winter rains. Place each acorn on its side, and cover with 1 inch of soil. If you have squirrels or gophers nearby, place the acorns 2 to 3 inches deep. During the first two summers it helps to water the acorns occasionally with a deep soaking. Under normal rainfall conditions they should take hold on their own.

NATIVE CALIFORNIA SCRUB OAKS.

TREE SELECTION GUIDE

	Evergreen Trees	Spring-Flowering	Fall Color	Well-Mannered Shade Tree	Small Accent Trees	Night Lighting Subjects	California Natives	Drought Tolerant	Oak-Root-Fungus Resistant
Acacia baileyana	•	•						•	
Acacia longifolia	•				•			•	•
Acacia melanoxylon	•							•	
Acer palmatum			•		•	•			•
Albizia julibrissin		•				•		•	
Alnus cordata				•					
Betula pendula			•		•				
Cedrus deodara	•			•				•	
Ceratonia siliqua	•			•				•	•
Cinnamomum camphora	•			•				•	
Cornus florida		•	•		•				
Eucalyptus nicholii	•			•				•	
Eucalyptus sideroxylon 'Rosea'	•	•						•	
Ginkgo biloba			•	•					•
Grevillea robusta	•	•		•				•	
Lagerstroemia indica		•			•	•		•	
Laurus nobilis	•			•	•			•	
Liquidambar styraciflua			•	•					
Liriodendron tulipifera		•	•	•					•
Magnolia grandiflora	•	•		•					•
Magnolia soulangiana		•			•	•			
Magnolia stellata		•			•				
Maytenus boaria	•				•	•			•
Olea europaea 'Swan Hill'	•			•				•	
Pinus canariensis	•			•				•	•
Pinus pinea	•			•		•		•	
Pistacia chinensis			•	•				•	•
Platanus acerifolia				•					
Podocarpus gracilior	•			•				•	
Prunus cerasifera 'Atropupurea'		•		•	•				
Prunus serrulata 'Kwanzan'		•			•				
Prunus subhirtella 'Pendula'		•			•				
Pyrus calleryana 'Bradford'		•		•					
Quercus palustris			•	•					
Quercus suber	•			•		•		•	
Rhus lancea	•			•				•	
Robinia ambigua 'Idahoensis'		•						•	
Salix babylonica									
Sapium sebiferum			•	•					•
Schinus molle	•					•		•	
Sequoia sempervirens	•			•			•		•
Ulmus parvifolia				•					•

NORTHERN CALIFORNIA'S BEST LANDSCAPE TREES

Note: Although zone 1 is indicated for many trees, this applies primarily to middle elevations of high mountain ranges. Even some of the hardiest plants cannot tolerate the thin, infertile soils and snow loads of the high country. Approximate height and diameter are indicated to show how much space to allow for design purposes. Rooting is one of the most critical issues, and those indicated as invasive or shallow rooting must be located far from septic tanks, water lines, sewer pipes, and paving. All trees benefit from root control devices if planted on city lots.

ACACIA

Acacias originate in arid Australia and all thrive in our dry climate. Although highly drought tolerant, acacias also have invasive roots, frost sensitivity, and brittle branching structures. Many people are allergic to the blossoms. Plant flowering acacias in those forgotten corners of the garden for a drought- and heat-tolerant source of bright yellow color. Use the others for shade and foliage in difficult spots where no other trees will grow.

Acacia baileyana

Bailey Acacia Zones 7 and 5
Evergreen, 30 feet tall, 20 feet wide. Full sun.
Drought-tolerant accent tree. Shallow rooting.

This is the most unique member of the large genus *Acacia*, with fernlike leaves and foliage a unique shade of blue-gray. Bailey acacia is not a long-lived tree, and has brittle branching. If grown with a single trunk it will develop into a round headed tree, but if broken or pruned it resorts to a rangy, shrubby form. Flowers are fuzzy, light yellow balls that appear in clusters from January to March. Like all acacias it is drought tolerant and not particular about soil type. A cultivar 'Purpurea' is superior, with contrasting burgundy-colored new growth.

Acacia longifolia

Sydney Golden Wattle Zone 7
Evergreen, 20 feet tall, 20 feet wide. Full sun.
Drought-tolerant accent tree. Shallow rooting.

Although often used as a shrub, this frost-tender acacia will become a small tree over time. Its long flat leaves are the source of its species name, and it too has the characteristic round yellow blossoms. Often used in coastal plantings due to its tolerance of salt air and alkaline, sandy soils. Its strong root system helps cover slopes and reduce erosion. In one case a close relative was used on a series of steeply cut slopes, and every two to three years each individual is topped to about 4 feet tall. This reduction in foliage promotes a deeper and more dense root system, which proved highly successful for landslide control. Resistant to oak root fungus.

TOP: *ACACIA BAILEYANA* 'PURPUREA'
LEFT: *ACACIA BAILEYANA* IN FLOWER.

Acacia melanoxylon

Blackwood Acacia Zones 3, 5 and 7
Evergreen, 40 feet tall, 25 feet wide. Full sun.
Drought tolerant. Shallow, aggressive rooting.

Although listed as hardy in zone 3, the freeze of 1990 devastated the blackwood acacia population in the central valley. Trees that weren't killed entirely died down to a few inches above the ground. With fast growth and tolerance of heat, smog, and poor soils, it is an excellent evergreen shade tree. Invasively rooted, it should not be located where paving or structures may be damaged. Foliage is dense, brownish green, and unattractive, messy flowers appear in late spring. Best use is on large homesites or avenues where there is enough space for it to spread both above and below ground.

Acer palmatum

Japanese maple Zones 1 to 7
Deciduous, 20 feet tall, 15 feet wide. Shade, part shade. Fall color accent tree. Shallow, fine rooting.

Japanese maples are striking small landscape trees with a brilliant fall color display. The shade and brilliancy of hue may vary with climate, and there is quite a bit of diversity among those grown from seed. An important tree for shade gardens, some varieties are small enough to be considered shrubs. Japanese maples tend to develop thin, whiplike twigs when young, and, to achieve the best sculptural character, the tips should be nipped back on a regular basis to promote a finer branching pattern. Visit the Japanese Tea Garden at Golden Gate Park in San Francisco to see well-shaped specimens.

Japanese maples are sensitive to inland heat and foliage will burn in late afternoon summer sun. Plant where sheltered by buildings or shade tree canopy for best results. These trees are more expensive than other types in the same-sized container, particularly unusual grafted varieties. It can be more economical to buy them with roots balled and burlapped where available. Various cultivars offer unique lacy or cut-leaf patterns. An important component in Oriental inspired gardens, it is a good companion for azaleas, camellias, dogwood, and many other acid-loving plants.

Albizia julibrissin

Mimosa Zones 2 to 7

Deciduous, 35 feet tall, 35 feet wide. Full sun. Drought-tolerant flowering shade tree. Shallow rooting.

The shape of the mimosa tree is similar to the broad-headed thorn trees of the African plains, and is complementary with both modern and Victorian architecture. Lacy, fernlike foliage provides light, filtered shade, and pink, power-puff flowers cover the branches in spring. Deciduous mimosa has a serious litter problem with leaves and flowers, compounded by long seed pods. Very drought and cold tolerant, mimosa can survive on natural rainfall, although it's considered a short-lived tree. This tree is at its best when planted in lawns where the mower can collect the litter and bag it conveniently for you. Avoid planting near patios, driveways, and especially swimming pools.

Alnus cordata

Italian Alder Zones 2 to 7

Deciduous, 45 feet tall, 25 feet wide. Full sun, shade. Shade tree. Shallow, invasive rooting.

In the wild, the California native alder grows in riparian areas near rivers and streams. The native, plagued by disease and short lived, is being replaced by the Italian alder where soils are poorly drained or perpetually wet. Its pyramid shape suggests planting in dense groupings. It is fast-growing, with a pointed, glossy leaf. Slightly less aggressively rooted than native alders, it bears the same light gray bark. One of the best northern California landscape trees for semiformal plantings.

Betula pendula

White Birch Zones 1 to 7

Deciduous, 30 feet tall, 15 feet wide. Sun coast, shade inland. Attractive bark accent tree. Deep rooting.

Although birch trees are planted all over northern California, they don't seem to grow very well in hot inland locations. Many small trees either grow poorly or die out, and sunburn on trunk and branches becomes a haven for borers. More successful when protected by a woodland of evergreen trees. Birches are better suited to areas with cold winters and cool summer nights, and where soil moisture is plentiful. They are loved for their papery white bark and weeping growth habit that varies with each individual. For best effect it should be planted in groves from three to five or more, where the combined density of foliage is sufficient to shade the root zone and reduce soil temperature.

Cedrus deodara

Deodar Cedar Zones 2 to 7

Evergreen conifer. 100 feet tall, 50 feet wide. Full sun. Shade tree. Deep rooting.

The old stands of deodar cedars in northern California with their soft, pendulous branches are strikingly beautiful. They are good examples of how large trees can modify the climate and growing conditions beneath them. Broad evergreen canopies cause lawns to die out and soil acidity to increase, creating perfect conditions for acid-loving plants. Tolerant of poor soils and drought conditions, ample watering makes them grow more quickly. Deodar cedars are not subject to insects or disease and they make good lawn trees. Do not underestimate the mature size because these cedars will crowd out or deform smaller trees forced to compete for light and water. Supply additional water from the garden hose to stimulate growth of young trees planted in lawns.

Ceratonia siliqua

Carob Tree Zones 3, 5 and 7

Evergreen, 35 feet tall, 30 feet wide. Full sun. Shade tree. Deep rooting.

Even in the milder zones of the central valley, the carob trees suffered foliage burn in the 1990 freeze. Despite complete defoliation, most trees totally leafed out again the following summer. This is a valuable landscape tree that has very neat growth habits and foliage. It can be encouraged into formal standards or allowed to become more irregular for natural plantings that make good subjects for night lighting. It is a frost-tolerant substitute for *Ficus nitida*, a common southern California street tree. The carob tree has insignificant yellow flowers that mature into long pods, which can be a litter problem. These pods are the source of the chocolate substitute, carob.

Pods are highly nutritious and used as fodder for livestock in many countries.

Cinnamomum camphora

Camphor Tree Zones 3, 5 and 7
Evergreen, 40 feet tall, 30 feet wide. Full sun. Aromatic foliage shade tree. Heavy, invasive rooting.

The camphor tree is easily identified by the strong scent of the foliage when crushed, and is the source of camphor oil. It is a pest-free, spreading shade tree that is not particular about alkaline soil, heat, or water supply. Slow-growing but aggressive roots will damage paving, and ultimate size is not suitable for small sites. The thickness of its foliage head creates dense shade, and leaves do not readily break down for leaf mold, compost, or amendments. Although evergreen, it will drop leaves constantly along with black berries in summer, which restricts its use near swimming pools. The camphor tree has a very uniform growth rate and makes an excellent street tree if root control devices are installed.

Cornus florida 'Rubra'

Pink Flowering Dogwood Zones 1 to 7
Deciduous, 25 feet tall, 20 feet wide. Shade, part shade. Flowering and fall color accent tree. Deep rooting .

High in the Sierra Nevada foothill gardens, the pink flowering dogwood achieves its best color and growth. But even in hot valley locations it does well when shaded by buildings or tall tree canopies. This slow-growing tree offers both spectacular flowers and fall color. Even a very young tree will burst into bloom in late spring with varying shades of coral pink; perfect for small patios or near windows where it can be thoroughly enjoyed. As temperatures fall in autumn, the dogwood shows its bright red leaves in cooler elevations of the foothills. A good small tree to provide interest for gardens beneath older shade trees, dogwood blends in with azaleas and other acid-loving plants. California native dogwood, *Cornus nuttallii,* has white flowers and is not often grown because of sensitivity to root disturbance and irrigation water.

CORNUS FLORIDA 'RUBRA'

EUCALYPTUS

These Australian natives have long been one of the most popular trees in California due to rapid growth and resistance to pests and disease. They exude an aromatic oil from their roots and leaves into the soil to discourage germination of other plants that may compete for their water. This sometimes makes establishment of other landscape plants around eucalyptus difficult.

Eucalypti grow too fast to develop adequate structural integrity, and this is illustrated by the fact that numerous limbs drop from old stands after high winds. In hardpan soils the trees will develop shallow "pancake" root systems, and after heavy rains tall specimens may blow over. For the first few years after planting, landscapers have begun pruning off the top 30 percent of the trees' annual growth in order to encourage the trunk and root systems to become stronger. In many cases eucalypti are used in two-phase tree programs to provide immediate effect until the more long-lived shade trees mature. The eucalypti are then removed to allow the shade trees to develop without crowding.

There are so many species of eucalyptus sold for windbreaks, evergreen screens, and shade trees that many are of unknown origin. At one time they were planted in wood lots in California to provide fuel for steam locomotives, but were later abandoned when the wood proved unsuitable. Cuttings from these stands are frequently propagated and sold unidentified. It is important to know the exact species of eucalyptus in order to avoid trees far too large for residential landscapes.

For the gardeners who enjoy the florist's eucalyptus, it is sold as *Eucalyptus pulverulenta,* common name: silver mountain gum. It is a very small, sprawling tree that has limited landscape value and is not widely grown because of sensitivity to frost.

THE SOFT COLORING OF EUCALYPTUS BARK.

Eucalyptus nicholii

Nichol's Willow-Leaved Peppermint Zones 3, 5 and 7. Evergreen, 40 feet tall, 30 feet wide. Full sun. Shade or screen tree. Shallow, invasive rooting.

This tree does not achieve gigantic proportions, and weeping foliage makes it one of the most graceful species for landscaping. It has the typical eucalyptus bark that peels off occasionally to reveal the buff tones of its smooth trunk. *Nicholii* should be topped vigorously when young to promote stronger branching structure.

Eucalyptus sideroxylon 'Rosea'

Pink Ironbark Zones 3, 5 and 7
Evergreen, 45 feet tall, 20 feet wide. Full sun. Aromatic shade or screen tree. Shallow, invasive rooting.

This eucalyptus is unique because of its dark red rough-textured bark and large pink flowers. The foliage and small stems also have a rosy tint. Pink ironbark is slower growing, but has become popular due to its strong branching structure. Like all members of its family, this tree is tolerant of poor soil, low water supply, and persistent winds.

Ginkgo biloba

Maidenhair Tree Zones 1 to 7
Deciduous, 70 feet tall, 50 feet wide. Full sun. Fall color shade tree. Deep rooting.

The ginkgo tree is a living fossil and has changed little in the last 125 million years. It has a primitive branching structure that makes it technically a conifer, despite its broad, fan-shaped leaves. The ginkgo tree is notorious for slow growth, and it has been documented as growing only 10 feet in nine years. But its beautiful leaves and brilliant gold fall color make the ginkgo well worth the wait. Ultimately it becomes a very large shade tree tolerant of a wide variety of conditions. The female tree of this species produces messy fruit with an offensive odor, and **only male trees** should be used in landscapes.

Grevillea robusta

Silk Oak Zones 3, 5 and 7
Evergreen, 60 feet tall, 25 feet wide. Full sun. Drought tolerant shade tree. Invasive rooting.

Yet another drought-tolerant Australian native, the silk oak offers fast growth, but will become brittle and lose

MATURE EUCALYPTUS GROWN WITHOUT PRUNING SHOW THE TREE'S NATURAL SHAPE.

branches in winds. Its lacy foliage is complemented by exotic golden orange flowers that bloom only at the top of the tree. Faded flowers and seed pods are a moderate litter problem. Can be sensitive to transplanting and has been known to suddenly defoliate, but leaves soon grow back. Experienced damage in 1990 freeze, which killed the entire top of some trees, and temporarily defoliated the rest.

Lagerstroemia indica

Crape Myrtle Zones 2 to 7

Deciduous, 20 feet tall, 15 feet wide. Full sun.

Flowering accent tree. Shallow rooting.

The crape myrtle flowers in late summer when few other trees are blooming. Its flowers in shades of pink, violet, and watermelon red are borne on spires at the ends of every branch. Slow growth makes it ideal for small landscapes or courtyards. The crape myrtle has sinuous branches that are wrapped in a smooth bark like that of eucalyptus, with patches of soft tan and gray. Leaves may mildew where there is too much shade or moisture. Prune back branch tips after flowers have dropped off to promote new growth that will support flowers in the coming year.

A close-up of *Grevillea* flowers borne on the upper branches of the tree.

A very large, mature crape myrtle tree.

Ginkgo biloba in fall color.

Close-up of brilliant crape myrtle flowers.

A YOUNG *LIRIODENDRON* TREE SHOWING SYMMETRICAL FORM AND FALL COLOR.

Laurus nobilis

Sweet Bay, Grecian Laurel Zones 2 to 7
Evergreen, 25 feet tall, 20 feet wide. Full sun. Drought tolerant, aromatic foliage. Deep rooting.

The leaves from this tree are the traditional "laurels" of ancient Greece, and is the commercial source of bay leaves for cooking. The Romans sheared them to release the strong scent into courtyard gardens. It's a natural for California landscapes because of dense foliage that can be sheared into various shapes or left to grow into its open, upright form. Protect the trunk from sunscald until foliage head is large enough to provide shade. Good companion for other drought-tolerant and California native plants.

Although not the same genus, another tree *Umbellularia californica,* the native California bay, is almost identical to sweet bay. It is very drought-tolerant, extremely long-lived and much less formal, often having multiple trunks. The leaves are also aromatic and suitable for use as seasoning. The California laurel is a good evergreen tree for planting with other natives and water thrifty plants.

Liquidambar styraciflua

American Sweet Gum Zones 1 to 7
Deciduous, 35 feet tall, 25 feet wide. Full sun. Fall color shade tree. Shallow rooting.

Liquidambar is one of the most reliable sources of fall color for warm regions of California where temperatures fail to stimulate color in other species. It is a tall and narrow tree, the canopy providing only limited shade. Growth rate is moderate, but may be quicker with plenty of water. Beware of surface roots that can damage paving. Litter from golf-ball-sized, hard seed pods occurs in late fall, and some individuals will produce more pods than others. Over twenty different named clones provide a varying array of fall color, from predominately yellow to fiery reds and purple.

Liriodendron tulipifera

Tulip Tree Zones 1 to 7
Deciduous, 75 feet tall, 35 feet wide. Full sun. Fall color shade tree. Deep rooting.

This is one of the most well-behaved species for use as a street tree, because it has no bad habits and rooting does not threaten paving. The tulip tree is a very slow grower for the first 5 to 7 years, but then takes off rapidly

MAGNOLIA GRANDIFLORA WITH MULTIPLE TRUNKS.

until it reaches maturity. Leaves are large and lyre shaped, providing shade that is sufficiently dense to reduce temperatures beneath them. Baseball-size yellow tulip-shaped flowers, the source of its name, occur on upper branches as the tree matures. Very long lived and requires plenty of room to develop properly.

MAGNOLIA SOULANGIANA

Magnolia grandiflora

Southern Magnolia Zones 3, 5 and 7

Evergreen, 60 feet tall, 50 feet wide. Full sun, part shade. Flowering shade tree. Deep rooting.

There are many beautiful old specimens of this classic magnolia on sites of Victorian homes in the central valley. Its large, stiff leaves are glossy on one side and fuzzy brown on the other. Large white, fragrant flowers bloom off and on during a long season from April to July. Litter from the petals and resulting seed structures can be a problem near paving. Foliage renews every other year or so, resulting in considerable leaf drop. This magnolia is sensitive to reflected heat and low moisture levels, which drastically reduce the already slow growth rate. Performs best in deep valley soils with a high water table. Keep evenly moist.

MAGNOLIA SOULANGIANA FLOWERS.

Magnolia soulangiana

Saucer Magnolia Zones 1 to 7

Deciduous, 20 feet tall, 20 feet wide. Sun coast, part shade inland. Flowering shade or accent tree. Deep rooting.

When the saucer magnolia comes into bloom in early spring it is a sight to behold, with very large white or pink tulip-shaped flowers. The tree is literally clothed in color that precedes foliage. Our inland summers and hot winds are a problem for the saucer magnolia, particularly when young. Early morning moisture or sprinkler water on leaves causes burning and discoloration. May also be damaged by too much hot afternoon sun, making a north or east exposure a must. Root system is fibrous and sensitive to disturbance from planting shrubs within its dripline. Take extra care in transplanting to keep rootball intact. Growth rate is slow; keep soil evenly moist and mulch to cool roots in summer. Many known cultivars with varying flower shape, size, and color.

A YOUNG MAGNOLIA STELLATA.

Magnolia stellata

Star Magnolia Zones 2 to 7

Deciduous, 10 feet tall, 15 feet wide. Full sun, part shade. Flowering accent tree. Deep rooting.

The little star magnolia is often forgotten in favor of more colorful flowering trees. This is unfortunate because a close look at the fancy white starlike flowers will make anyone an instant fan. This magnolia is very easy to grow and responds to careful pruning that transforms its shrubby tendencies into a much neater form. Blooms very early in spring along with primroses; prune after flower-

MAYTENUS BOARIA

OLEA EUROPAEA 'SWAN HILL'

ing. Roots are sensitive to disturbance; keep evenly moist. Plant on north and east exposure to prevent foliage burn. Excellent for small urban gardens and a good choice to make beginner gardeners look like pros.

Maytenus boaria

Mayten Tree Zones 3, 5 and 7

Evergreen, 20 feet tall, 15 feet wide. Full sun, part shade. Accent tree. Deep rooting.

For landscapes that are very short on space, the dainty mayten tree may be the perfect solution. Occasionally you may find a mature specimen that shows its true beauty, with slender weeping branches covered in tiny, light green leaves. Consider it a miniature evergreen weeping willow with none of the bad habits, suitable for patios and courtyards. Although drought tolerant, the mayten tree grows very well in lawns, its rooting being deep enough to avoid competing with the roots of grasses. Excellent subject for night lighting. Buy in larger sizes because growth rate is very slow, particularly in the early years.

Olea europaea 'Swan Hill'

Fruitless Olive Zones 3, 5 and 7

Evergreen, 25 feet tall, 20 feet wide. Full sun. Drought-tolerant shade tree. Moderate rooting.

The olive has been a part of the California landscape since mission days when it was the tree of choice for both shade and fruit. Drought tolerant, indifferent to soils, and susceptible to very few diseases or pests, the olive makes a beautiful landscape tree. Mature trunk and branches become thick and gnarled, an excellent subject for night lighting. This hybrid lacks both flower and fruit, which eliminates staining and litter problems. Fruit production in existing olive trees can be reduced by expensive spraying during the flowering cycle, but timing is critical to its effectiveness. Grows best in warm inland areas. Good companion for other drought tolerant plants and California natives.

Pinus canariensis

Canary Island Pine Zones 3, 5 and 7

Evergreen conifer, 70 feet tall, 25 feet wide. Full sun. Drought-tolerant shade tree. Deep rooting.

The Canary Island pine is one of the most graceful pines for landscaping, with soft needles sometimes 12 inches long and an open, tiered growth habit. It is marginally hardy in the central valley, and during the 1990 freeze many completely defoliated, but needles returned the following spring. Like all pines it is drought tolerant and prefers warm dry conditions. Lower branches naturally die out as it matures, making an excellent shade tree. A unique feature is its ability to sprout from the ends of cut branches. Spindly when young. Litter from 8-inch cones.

Pinus pinea

Italian Stone Pine Zones 3, 5 and 7

Evergreen conifer, 60 feet tall, 40 feet wide. Full sun. Drought tolerant shade tree. Deep rooting.

A visit to the California state capitol in Sacramento will show how truly magnificent this tree is when mature. It can also be found in old plantings throughout the northern state with the characteristic broad foliage head atop an immense trunk. Typically drought tolerant, the Italian stone pine eventually grows on natural rainfall or groundwater into a gigantic tree that shades a vast area. An excellent tree for the coast, it is not damaged by the persistent winds. Good for Mediterranean or Spanish architecture and companion for California natives and other drought-tolerant plants.

Pistacia chinensis

Chinese pistache Zones 3, 5 and 7
Deciduous, 40 feet tall, 30 feet wide. Full sun.
Fall-color shade tree. Deep rooting.

Few trees can rival the pistache for brilliant fall color, with its many shades of bright orange-red. Very drought tolerant, it is a slow grower and branches can become lanky. Foliage head is made more dense if lightly pruned and thinned while young. Trees can be either male or female, producing red nut clusters that are ornamental, but create litter. Nuts are inedible and used commercially for oil. Prefers direct sun and is resistant to reflected heat. Leaves are compound, disintegrating into slender leaflets, making the tree unsuitable for planting near swimming pools.

PINUS PINEA

Platanus acerifolia

London Plane Tree Zones 2 to 7
Deciduous, 60 feet tall, 35 feet wide. Full sun.
Shade tree. Shallow, invasive rooting.

Plane trees are commonly planted throughout northern California despite the perpetual struggle with both anthracnose and powdery mildew. Both diseases cause leaves to turn brown and drop prematurely during the summer. Spraying can reduce the problem but not eliminate it. Variety 'Bloodgood' is resistant to anthracnose, and 'Yarwood' is resistant to mildew, but neither is resistant to both. Water-loving trees, they are fast growing, but very aggressive roots become a liability that can easily heave paving and damage foundations. Under some conditions they can also survive limited drought. Trees litter with unseasonal leaf drop and golf-ball-size seed pods that disintegrate into tiny fluffy seeds that are a problem for swimming pools. Not recommended, but existing trees should be preserved and sprayed annually to discourage disease.

A close relative, *Platanus racemosa* is our native sycamore that grows in dry washes of southern California, where it feeds off water trapped deep in the soil. Although it will grow in the northern state, it is also subject to diseases. In contrast to the rigid plane tree, the native sycamore is very irregular and loved for its rustic character, textured bark, and immense leaves.

PISTACIA CHINENSIS

Podocarpus gracilior

Fern Pine Zones 3, 5 and 7
Evergreen, 50 feet tall, 30 feet wide. Full sun, part shade. Screen or shade tree. Deep rooting.

Despite its size at maturity, landscapers persist in planting this tree beneath the eaves of houses. The result is constant pruning and shearing to keep it small. But when the fern pine is allowed to grow naturally it becomes a very beautiful tree, with foliage colors in various shades of blue, gray, and green. Staking for support when young reduces the tendency to sucker. Many trees were lost entirely during the 1990 freeze and they should be planted only in mild coastal areas. Slow growth rate can be speeded up with plenty of deep watering. An excellent pest-free screen or patio tree.

NOTE: Both plums and cherries are members of the genus Prunus and the botanical names can be confusing.

Prunus cerasifera 'Atropurpurea'

Purple Leaf Plum Zones 1 to 7
Deciduous, 30 feet tall, 20 feet wide. Full sun.
Purple foliage, flowering accent tree. Moderate rooting.

Our warm California climate prevents growing the purple-leafed beech, but this flowering plum makes a

PRUNUS SERRULATA 'KWANZAN'

PRUNUS SUBHIRTELLA 'PENDULA'

great substitute. Its foliage is a rich purple that provides contrast against green leaf backgrounds, and full-sun exposure will promote a much richer hue. In spring it bursts into a mass of light pink flowers that often occur at the same time as the white blossoming flowering pear. Durable, it tolerates heat and some drought, and has a compact size suitable for small gardens. The flowering plum has many traits in common with the fruiting varieties and tends to cross branch, sucker, and develop water sprouts, which are best removed while dormant. Many cultivars including 'Hollywood,' 'Thundercloud,' and 'Vesuvius.' They have either very small fruit or none at all. Insist on a labeled variety to insure against unwanted fruit.

Prunus serrulata 'Kwanzan'

Flowering Cherry Zones 1 to 7
Deciduous, 30 feet tall, 20 feet wide. Full sun.
Flowering accent tree. Moderate rooting.

This is the tree used in the famous cherry tree plantings of Washington, D.C., that cause such a stir when they bloom each spring. Although there are many other varieties of flowering cherry, this is the most reliable and frost hardy. Its flowers are fragrant, deep pink, and fully double, with up to thirty petals each. In warmer zones of California it may not be as long lived as in cold winter areas. All cherries are subject to sunscald. The unique and attractive bark of the trunk should be protected until the foliage canopy has grown large enough to provide shade.

Prunus subhirtella 'Pendula'

Weeping Japanese Cherry Zones 2 to 7
Deciduous, 15 feet tall, 15 feet wide. Part shade.
Weeping, flowering accent tree. Deep rooting.

When this little cherry blooms it will be the focal point of the landscape for a few weeks each spring. The drooping branches become wreathed in pink flowers that appear like tendrils of long flowing hair, and to make the most of this quality it should be located where no other tree will crowd it and disturb the symmetrical form. Avoid direct exposure to hot winds or afternoon sun. The tree you buy in the nursery is created by cleft grafting three or more separate pieces of weeping scion wood into the top of a tall rootstock. This is why the trunk is so large and the branching occurs abruptly at the top.

Old-time gardeners trained the branches into a flat-topped umbrella shape by weighting more upright limbs with stones or little bags of gravel. Because of the multiple grafts, weeping cherries can lose scion wood if transplanted in very hot, windy weather or if the rootball is damaged. Protect the trunks from sunscald, and if any of the grafts die immediately after planting, contact the nursery where it was purchased and request a replacement.

PYRUS

For many years *Pyrus kawakamii* was the only flowering pear used in landscaping. Its main drawback was susceptibility to fire blight, a disease that afflicts members of the rose family and is spread by pruning equipment. The newer Bradford pear is resistant to fireblight, but isn't as beautiful as *kawakamii.*

Pyrus calleryana 'Bradford'

Bradford Pear Zones 1 to 7
Deciduous, 40 feet tall, 25 feet wide. Full sun.
Flowering accent or shade tree. Deep rooting.

The Bradford pear is an excellent tree for home landscaping because it grows quickly into a moderately sized shade tree. In spring it is covered with little white flowers at about the same time as the flowering plum. This variety has a noticeably upright branching structure when young and requires little special care except removal of suckers or water sprouts. Fire blight resistant.

PYRUS CALLERYANA 'BRADFORD'

QUERCUS

The large family of oaks are the most disease resistant and reliable trees in landscaping today. Unfortunately they are painfully slow growing, although some species are more active than others. Most require from twenty to twenty-five years to develop good character. As a rule they root deeply when young as a means of quickly reaching ground water to survive dry spells. California native oaks are difficult to grow in containers for this reason, and it's advisable to buy trees as young as possible in order to take advantage of this survival mechanism.

All oaks produce acorns and wind-pollinated catkins that create a litter problem. They should not be planted near swimming pools and do best where the acorns can remain scattered around the tree to encourage wildlife. The three oak species fully described below have been selected to represent a cross section of characteristics. The following list includes those landscape-quality oak trees that are also suitable for northern California gardens:

Quercus coccinea	Scarlet Oak
Quercus douglassii	California Blue Oak (native)
Quercus ilex	Holly Oak
Quercus lobata	Valley Oak (native)
Quercus rubra	Red Oak

CLOSE-UP OF CORK OAK BARK.

Quercus palustris

Pin Oak Zones 1 to 7
Deciduous, 80 feet tall, 35 feet wide. Full sun.
Shade tree. Shallow rooting.

This tree belongs to the group that may loosely be termed "eastern" oaks because they grow very upright, with a pointed top and single trunk. Their uniformity of growth is great for boulevard plantings or as street trees. leaves fall cleanly, but in most parts of California they persist until spring. Pin oaks require a good water supply to grow properly and are an excellent choice for lawn plantings.

Quercus suber

Cork Oak Zones 2 to 7
Evergreen, 70 feet tall, 65 feet wide. Full sun.
Unusual bark, drought-tolerant shade tree.
Deep rooting.

The thick, spongy bark of this tree is the source of commercial cork, and children find its texture irresistible.

Cork oaks are excellent trees for landscaping because of their evergreen, pendulous foliage and well mannered growth habits. Very slow growing, they are tolerant of drought, heat, smog, and wind but sensitive to extreme frosts. Cork oaks are good street trees or companion plants for Mediterranean inspired gardens, and they grow under similar conditions as those of California natives.

Rhus lancea

African Sumac Zones 3, 5 and 7
Evergreen, 25 feet tall, 20 feet wide. Full sun.
Drought-tolerant shade tree. Moderate rooting.

African sumac is not a large tree, and with its spreading crown has become a popular multiple-trunked specimen. However, it is also very attractive with a single trunk and is used extensively as a street and parking lot tree throughout California. Foliage is aromatic in hot weather and branches are slow growing and look like willow. Insignificant flowers have a scent that may be offensive to some. Sumac is one of the best small broadleaf evergreens for very hot, dry environments, and in some areas it may survive after irrigation has been phased out.

Robinia ambigua 'Idahoensis'

Idaho Locust Zones 2 to 7
Deciduous, 50 feet tall, 30 feet wide. Full sun.
Drought-tolerant, flowering shade tree.
Invasive rooting.

The Idaho locust is one of the best flowering trees for drought-tolerant gardens, with its long, wisteria-like clusters of generous rose pink blooms. Drought conditions cause this tree to have sparse foliage and small flower clusters, but it grows rapidly and flowers profusely under regular irrigation. Flowers draw bees and are followed by flat brown seed pods which hang on until winter. Some trees have thorns. All locust species should be kept where invasive roots and litter won't spoil patios or swimming pools.

Throughout California, the Idaho locust's close relative, *Robinia pseudoacacia*, the black locust, has naturalized and spreads by seeds and root suckers into extensive groves that coexist with native vegetation. This proves how adaptable and rugged the locust can be. The most common cultivar is 'Purple Robe,' which is being substituted with the more long lived and less invasive Idaho locust.

SALIX BABYLONICA

SALIX—WILLOWS

There are over 300 species of willow in America, but only two are commercially grown for landscape trees. Willows are all river bottom trees and require lots of water to grow properly. Rooting is highly invasive and care should be taken to avoid planting them near water lines, sewers, or septic systems. In their greedy hunt for water, roots have the ability to heave pavement and crack foundations.

Like poplars, willows grow well from unrooted cuttings or poles during the dormant season. Many native species can be used for vegetating banks along rivers or streams to reduce erosion or undercutting. The fibrous roots help to bind sandy soils and stabilize them. If poles are anchored into the soil lying perpendicular to the slope, they will root and sprout along the entire length of the pole and filter sedimentation from runoff water.

Salix babylonica

Weeping Willow Zones 1 to 7
Deciduous, 40 feet tall, 30 feet wide. Full sun.
Weeping shade tree. Invasive rooting.

Few trees can compete with weeping willows for such graceful branching habit and rapid growth. Unfortunately this fast growth also contributes to a shorter than normal lifespan. Weeping willows have fibrous roots that can become very dense if grown in a lawn with surface irrigation, and in most cases few plants will survive beneath the canopy. Although popular trees near ponds or other water features, their constant shedding of foliage will quickly foul the water as leaves decompose. Branches are brittle and will break off in high winds. Weeping willows are a favored tree for country, Victorian, or historic garden themes.

Sapium sebiferum

Chinese Tallow Tree Zones 3, 5 and 7
Deciduous, 35 feet tall, 30 feet wide. Full sun.
Fall-color shade tree. Moderate rooting.

One of the newer trees used in California landscapes, the tallow tree is best known for its brilliant fall color in shades of red, yellow, and orange. It is fast growing in most soils and develops a broad, rounded crown that provides plenty of shade. Yellow flower spikes turn into small clusters of light gray fruit that the Chinese use for making candles and soap, hence the name. The tallow tree grows well in lawns and prefers a good water supply. It resists disease and pests and makes a reliable shade tree.

Schinus molle

California Pepper Zones 5 and 7
Evergreen, 35 feet tall, 35-plus feet wide. Full sun. Weeping shade tree. Invasive rooting.

The first pepper trees came to California with the padres and soon became a common sight in mission gardens. It is a beautiful shade tree with gnarled branches and light green weeping foliage that is aromatic and most beautiful in breezy climates. Like eucalyptus, it exudes a strong oil that makes growing other plants beneath the canopy difficult. In northern California the pepper is frost tender and does best near the coast, but many good sized trees are growing inland. During the 1990 freeze all those inland defoliated but soon the leaves returned, with some branch die-back. The tree is made even more interesting by the ornamental clusters of bright red pepper seeds, which are often used for dried arrangements. Extremely drought tolerant, it requires irrigation to get started, but will soon grow on natural rainfall as it becomes established.

California pepper in a dryland setting.

A very old California pepper showing the gnarled branching structure.

Sequoia sempervirens

Coast Redwood Zones 3, 5 and 7
Evergreen conifer, 80-plus feet tall, 30 feet wide. Full sun, part shade. California native shade tree. Shallow, dense rooting.

Redwoods are northern California's favorite conifer trees. Anyone who has visited the groves on the north coast knows how large they grow and how much shade they cast in their natural habitat. When used as landscape trees, they perform much better when planted in groups, as their roots require the same degree of shading to prevent overheating in the summer. When planted in lawns, it's a common practice to remove the lower limbs to make mowing easier, but this is not healthy for the trees and reduces the growth rate. It is better to apply a thick mulch around the base and keep the lawn edge further away from the trunk. Redwoods do poorly and may even be permanently stunted when planted inland, where there is considerable reflected dry heat and summer temperatures are high. Provide plenty of water, especially in hot weather.

Ulmus parvifolia

Chinese Elm Zones 2 to 7
Evergreen, semideciduous, 60 feet tall, 40 feet wide. Full sun. Weeping shade tree. Shallow, fibrous rooting.

The Chinese elm is only evergreen in mild climates. In most parts of northern California it is semideciduous, with a partial leaf drop when the first frosts hit. It is one of the very best shade trees, fast growing, with a broad canopy of thick, pendulous foliage. Over time it may become a bit top heavy, but thinning the branches will solve the problem. (Beware of tree companies that ruin these trees by dead-heading them to insure future pruning contracts.) The bark is also noteworthy with a richly colored, patchy texture. Although it is an elm, this tree has good resistance to elm leaf beetle and Dutch elm disease.

CHAPTER FOUR

The Stability of Shrubs

Shrubs are the backbone of a landscape and represent the largest and most versatile group of garden plants. Permanent and long lived, they provide a low-maintenance background of foliage and seasonal color. A diversity of shrubs can be used to solve problems while providing year-around interest.

Our mild climate here in California allows a huge selection of landscape shrubs to choose from. This diversity can seem overwhelming to gardeners as well as professionals, who also have problems identifying the "miscellaneous green shrub" when not in flower. The key is to create a mental association with each plant

FACING PAGE: IN THE WARMER COASTAL LOCATIONS FUCHSIAS BECOME LARGE SHRUBS WHEN SHELTERED BY WINDBREAKS. ABOVE: RHODODENDRON HYBRIDS.

that distinguishes it from the others, and to understand why it is important in landscaping.

NORTHERN CALIFORNIA TIP

Many large perennials that become woody when mature are sold in 5-gallon containers. This size container is expensive and should be reserved for shrubs. But growers make a higher profit from these short-lived perennials, which die out after a few years. It's better to buy woody perennials like euryops daisies or lantana in 1-gallon or even smaller containers because they grow fast enough to quickly catch up to the far more expensive 5-gallon size.

SELECTING THE RIGHT SHRUB FOR THE RIGHT PLACE

There is a proper shrub for every nook and cranny of a landscape. Choosing the correct plant means understanding how it grows and what it has to offer. It demands we know how large the plant will become and whether it is evergreen or deciduous. Will it survive in full sun or shade, wet ground or drought? Does it flower or have colorful berries, and is its foliage attractive all year around?

WATCH OUT FOR LARGE SHRUBS

The landscape maintenance industry thrives on gardens with overgrown shrubs. Constant pruning translates into lots of labor and clean-up time. Escallonia shrubs look very innocent in 5-gallon containers, but they soon grow into small trees as wide as they are tall. Make absolutely sure you know how large a shrub will be at maturity, especially when working with limited space around buildings or in tight planters.

Seek Out the Dwarf Hybrids

Plant breeders have developed some excellent dwarf versions of popular landscape shrubs. These cultivars need no shearing, and are just as long lived as their bigger relatives. Monster escallonia has been improved with 'Newport Dwarf.' Pittosporum is down-sized by the hybrid 'Wheeler's Dwarf' which mounds no higher that about 30 inches and spreads out nicely. Rhaphiolepis, the traditional parking lot shrub, offers the small 'Ballerina.' Look carefully at the plant labels on shrubs to make sure you are buying a dwarf, because in containers they appear almost identical to the larger species.

VISUAL QUALITIES OF SHRUBS

In colder climates, the frost-hardy deciduous flowering shrubs are the mainstay of landscapes. Unfortunately the bare twigs are leafless while dormant and many Californians have abandoned them for less colorful evergreens. Yet few of us can resist a brilliant mass of gold from early forsythia or the haunting fragrance of lilac.

You can have the best of both worlds by using a mixture of evergreens and deciduous flowering shrubs. Evergreens make a rich and constant background which compensates for the bare shrubs in winter. Later, the intense color of deciduous shrubs is enhanced when played against this deep green field. Diversity makes gardens more exciting as they change with the seasons.

Fruit, Flowers and Thorns

The winter landscape depends on colorful berries to provide interest, especially in the snow. Berries stand out cheerfully and also draw hungry birds into the garden. But during other seasons this type of fruit can become a liability as it stains pavement and birds aid in seed dispersal. In some cases the berries may also attract flies.

Don't plant shrubs with thorns near doorways, gates, or frequently used corners. When large objects must be maneuvered through tight openings, the task is made more difficult when thorns restrict movement. This also applies to access to utility meters, heaters, and air conditioning units. If a serviceman must remove the side panels to service your unit, a thorny plant nearby can make the task more difficult and costly.

CONSIDERATIONS FOR CALIFORNIA NATIVE SHRUBS

Most native shrubs have adapted to our long dry summers. They require excellent drainage but are not picky about soil fertility. They seem to thrive best on slopes where water runs off quickly. Most natives require occasional deep watering during their first two years to ease the adjustment after planting. The biggest problem is finding California native shrubs to buy. Most species are difficult and slow to propagate, while demand is high. They do not grow well in containers, which tend to overheat in the summer, making them risky stock for retail nurseries.

HOW SHRUBS ARE USED IN A LANDSCAPE

Designers use shrubs to make a landscape respond to the user's needs. Before you select a shrub, you should know how it will function in your landscape, and what kind of visual quality it provides.

Shrubs as Cover-Ups

Broadleaf evergreen shrubs provide a more lush appearance with many shades of green and varying leaf texture. Conifers, a term given to needled evergreens, are softer, with fine textured leaves and more arid character. Both are perfect for screening less attractive parts of a landscape. Informal hedges restrict views of utility areas, clothes lines, garbage cans, and bicycle parking. One or two well placed evergreens will cover up a gas, electric, or water meter. A border of evergreens breaks up long fence lines, and extra tall shrubs may even block the neighbor's window. Planting around the house foundation protects the base of each wall from rain-splashed mud or hard-water discoloration.

Shrubs as Background Plants

Without a lush, green background, flowers lose their brilliance. To make your efforts with annuals and perennials more effective, the stable plantings of leafy shrubs must be firmly in place. Dark and shady areas lighten up with lime green, yellow, or variegated foliage. The deep greens of large-leaved foliage plants help to reduce glare from pools or pavement.

Shrubs for Seasonal Color

One forsythia shrub can provide a larger mass of brilliant yellow than a whole planter full of pansies. Forsythia flowers on its own year after year without any help from us. This is the key to obtaining lots of color in a low-maintenance landscape.

Some of the best deciduous spring-flowering shrubs include lilac, bridal wreath, flowering quince, and forsythia. Deciduous shrubs which flower later in the season are rose of Sharon, crape myrtle, and hydrangea. Azaleas, rhododendron, and camellias are the best heavy flowering evergreen shrubs. Still more shrubs with a bonus of drought tolerance reward us with brilliant color from western redbud, orchid rockrose, and lavender. Don't hesitate to use a heavy hand with flowering shrubs so that even a drought tolerant, low-maintenance landscape can be intensely colorful.

Shrubs that Establish Character

Certain species of shrubs are associated with a particular kind of garden style. For example, tight formal designs will be enhanced by clipped hedges of boxwood. Aucuba, the gold dust plant, with its exotic spotted leaves lends a distinctly Asian appearance. Deep green fragrant gardenias make wonderful subtropical plants for evening gardens.

The relaxed character of rockroses is casual enough for the western ranch house. Nandina is a natural for Oriental flavor, along with azalea and xylosma. For a Latin effect, flowering pomegranates, dwarf citruses, and oleanders make red tile and stucco come alive. When a strong theme or character is important, do a landscape justice by taking time to select just the right shrubs.

HOW TO PLANT AND AVOID COMMON MISTAKES WITH SHRUBS

Shrubs are surprisingly forgiving and easy to plant. As with all container-grown plants, the condition of the root system is essential to future success. Watch out for roots growing on the surface of the soil or out the drain holes.

PLANTING SHRUBS

Woody container grown shrubs are planted exactly the same as a tree except that they require no support stake. Refer to the detailed planting instructions for trees in chapter 4.

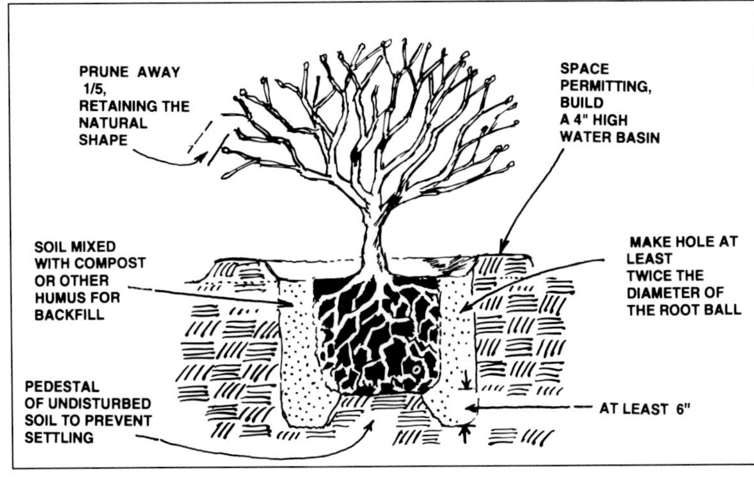

Special Needs of Acid-Loving Shrubs

The BIG 3, camellias, azaleas, and rhododendrons, prefer the acid soil and partial shade of a forest floor. They have adapted with wide, shallow, fibrous root systems to feed off the top 6 inches of soil where the nutrients lie. As these shrubs mature, their root systems spread wider to feed off a greater surface area. The best way to plant one is to dig a hole at least three times the diameter of the rootball or even wider if you can. But make it only deep enough to accommodate the rootball. Backfill around the rootball and the entire hole with azalea planting mix to insure the proper soil conditions and encourage more rapid rooting and top growth. If you buy a pot-bound plant, it is worthless because this kind of root system rarely recovers after planting.

Planting California Natives

Native shrubs can be very particular about root disturbance and soil moisture, which makes them tricky to plant. More natives die from rough handling or over-wet soil conditions than any other cause. It's best to arrange natives together in zones with their own control valve to better regulate sprinkler water delivery. Beware of restrictive layers beneath soil that cause water to pool underground, even though the surface of the soil around the shrub appears to be dry. Before selecting and planting a native shrub, make sure you have excellent drainage in winter as well as during the other seasons.

Transplanting Existing Shrubs

The best time to transplant garden shrubs is while they are dormant. It can be difficult to know when to transplant evergreens because here they have only a slight dormant period, if any at all. Whenever a shrub is transplanted, the root system takes a beating. To compensate, cut back a proportional amount of top growth to achieve a better balance of roots to foliage.

Some shrubs are risky to transplant. Most California natives don't tolerate root disturbance, and cannot be transplanted no matter what size rootball is excavated. Acid-loving plants are also difficult because of their spreading, shallow root systems. Before you risk a shrub by transplanting, consult a garden center expert to find out if that species will tolerate the move.

REGULAR CARE OF LANDSCAPE SHRUBS

Most shrubs are delightfully care free, and in fertile soil they ask only for regular watering. But deciduous flowering shrubs must be pruned at the right time each year to insure a bountiful crop of blooms. Evergreens look neater if given an occasional mild shaping, and of course formal hedges require frequent shearing to maintain their prescribed forms.

THE BASICS OF PRUNING SHRUBS

The most commonly planted shrubs here in northern California require no pruning at all. Never prune a shrub unless you know exactly what you are trying to do. Electric hedge clippers are so easy to use they encourage wholesale shearing of all shrubs, whether they need it or not.

COMMON GARDEN QUESTION

"Why are my azaleas suddenly turning yellow after growing so well for many years, even though I've kept them fed and watered?"

Water supplies in many parts of California contain a large amount of soluble salts and other high-pH minerals. When applied as irrigation water on slow-draining heavy soils, the salts gradually build up and raise the soil pH far above the tolerance of azaleas and other acid-loving plants. Once the soil has changed there is no choice but to replace the azaleas with other plants more tolerant of higher pH levels.

The Art of Natural Pruning

There is a tendency for many homeowners to feel that shrubs not sheared into neat, geometric shapes look messy. This frame of mind creates perpetual chores. If a shrub is too large, it should be reduced not with an attack of hedge clippers, but through the art of natural pruning.

Very light natural pruning helps shrubs to develop a fine pattern of branching. Every time you cut off the growing tip of a twig, it will regrow by branching out into numerous new twigs. When azaleas are trimmed back this way after flowering, they bloom twice as much the following year from the newly produced growing tips.

In natural pruning, twigs and branches are removed from inside the foliage, not outside where the stumps are visible. A shrub that is naturally trimmed since infancy will have a much finer branching structure, and willl require far less attention as an adult. Stand back and observe the general outline of the plant. If one portion sticks out, look inside the branches and see which twigs support that growth. Remove only those twigs, making the cut as close to the framework branches as possible.

Pruning Deciduous Flowering Shrubs

Deciduous flowering shrubs are pruned to stimulate more blooms, but they still bloom if left untouched. Prune back $^1/_3$ of each branch for spring flowering so new branches will develop over the summer to bear the next spring's crop of buds. Summer-flowering shrubs should be pruned back the same way either in late winter or very early spring. This stimulates growth of new branches, which bear more numerous blooms later in the same season.

WHEN TO PRUNE DECIDUOUS FLOWERING SHRUBS

Botanical name	Common name
Spring flowering shrubs: Prune after flowering.	
Cercis occidentalis	Western redbud
Chaenomeles	Flowering quince
Cornus florida	Shrub dogwood
Forsythia	Forsythia
Spiraea prunifolia	Bridal wreath
Syringa	Lilac
Viburnum carlcephalum	Snowball
Summer flowering shrubs: Prune before flowering in spring.	
Buddleia	Butterfly bush
Hibiscus syriacus	Rose of Sharon
Hydrangea	Hydrangea

Shearing Hedges

Start shearing hedges when the shrubs are very small to produce a fine branching pattern capable of supporting leaves evenly over the entire plant. Shearing should continue as the plants mature to avoid lanky branches which later leave holes in the adult hedge.

Although most hedges appear to be square, they should actually be slightly narrower at the top than the bottom. This allows sunlight to reach the foliage on the lower parts of each shrub. If the top is too wide, the lower leaves are denied light and the hedge becomes barren at the bottom. If you live where there is snowfall, the top of the hedge should be rounded or nearly pointed to prevent buildup. The weight of the snow can crush the twigs or even cause the main branches to split off from the trunk.

T.L.C. FOR SHRUBS = GREAT PERFORMANCE

If you want to see your shrubs really perform with lots of flowers and new growth, give them extra food and water during the summer. Even though you may use a sprinkler system, shrubs on west and south sides of the house benefit from a gradual, deep soaking during hot days. Apply a thick mulch around a shrub within its dripline to retain soil moisture and keep roots cool. Mulching makes a big difference in growth rate and also helps control weeds.

If your garden is on less fertile, rapidly draining shale or sand, plants appreciate extra fertilizer. Use fertilizer with lots of phosphorus and potassium if you're looking for fruit, berries, or flowers. Use higher-nitrogen formulas to promote foliage and branching. Use special fertilizers on acid lovers, citrus, and roses. Well-fed shrubs grow faster and have an increased resistance to insect pests and diseases.

LANDSCAPE SHRUBS FOR NORTHERN CALIFORNIA

Although there is an endless number of shrubs suited to northern California landscapes, many of them are not commonly grown. Landscape designers are forced to work exclusively with those plants termed "available" in order to avoid endless substitutions during the construction process. The following list includes stable woody shrubs commonly available at garden centers throughout the state. You'll find some that are loosely termed herbs, which grow woody over time and make excellent small landscape shrubs that defy drought. Other shrubs may eventually grow into small trees if not properly shaped when young. Pay attention to the height and width dimensions provided.

Abelia grandiflora 'Edward Goucher'

Glossy Abelia   Zones 2 to 7   Frost to 15° F.
Evergreen, 5 feet tall, 5 feet wide. Full sun.

Excellent large flowering shrub that takes well to shearing, but also grows into a fountain shape if left alone. Not susceptible to diseases or insect pests, although blooms will draw bees. Abelia's size is usually underestimated, resulting in constant shearing to control growth. Summer flowers are white and tubular, leaves are small, glossy, with a pinkish tint. Best used as an informal hedge, tall screen, or as a single accent.

Arbutus unedo 'Compacta'

Dwarf Strawberry Tree   Zones 2 to 7
Evergreen, 6 feet tall, 8 feet wide. Full sun.

Originally from southern Europe, the dwarf strawberry tree is remarkably similar to other California native shrubs. It is drought tolerant, slow growing, and remains a shrub if kept trimmed, but eventually grows into a small tree with gnarled branching that is enhanced under night lighting. Leaves are dark green and flowers urn shaped, similar to those of the manzanita. Named for its bright red, strikingly attractive fruit about the size of a large shooter marble. Tolerant of both dry summers and smog.

Arctostaphylos densiflora 'Howard McMinn'

Vine Hill Manzanita   Zones 2 to 7
Evergreen, 6 feet tall, 8 feet wide. Full sun on the coast, part shade inland.

Upright shrub with dense foliage and mounding form. Leaves are nearly round and tend to be light, sometimes a mint green. Flowers in spring with clusters of tiny, bell-shaped white or blush pink blooms followed by red

SHRUB SELECTION GUIDE

	Evergreen Foliage	Flowering	Deciduous Flowering	Hedge Material	Unusual Foliage or Berries	Drought-Tolerant	California Native	Dwarf Variety	Fragrant Flowers	Aromatic or Herb
Abelia grandiflora 'Edward Goucher'	•	•		•		•				
Arctostaphylos densiflora 'Howard McMinn'	•	•			•	•	•			
Arubutus unedo	•	•			•	•				
Aucuba japonica	•				•					
Azalea Southern Indica Hybrids	•	•								
Buxus microphylla japonica	•			•						
Callistemon citrinus	•	•			•	•				
Camellia japonica	•	•								
Ceanothus hybrids	•	•				•	•			
Cercis occidentalis			•			•	•			
Chaenomeles japonica			•	•		•		•		
Cistus purpureus	•	•				•				
Cotoneaster lacteus	•				•	•				
Dodonaea viscosa 'Purpurea'	•			•	•	•				
Escallonia exoniensis 'Fradesi'	•	•		•						
Escallonia 'Newport'	•	•						•		
Forsythia intermedia			•	•		•				
Gardenia jasminoides 'Mystery'	•	•							•	
Grevillea noellii	•	•		•	•	•				
Hibiscus syriacus			•			•				
Hydrangea macrophylla			•							
Ilex aquifolium 'San Gabriel'	•				•					
Ilex cornuta	•			•	•					
Juniperus chinensis 'Pfitzerana'	•				•	•				
Lavandula angustifolia	•	•				•			•	•
Lavandula dentata	•	•				•			•	•
Ligustrum japonicum 'Texanum'	•			•	•	•				
Mahonia aquifolium	•	•			•	•	•			
Nandina domestica	•				•	•				
Nerium oleander	•	•		•		•				
Photinia fraseri	•			•	•	•				
Pittosporum tobira 'Variegata'	•			•	•	•				
Pittosporum tobira 'Wheeler's Dwarf'	•					•		•		
Punica granatum 'Nana'			•		•	•		•		
Pyracantha hybrids	•			•	•	•				
Raphiolepis indica 'Ballerina'	•	•				•		•		
Raphiolepis indica 'Jack Evans'	•	•		•	•	•				
Raphiolepis indica 'Springtime'	•	•		•	•	•				
Rhododendron Various Cultivars	•	•								
Rosmarinus officinalis	•	•				•				•
Santolina chamaecyparissus	•	•			•	•				•
Spiraea x *vanhouttei*			•	•						
Syringa vulgaris			•			•			•	
Xylosma congestum	•			•		•				

berries. One of the varieties most tolerant of the cultivated landscape.

Aucuba japonica 'Variegata'

Gold Dust Plant Zones 3, 5, 6 and 7
Evergreen, 8 feet tall, 6 feet wide. Shade or part shade.

An excellent background shrub for shade gardens, aucuba is slow growing and easy to keep at a modest size by regular pruning. If exposed to direct sun the top leaves burn and turn black. It's called gold dust because the glossy, vivid leaves are speckled with flecks of gold. When planted in deep shade, the flecks bring the illusion of light and provide contrast with other deep green shade plants. Flowers in midspring with small purple flowers that ripen into bright red fruits. Other varieties offer variegated leaves and dwarf cultivars, both of which may not be available in nurseries.

Azalea Southern Indica Hybrids

Sun Azalea Zones 2 to 7
Evergreen, frost to 10°F., 3 feet wide, 3 feet tall. Shade or partial shade.

Although azaleas are in the genus *Rhododendron*, they are rarely listed as such because most are called by their variety name, much like Hybrid Tea roses. The Southern Indica hybrids are the most durable azaleas, growing much faster and taller under less than ideal circumstances. They also tolerate the dry heat and high summer temperatures of valley and foothill zones. Plant in shade or with east and north exposures only. They are subject to chlorosis (yellowing of leaves) when soil or water is alkaline.

Buxus microphylla japonica

Japanese Boxwood Zones 3 to 7
Evergreen, frost to 10°F., 3 feet wide, 5 feet tall. Full sun or part shade.

This dainty-leaved boxwood is the best for California gardens because it tolerates our hot, dry summers. A slow grower, its tight foliage is usually sheared into low formal hedges or topiary. Leaves develop a reddish cast when exposed to low winter temperatures. Hardier cultivars for mountain landscapes are available but not common.

Callistemon citrinus

Lemon Bottlebrush Zones 3, 5, 7
Evergreen shrub or small tree, 10 feet wide, 15 feet tall. Full sun, drought tolerant.

Very popular with hummingbirds, bottlebrush is one of the most durable plants for the drought-tolerant garden. Seasonal, bright red flowers resembling bottle brushes appear at the ends of branches and cover the entire plant. Pea-sized ornamental seed pods remain on

LEAVES AND FLOWERS OF MANZANITA.

MATURE MANZANITA SHRUB IN FLOWER.

AUCUBA JAPONICA, GOLD DUST PLANT

SOUTHERN INDICA HYBRID AZALEAS

BUXUS JAPONICA HEDGES

CAMELLIA JAPONICA

CEANOTHUS SHRUB

the branches after seed is dispersed. Although it is slow growing, beware of its mature size which is more like a small tree. Its weakness is in cold tolerance, and it has been killed entirely in freezes below 20°F. An excellent choice for Southwest-inspired gardens, its breezy growth habit, flowers, and evergreen foliage combine to make bottlebrushes good for screening or as single specimens. Its cousin, *Callistemon viminalis,* is a small tree and more graceful, with weeping branches.

Camellia japonica

Japanese Camellia Zones 2 to 7
Evergreen, 6 feet wide, 12 feet tall. Shade or part sun.

This plant grows so well in the central valley that Sacramento has long held an annual camellia festival at bloom time. Although considered slow growing, old camellias can become very large at maturity. Easy to grow if protected from direct exposure to afternoon sun and kept moist but well drained, this shrub provides brilliant spring flowers in many shades from white to deep red. Keep spent blossoms picked up to discourage camellia petal blight, and discard (not in compost pile) any that have brown patches. Camellias are in the same genus as the shrubs which yield black tea. Old timers use the left-over contents of tea bags as a nutritious mulch. Camellias are surface feeders and do not tolerate cultivation within their dripline. Prune and fertilize after blooming. There are dozens of excellent hybrid Japanese camellias to choose from. For earlier blooms, the sasanqua camellia hybrids help extend the season.

Ceanothus hybrids

California Lilac Zones 2 to 7

Ceanothus is an evergreen California native shrub grown for its blue flowers and deep green foliage. A common member of chaparral plant communities, it requires fast drainage, direct sun, and restricted seasonal watering. A few cultivars of *Ceanothus* have been developed to enhance the foliage and flowers while reducing the sensitivity to irrigation and slow-draining soils. These make excellent background shrubs for both regular and arid landscapes. Because of spotty availability, choices may be limited, but there are many more good hybrids available for substitutes.

***Ceanothus* 'Concha'** 7 feet high, upright habit, small leaves, deep blue flowers, long bloom season.

***Ceanothus* 'Joyce Coulter'** 4 feet high, 7 feet wide, spreading habit, bright green leaves, medium blue flowers.

***Ceanothus* 'Ray Hartman'** 12 feet high, 14 feet wide, tall shrub or small tree, medium blue flowers.

Cercis occidentalis

Western Redbud Zones 1 to 7

Deciduous, 15 feet tall, 10 feet wide. Shrub or small tree. Full sun.

Redbud is one of the most adaptable California native shrubs and offers many unique qualities. Early in spring the entire shrub is cloaked in bright purple blossoms that stand out boldly against an evergreen background. It makes a good drought-tolerant substitute for flowering quince, and often blooms at the same time as the equally dry brooms, with their contrasting yellow flowers. Rounded heart-shaped leaves flutter with the slightest breeze, and as summer ends they take on a smoky magenta color before they drop. Like all natives, redbud is not particular about soil fertility and may survive the entire summer without supplemental watering. If planted very small and watered along with other ornamental plants in well-drained soil, it may adapt and grow faster with the added moisture.

Ceanothus flowers

Cercis occidentalis shrub in flower.

Chaenomeles japonica

Flowering Quince Hybrids Zones 1 to 7

Deciduous. Full sun.

No other plant offers such intense shades of coral and pink than flowering quince. It asks for no special care except a gentle pruning after bloom time to stimulate more wood for next year's flowers. There are many different cultivars that vary in size and flower color, classified either as tall, reaching at least 6 feet, or low, those that grow to only about 3 feet high. Some types may have thorns or bear hard, inedible fruit. It has no special needs but can be sensitive to alkaline soils. Old homesteads have rugged mixed hedges of both quince and forsythia that never fail to herald the coming of spring as they burst into bloom together.

Cercis occidentalis blossom and seed pod close-up.

Cistus purpureus

Orchid Rockrose Zones 2 to 7

Evergreen, 4 feet tall, 5 feet wide. Full sun.

This rockrose is the best landscape variety because of its bright pink flowers and extended bloom time. A star performer for xeriphytic gardens, it grows fast, tolerates heat, neglect, and drought. Plants can become foliage heavy, and the branches may break apart in the center. Having a moderate life span, it should not be considered a long-lived shrub. Regular pruning will keep growth checked and encourage stronger branching.

Cotoneaster lacteus

Red Clusterberry Zones 3, 5, 6 and 7

Evergreen, 8 feet plus tall, 6 feet wide. Full sun.

All of the cotoneaster clan have become popular because of their durability, cold hardiness and tolerance of dry conditions. Red clusterberry can become an attrac-

Chaenomeles japonica in flower (red), forsythia behind.

CISTUS PURPUREUS SHRUB

CISTUS PURPUREUS FLOWER

FORSYTHIA SHRUBS

tive small tree over time. It also makes a good background shrub, made more attractive when branches are thinned to reveal its arching habit. Leaves are a dull green that is enhanced as thick clusters of red berries mature. Tolerates moderately alkaline soil.

Dodonaea viscosa

Hopseed Bush Zones 3, 5 and 7
Evergreen, 14 feet tall, 5 feet wide.

Hopseed bush has long been a part of the California landscape because it will grow fast and is drought tolerant. It is best used as a background plant, hedge, or screen. Papery flowers are insignificant but do create litter and the shrub should not be planted near swimming pools. Suffers frost damage in temperatures lower than 20°F. The variety 'Purpurea' has purple-bronze foliage which becomes more vivid in the fall. Highly flammable.

Escallonia exoniensis 'Frades'

Escallonia Zones 3, 6 and 7
Evergreen, 8 feet tall, 6 feet wide. Full sun, part shade.

This escallonia is one of the most commonly used shrubs in California landscapes because of its bright green foliage and small red flowers. It grows very large in just a few years and usually ends up being sheared to a manageable size. This escallonia is not particular as to soil, temperature, or exposure and is a very reliable background shrub.

Escallonia 'Newport'

Newport Dwarf Escallonia Zones 3, 6 and 7
Evergreen, 18 inches high, 3 feet wide. Full sun, part shade.

A valuable dwarf form of escallonia that is excellent anywhere that size is important. Low mounding shrubs with tiny light green leaves that can become a small hedge or border plant. Tends to be brittle and is best planted from 1-gallon containers to avoid damage when transplanted.

Forsythia intermedia

Forsythia Zones 1 to 7
Deciduous, 10 feet tall, 6 feet wide. Full sun.

Forsythia is the first shrub to bloom in early spring. Before foliage appears, the entire plant is covered with yellow blossoms that are a great source of seasonal, low-maintenance color. It is not particular about soil and will tolerate inland heat. Forsythia is a spring-flowering shrub and should be cut back about 30 percent *after* flowering. When it gets old and rangy, forsythia can be rejuvenated by cutting back the entire branching structure to start over. Good companion for flowering quince.

Gardenia jasminoides 'Mystery'

Gardenia Zones 3, 5 and 7

Evergreen, 6 feet tall, 4 feet wide. Full sun coastal, part shade inland.

Few flowers can rival gardenia for richness of fragrance. Plant it close to outdoor living spaces for best effect. 'Mystery' is a good sized shrub with attractive foliage even when not in bloom. Gardenias are acid-loving surface feeders with needs similar to those of the rhododendron clan. In many areas it suffers from chlorosis, a yellowing of the leaves caused by alkalinity in the soil or water. It will tolerate a surprising amount of sun and does not bloom well when growing in deep shade. Flowers measure up to 4 inches across. Mulch to keep roots cool and moist inland, and protect from persistent coastal winds. Varieties 'Radicans' and 'Veitchii' are lower growing and best suited to small gardens.

Hibiscus syriacus shrub with iris in foreground.

Grevillea 'Noellii'

Grevillea Zones 2 to 7

Evergreen, 4 feet tall, 5 feet wide. Full sun.

When a landscape is abandoned, most plants die except grevillea, which seems to thrive on neglect. This shrub has yellow-green, thick needlelike foliage, and its shape is dense but with a feathery outline. Small pink flowers appear in the spring at the end of each branch. Grevillea is a reliable, low-maintenance and deer-resistant shrub that grows rapidly and may overwhelm slower-growing plants nearby. Good companion for California natives or drought tolerant conifers such as cedar and juniper.

Hibiscus syriacus

Rose of Sharon Zones 1 to 7

Deciduous, 12 feet tall, 5 feet wide. Full sun, part shade.

Where winter frosts prevent growing the subtropical hibiscus, this shrub makes an excellent substitute. Flowers are large, tubular, and cultivars offer white, blue, and purple colors. Very upright in form, rose of Sharon makes a good single accent that keeps its shape. Can be drought tolerant and requires little care, flowering in late summer. Prune in winter, before spring growth begins. Nearly pest free, it is also one of the few shrubs resistant to oak root fungus.

Potted blooming hydrangeas.

Hydrangea macrophylla

Garden Hydrangea Zones 2 to 7

Deciduous, 6 feet tall, 4 feet wide. Shade or part shade.

This old-fashioned plant is one of the star performers in the shade garden, flowering in late spring. It has broad, deep green leaves and huge flower heads that keep their color when dried for flower arrangements. Flower color may vary with the level of soil acidity. The addition of aluminum sulfate to the soil causes flowers to take on blue tones, while liming the soil stimulates reddish coloring. Cut back old branches in winter to stimulate new growth.

ILEX

The family of hollies is huge and includes many different species and hybrids. New hybrids are self-fertile, but older varieties require both male and female plants in order to bear fruit, which occurs on the females only. Attracts birds, and berries may cause staining of pavement.

ILEX AQUIFOLIUM

Ilex aquifolium 'San Gabriel'

English Holly Zones 2 to 7

Evergreen, 10 feet tall, 5 feet wide. Sun or part shade inland.

One of the most popular varieties for Christmas greens. San Gabriel provides seedless red berries and does not require a pollinator. All *aquifoliums* are sensitive to inland heat and should be planted in moist areas shaded from afternoon sun. Prefers slightly acid soil. Mulch to keep roots cool. Shape by gentle pruning when plant is young. Resistant to oak root fungus.

Ilex cornuta

Chinese Holly Zones 2 to 7

Evergreen,10 feet tall, 5 feet wide. Part shade. North and east exposures.

Less traditional in appearance, Chinese holly has large, four-cornered leaves. It is one of the most rugged hollies, tolerant of heat, dry conditions, and marginal soils. Foliage is deep green and plants make good background shrubs. 'Burford' and 'Dwarf Burford' most commonly planted and vary in size according to variety. This holly requires long, warm summers to set fruit, and shearing eliminates berries entirely.

JUNIPER

When in doubt, plant a juniper! There is no plant as adaptable as this evergreen, although it has been used to

ILEX CORNUTA

excess. One of the few plants that can survive in alkaline or infertile soil, it continues to thrive even after irrigation has been eliminated. Older plants can be creatively pruned into Oriental "bonsai" forms to expose gnarled branches. Dozens of varieties are available with yellow foliage for contrast against evergreen backgrounds.

Juniperus chinensis 'Pfitzerana'

Pftizer Juniper Zones 2 to 7

Evergreen Conifer, 6 feet tall, 18 feet wide.

Full sun, part shade.

Pfitzer is an excellent fast-growing shrub that makes a solid barrier for screening. Tends to die-out on the bottom to expose trunk. Foliage is gray-green and plants have a graceful, arching habit. For same plant with gold foliage, consider variety 'Pfitzerana Aurea.'

Lavandula angustifolia

English Lavender Zones 2 to 7

Evergreen herb, 4 feet tall, 3 feet wide. Full sun.

Lavender has become a very popular small shrub because it has so much to offer. Requiring fast draining

JUNIPERUS 'PFITZERANA'

soils, it will survive on minimal watering when established, making it a good choice for rock gardens or embankments. Lavender has a soft gray-green foliage that is highly aromatic. It becomes woody with age and flowers in purple spikes at the end of each branch. Cut back after flowering to discourage legginess and promote more compact growth. Plant alone or in masses, as an informal hedge or border.

Lavandula dentata
French Lavender
Slightly smaller than English lavender, this one is a bit more drought and heat resistant, with a mounding growth habit. Long flowering period. Tends to cascade over walls or the sides of planters.

Lavandula dentata

Ligustrum japonicum 'Texanum'
Waxleaf Privet Zones 2 to 7
Evergreen, 12 feet tall, 5 feet wide.

Privet is a fast-growing evergreen screen shrub that is good for background foliage. Its leaves are medium green and will take shearing into hedges or other shapes. Clusters of creamy white flowers in late spring become dark berries that will stain paving. Birds spread the seed everywhere, and the seed is quick to take root and become a persistent weed. In hot inland areas privet may show some leaf burn, and heat tolerance is improved with occasional summertime deep watering.

Mahonia aquifolium
Oregon Grape Zones 2 to 7
Evergreen, 4 feet tall, 2 feet wide. Part shade.

Mahonia is native to northern California, where it grows in coastal forests beneath the canopies of redwood trees. Leaves are hollylike with spiny edges, and new growth may have a bronzish cast. Flowers are small, bright yellow, and appear in late spring, followed by purple berries. It is best grown in a partially shaded location to obtain large leaf size and color. Its long-stemmed, lanky form is one of the few plants suited to narrow spaces. A good companion for some woodland native plants.

Nandina domestica

Nandina domestica
Heavenly Bamboo Zones 3, 5 and 7
Evergreen, 5 feet tall, 3 feet wide. Full sun; part shade inland.

Nandina is most attractive when planted in Asian-inspired gardens. It is easily identified by its tangerine-colored foliage and tall, lanky shape. Like mahonia it is excellent for narrow spaces and can be easily pruned to control growth. New leaves are bright orange-red and become more green as they mature. Flower clusters on top of the plant bloom in late summer, followed by sprays of red berries suitable for winter decorations. Good as single specimen, hedge, or in groups. Variety 'Compactum' is a dwarf form only 3 feet tall and 18 inches wide.

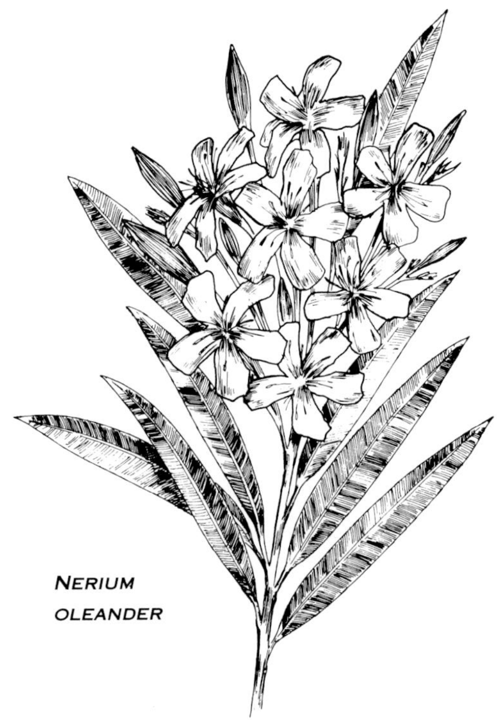

Nerium oleander

Nerium oleander

Oleander Zones 2 to 7

Evergreen, 12 feet high, 10 feet wide.

Oleander has been tested on the highways of California and has proven to be one of the best evergreen shrubs for less than ideal conditions. Unfortunately it is so common many dismiss it as second-rate, but no other plant gives so much for so little effort. It tolerates salt, drought, heat, wind, and infertile soils. Flowering in June and July with many shades of white, pink, and red, oleander is a rank grower that regenerates branches and foliage at a startling rate. Don't underestimate how quickly and efficiently this shrub can screen off views and create privacy barriers. If older plants become too woody, rejuvenate by cutting all growth back to basic branches. All parts of the plant are highly poisonous; avoid planting near areas frequented by children, pets and livestock. Dwarf varieties 'Petite Pink' are only 6 feet tall and 6 feet wide.

Pittosporum 'Wheeleri'

Photinia fraseri

Toyon Zones 2 to 7

Evergreen, 10 feet tall, 6 feet wide, Full sun, part shade.

With its glossy bright red new foliage and green mature leaves, photinia offers changing beauty all year around. The best screening shrub today, it has no known pests or diseases, is heat tolerant and grows densely enough to become a formidable barrier. Good for background planting, and can be pruned into small trees. Clusters of white flowers in early spring have pungent odor that may be objectionable to some.

Pittosporum tobira 'Variegata'

Mock Orange Zones 2 to 7

Evergreen, 5 feet tall, 5 feet wide. Full sun, part shade.

Probably the most common shrub in California landscapes, Pittosporum and this variegated variety are valued for attractive foliage and low maintenance requirements. Best used in part shade where the light coloring suggests sun dappling. This shrub tolerates dry conditions, heat, and frost, making it a low-risk selection for novice gardeners. If low on water, the leaves of all tobiras will cup under to reduce the amount of surface exposed to direct sunlight. Plants may grow taller after many years, but gentle shaping when young helps to promote lower branching and better form. The common name mock orange denotes the fragrance of clusters of tiny white flowers that appear in spring, followed by clusters of hard, green marble-sized fruit.

Pittosporum tobira 'Wheeler's Dwarf'

Wheeler's Dwarf Tobira Zones 3, 5 and 7

Evergreen, 30 inches tall, 4 feet wide. Full sun, part shade.

Here is a dwarf shrub that is so versatile it can be found in almost every California landscape. The low, mounding profile insures it won't block windows or overwhelm nearby perennials. Although very tolerant of heat and direct sun, its leaf color will be darker if partially sheltered in the afternoon. Fast growth and brittle branches make 1-gallon the best size to buy. Good companion for azaleas in the Oriental garden.

Punica granatum 'Nana'

Dwarf Pomegranate Zones 2 to 7

Deciduous, 3 feet tall, 3 feet wide. Full sun.

A colorful dwarf shrub, this pomegranate with its luscious tangerine red flowers followed by miniature fruit is loved by hummingbirds. Its tree-size cousin, the pomegranate, held a special place in mission gardens of early California and this dwarf form becomes a more versatile way to lend that same arid character to smaller landscapes. Highly tolerant of heat, drought, and saline soils, this little shrub is not used as frequently as it should be. Plants bloom better in full sun, and the miniature pomegranate fruit can be picked and dried to use in Southwestern-inspired Christmas decorations.

PYRACANTHA

Pyracantha

Firethorn

Throughout northern California you can find *pyracantha* shrubs growing as volunteers along roadways, in pastures, and on the sites of old homesteads. It is primarily valued for the red berries that mature in the fall and hang on through Christmas. There are dozens of cultivars that vary in size and berry color. *Pyracantha* makes a good barrier hedge because plants bear sharp thorns and can spread rapidly. It can also be trained into an espalier when grown against any vertical surface. Berries draw birds. To control size, prune in spring after berries have faded. Like all members of the rose family, it is susceptible to fireblight, and pruning equipment should be sterilized with alcohol or bleach before and after cutting each plant.

RAPHIOLEPIS

RAPHIOLEPIS PATIO TREE

Raphiolepis

Indian Hawthorne

Parking lots throughout California have some form of this shrub planted in the islands and medians. It has a well-deserved reputation for thriving under very poor conditions. Many different cultivars offer a variety of sizes and bloom color ranging from white to dark pink in spring or summer. Dark purple or black berries follow but

RHODODENDRON HYBRIDS

ROSEMARINUS OFFICINALIS SHRUB

ROSEMARY BLOOMS

most varieties have very few. Foliage color varies from medium green to bronze on the new growth, and cold weather sometimes promotes the purplish tint. Growth is compact and plants retain a neat appearance.

Raphiolepis indica 'Ballerina'
Zones 2 to 7. Evergreen. 2 feet high, 4 feet wide. Full sun, part shade.
Made popular by its small, controlled size, 'Ballerina' is a perfect shrub for tight spots in low-maintenance gardens. It is a good companion for other dwarf shrubs and perennials because when not in bloom, it makes a good small scale background shrub.

Raphiolepis indica 'Jack Evans'
Zones 2 to 7. Evergreen. 4 feet tall, 5 feet wide. Full sun, part shade.
A midsized shrub that remains compact and makes a good hedge, 'Jack Evans' offers bright pink flowers. Foliage has a bronze tint and makes a good midheight background shrub for borders. Best used as an informal hedge, but will tolerate shearing. Other widely available cultivars of *Raphiolepis* include: 'Springtime,' 'Clara,' 'Majestic Beauty,' 'Pink Lady,' and 'Pinkie'.

RHODODENDRON

This relative of the azalea offers spectacular bloom displays on much larger plants. One species is a native that thrives in the shade of coastal redwood forests, proving that they can be grown with very little care. The key is to provide an environment where plants are protected from direct sunlight and drying winds. As surface feeders, the root systems of rhododendrons are vulnerable to overheating, but mulching with pine needles or oak leaves provides insulation and lowers pH. Do not disturb or cultivate the soil around the bottom of rhododendrons. Where summers are long and hot, they must have plenty of shade and moisture. Alkalinity in the soil or water system may prevent successful growth. Because there are over 800 species of rhododendron, it's best to ask the expert at a reputable garden center for those hybrids best suited to your local microclimate.

Rosmarinus officinalis

Rosemary Zones 2 to 7

Evergreen herb, 4 feet high, 3 feet wide. Full sun.

Although rosemary is a culinary herb, it is also a small woody shrub which can be very useful in the drought-tolerant garden. In Roman times it was grown in courtyard gardens and sheared often to release the scent of its aromatic foliage. The natural growth habit of rosemary is relaxed and rangy, with upright, spiky branches that bear small blue flowers. Rosemary attracts bees when in bloom. Foliage may be used in cooking when used fresh or dried. Do not confuse this rosemary with 'Prostratus,' its groundcover relative.

Spiraea 'Little Princess'

Spiraea x *vanhouttei*

Bridal Wreath Spiraea Zones 1 to 7

Deciduous, 6 feet tall, 6 feet wide. Full sun, part shade.

This is an old-fashioned, deciduous flowering shrub named for its habit of blooming during the wedding season. Small white flowers densely cover the entire length of each of its arching branches which are woven into wedding wreaths and garlands. Head back and prune after flowering to create more wood for next year's blooms. Bridal wreath's foliage is small and dark green, which may take on reddish fall tones before leaves drop, depending on local temperatures. Not particular about soils or care, spiraea often remains for many years after old farm houses are abandoned. Dwarf variety 'Little Princess' is only 18 inches tall and 24 inches wide with broad pink flowers on a low, mounding shrub.

Syringa vulgaris

Common Lilac Zones 1 to 7

Deciduous, 15 feet tall, 5 feet wide. Full sun, part shade.

Lilac is loved for its intensely fragrant blossoms, which are either cut for indoor arrangements or left on the plant for their landscape value. Old plants become small trees if left to grow naturally, but regular shaping can keep them much shorter. Lilac blooms better in the foothills and mountain zones, where colder winters insure complete dormancy. Various cultivars offer flower colors in pink, white, lavender, and purple. Plants won't bloom for the first two or three years, but with patience they will perform admirably. May suffer from mildew in areas of ground or coastal fog.

Syringa vulgaris, purple blooms

Xylosma congestum

Xylosma Zones 3, 6 and 7

Evergreen, 15 feet tall, 8 feet wide. Full sun, part shade.

Xylosma is one of California's most beautiful background foliage shrubs. It grows slowly at first, but will become a small tree over time. Bright green, glossy leaves hang on very graceful, almost weeping branches that lend themselves to creative pruning. Xylosma frequently sheds its leaves, and insignificant flowers attract bees, making it a poor choice around swimming pools or children's play areas. It's not fussy about soil, heat, or water, and its lush appearance is a welcome addition to drought-tolerant landscapes. A smaller variety 'Compactum' is still fairly large, measuring about 6 feet tall and 4 feet wide.

CHAPTER FIVE

VINES AND GROUNDCOVERS

Groundcover plants and vines share many similar qualities. If not trained to a vertical surface, a vine will sprawl along the ground, acting like a groundcover. It is chiefly the use of a plant in gardens that dictates its final classification.

VINES

Vines are the most creatively used plants in the garden. Unfortunately, a few destructive species have given them a bad reputation. The idea of gardening on vertical surfaces provides an opportunity to dress up bare walls and fences with soothing green foliage and colorful flowers.

ABOVE: BOUGAINVILLEA AND MORNING GLORY VINES.

CLASSIFYING VINES

In order to use vines successfully, it's important to distinguish the various types, how they grow, and how they can damage structures. This helps to select the right plant for the right place so that its special qualities can be used for maximum effect.

Self-Clinging Vines

Some vines have a built-in means of attaching themselves to surfaces, called holdfasts, which function in two ways. One group uses tiny rootlets that attach themselves by invading rough surfaces like mortar or masonry. This method is dangerous because the rootlets must penetrate the surface to gain a foothold. The second and less destructive group has disk-shaped suction cups that do not penetrate the surface and are capable of adhering to much smoother materials.

Clinging vines must be torn down off the walls of a house for painting, which is hard work, and ruins many years of growth. Damage is more likely to occur on masonry and stucco walls that are cracked, old, or exceptionally porous. Rootlets prefer to penetrate the mortar joints rather than dense masonry units, and when removed they pull out chunks of mortar. For this single reason, many homeowners won't allow clinging vines in the landscape.

All ivies do not not have the same effects, however. English ivy rootlets are the most damaging to masonry, and its runners invade roofing systems through narrow openings. The diameter of each runner increases as it ages to separate joists, siding, and rafters. Boston ivy, not related to English ivy, is the most gentle of the clinging vines because it attaches by clusters of suction cups. It is deciduous, which makes removal much easier during the winter when the runners are fully exposed. This ivy also does not grow to such large diameters and structural damage is rare.

NORTHERN CALIFORNIA TIP

Deciduous vines are a good way to reduce energy bills. When planted on the south and west walls of houses they offer a passive solar advantage. In summer their leafy foliage shades and insulates the wall to help reduce air conditioning costs. When the leaves are shed in winter, the warming sun is able to directly contact the wall and radiate heat into the house. Training deciduous vines over the tops of windows on hot southern and western exposures reduces the amount of direct solar exposure on the glass, while sunlight is still able to brighten rooms in winter.

Non-Clinging Vines

Most vines cannot cling by themselves and must have other means of support. Grape vines, for example, have stringlike shoots that curl tightly around a support upon contact. Twining vines, such as star jasmine, naturally weave themselves around and through the support. The remaining vines do not climb on their own and require hand-tying to nails or a trellis.

Deciduous vs. Evergreen Vines

Deciduous vines

- Easier to control.
- Unattractive in winter.
- More frost tolerant.
- Fall color.
- Passive solar.

Evergreen vines

- More invasive.
- Foliage attractive in winter.
- May not flower.
- Insulate house walls.

USING VINES IN THE LANDSCAPE

Vines are used in landscape design as either problem solvers or purely for their aesthetic value.

Vines as Cover-ups

Vines are the perfect solution for covering unattractive walls, fences, or buildings. Architects joke about vines being the only way to hide their mistakes. Plain block walls can be completely covered with clinging vines such as creeping fig or Boston ivy. Long spans of wood fence makes good supports for flowering vines as long as they are strong enough to support the weight of a mature plant.

Having to paint the house need not discourage you from growing vines on unattractive walls. When the vine is planted, attach a grid or fan-shaped prefabricated wood trellis to the wall and train the vine to it. If painting is required, simply detach the trellis and the vine pulls away from the surface temporarily.

Vines for Overhead Shading

Vines chosen for overhead structures must be able to produce enough foliage to create sufficient shade while tolerating direct solar exposure on top. Deciduous vines require the annual fall leaf cleanup chore, but they provide shade in the summer and let sunlight through in the winter. Be aware that flowering vines can attract bees and hummingbirds. Those that develop fruit or seed pods can stain pavement, drop messy litter, and possibly draw fruit flies.

RULE OF GREEN THUMB

A new product uses silicone glue to bond a small plastic bracket to masonry surfaces. The bracket looks like a clear, round flat plastic coat button disk with an eye on the back. Plant tie wire can be inserted through the eye and tied to the vine. If you can't find this package at your local garden center, make your own. Visit a fabric store and find big coat buttons that are flat on the front, with the eye protruding from the back. Use exterior silicone glue and the ties off your bread bags. Apply a marble-sized blob of silicone on the wall, press the face of the button into the glue, and press firmly. Let the glue dry overnight and it should be ready for tying in the morning.

Using Fragrant Flowering Vines

To make the most of fragrant flowering vines, plant them near outdoor living spaces or where foot traffic passes frequently. If there is a prevailing breeze, it helps to plant the vine just upwind. Make sure you like the fragrance of a flowering vine before you plant it on an arbor or near an often-used patio. The scent may become overpowering when the vine is mature and in full bloom.

Groundcover Vines

Sometimes the definitions of vines and groundcovers overlap. When not trained to a vertical surface, vines will crawl along the ground and sometimes root as they go. In this form their vigorous growth makes an excellent covering to reduce erosion on slopes. They also do well cascading off the tops of retaining walls.

Special Considerations for Vines

It pays to be fully aware of how fast a vine will grow and its potential mature size. Some vigorous vines such as wisteria can invade trees and shrubs very quickly. Although a vine may be grown in full sun, reflected heat from walls or adjacent paving can scorch leaves, especially when the plant is young. Also make sure you know how the vine will behave when mature, because, like creeping fig, some experience changes to their foliage as adults.

GROWING AND TRAINING VINES

Vines require help to become the beautiful specimens we admire. They should be trained carefully in the desired direction while young and flexible. Once the main stems have grown rigid with age, they can be difficult to change.

Planting a Young Vine

Vines can be purchased in either 1-gallon or 5-gallon containers, and are planted just like a container-grown tree or shrub. In the nursery it has been trained to a small stake that is anchored in the rootball. The stake should be removed after planting so the runners can be trained to the designated surface. Even if the vine is self clinging, it will need to be tied up at first to place the rootlets or suction cups close enough to the surface. The runners must be untangled and arranged on the wall or trellis in a fan shape so each leaf is exposed to maximum light and air circulation. This arranging of runners or branches is sometimes called "espalier" after a French method of artistically growing all kinds of plants on vertical surfaces.

If you plan to grow the vine on an overhead structure, select the best two or three runners and prune back the rest. Attach these to the support post so they receive all the growth energy. Once they reach the top of the structure, pinch back the tips so they branch outward into many new runners which will cover more area.

Ways to Attach and Train Vines

Attaching vines to a trellis is easy because the runners are tied manually. Don't pull the runners tightly because they may crack or split, and eventually die-back. Tie each runner loosely with plastic nursery tape so it is able to grow in diameter without being girdled. For wood fences or siding, attach the ties to small galvanized nails or brass screw-in hooks. Once the vine matures, it may hold itself up by cascading over the top.

It has always been difficult to get vines started on masonry surfaces. Concrete nails are an option, but they can damage stucco or loosen mortar as they require quite a pounding to penetrate these hard surfaces. One option is to run strong wire horizontally along the wall at 18-inch intervals anchored with nails at each end. Then tie the vines to the wires until established.

Pruning Vines

Tying and training vines is a task that may continue throughout the life of the plant. More rapid growers should be continually shaped throughout the year to

COMMON LANDSCAPING MISTAKES

Everyone loves the purple flowers of wisteria, but it can be a rampant grower. Do not allow it to grow into trees or tall shrubs. Once it has gained a foothold and the runners are thickening into woody branches, it may be nearly impossible to remove without damaging the tree. Most vigorous, fast-growing vines can be equally as invasive and should be handled with care. Think twice before planting wisteria, English ivy, Japanese honeysuckle, and grape vines.

maintain control. If neglected, a vine can grow into itself and runners above shade those beneath, causing them to defoliate and eventually die out. Don't allow them to grow out of reach from your ladder. Keep vines off the roof so they don't interfere with rain gutters or begin to pry up shingles. Do not allow any vine to climb into trees or large shrubs. Tree bark requires oxygen to remain healthy, and when sheathed in ivy or other clinging vines the tree is gradually weakened.

In general, keep all dead, broken, or diseased wood pruned out of vines. Be careful when thinning because runners without foliage lower on the vine may be actively growing and blooming at their tips. It's best to start at the leafy ends and work your way back to the trunk to avoid cutting an important runner. Keep in mind that the leaves of creeping fig vines changes when plants mature. This secondary, leathery growth should be sheared off cleanly to reveal the more attractive small leaves beneath.

CAMPSIS RADICANS

VINES FOR NORTHERN CALIFORNIA GARDENS

Campsis radicans

Trumpet Creeper Zones 1 to 7
Deciduous flowering, to 30 feet. Full sun, part shade. Twining.

This rugged vine thrives even in poor soil and under drought conditions, but it grows much faster with more water and fertilizer. It blooms with clusters of bright orange, 3-inch long trumpet-shaped flowers which are very similar to many less hardy tropical vines. *Campsis* is better for large landscapes where there is plenty of room for its rapid growth and spreading by underground roots. A good choice for planting on split rail fences or to provide shade for arbors, it is large enough to cover gazebos or other outbuildings. Buy trumpet creeper in 1-gallon containers because it is best trained when young.

Clematis armandii

Evergreen Clematis Zones 1 to 7
Evergreen flowering, to 15 feet. Shade, part shade, full sun on the coast. Twining

This is the most forgiving, and only evergreen, member of the clematis vine family. It grows well even in the central valley heat as long as it is adequately shaded and watered. In April and May it flowers with abundant, white single blooms that grow to nearly 3 inches across. These are so fragrant they perfume the air around the vine, making it a good selection for patios or gateways. The long narrow leaves are a leathery deep green and hang gracefully on the delicate vine runners. Evergreen clematis is great for running along the tops of fences or trained onto a trellis. Although very frost hardy, it may be killed down to ground level in severe weather but grows back in spring. May not thrive in the highest Sierra elevations.

VINE SELECTION GUIDE

	Self-Clinging	Flowering	Foliage Vine	Evergreen	Invasive
Campsis radicans		•			•
Clematis armandii		•		•	
Clematis jackmanii 'Superba'		•			
Clytostoma callistegioides		•		•	
Ficus pumila	•		•		
Gelsemium sempervirens		•		•	
Hedera helix	•		•	•	•
Jasminum polyanthum		•		•	•
Lonicera japonica		•		•	•
Parthenocissus tricuspidata	•		•		•
Rosa banksiae		•		•	
Trachelospermum jasminoides		•		•	
Wisteria sinensis		•			•

Clematis jackmanii 'Superba'

Jackman Clematis Zones 1 to 7
Deciduous flowering, to 15 feet. Sun or part shade. Twining.

This is one of the most successful deciduous clematis hybrids for northern California. Its blooms are a rich royal purple, borne on slender stems in July and August. Runners are slender and require support or they will twine around each other into a tangled mass. In cold areas it may freeze to the ground but comes back completely in spring. All deciduous clematis prefer to have their shallow roots in the shade with a thick layer of mulch to keep them cool. Foliage and runners require plenty of sun but suffer from reflected heat on south- or west-facing building walls.

CLEMATIS JACKMANII

Clytostoma callistegioides

Violet Trumpet Vine Zones 3, 5 and 7
Evergreen/semideciduous flowering, to 20 feet. Part shade, full sun on coast. Tendrils.

Masses of lavender trumpet-shaped flowers make this a stunning vine against white lattice or arbors. Its gentle growth habits are susceptible to dry winds but rarely get out of control and it fits well in tight spaces. Where winters are cooler it may lose part or all of its foliage, and root damage occurs at 10°F. Excellent selection for chain link or woven wire fences, where it will self cling and flower repeatedly from midspring to fall. Not used often enough in northern California, it is an excellent alternative to tender tropical vines.

CLEMATIS ARMANDII

Ficus pumila

Creeping Fig Zones 3, 5 and 7
Hardy to 24°F. Evergreen, to 15 feet plus. Shade, part shade. Self clinging.

Creeping fig is exceptional for its ability to create a wall of foliage only an inch or two thick. It prefers north and east sides of buildings, and grows fastest where conditions are cool and moist. Runners self cling with rootlets that aren't as damaging as English ivy, but when removed, bits of root remain stuck to the wall. Mature foliage is large and leathery, bearing little resemblance to small juvenile leaves. Mature growth also has much thicker stems that grow outward, perpendicular to the wall and must be sheared off close to the smaller juvenile leaves to maintain a neat appearance. If vine grows out of reach, there will be a problem with removing mature growth. When first planted, tie up runners to the surface by hand until holdfasts have a chance to attach themselves.

Gelsemium sempervirens

Carolina Yellow Jessamine Zones 2 to 7
Evergreen flowering, to 20 feet. Sun, part shade. Twining.

This vine is best suited for disguising ugly chain link fences. It is not a very rapid grower, but the runners are strong enough to support a tremendous amount of foliage, which can cascade over walls or board fences, and is suitable for shading when trained to overhead structures. It blooms once a year, in early spring, when the entire plant is engulfed in bright yellow tubular flow-

HEDERA HELIX

LONICERA JAPONICA HYBRID

ers that are highly fragrant. May draw bees during bloom time and is also poisonous, so beware of use around swimming pools or play areas. When not in bloom the glossy foliage remains attractive and may require occasional thinning to reduce accumulated woody undergrowth. Not particular about soil quality, it is also relatively drought tolerant.

Hedera helix

English Ivy Zones 2 to 7

Evergreen, to 20 feet plus. Part shade, full sun on coast. Self clinging.

There are over 100 different varieties of English ivy, offering varying leaf size and shape, and unusual variegated cultivars. Think twice before planting ivy as a vine or groundcover. Once considered the ideal plant for California, it has proven to be unruly and invasive, rapidly climbing trees, overwhelming shrubs, and invading structures. Rootlets are tenacious and may damage masonry, stucco, and mortar. Difficult to remove once established, it may also become a haven for rats and other rodents. When exposed to direct sun, leaves burn and massed plantings may die out in patches. As ivy ages, the diameter of runners becomes larger and may damage lattice or other surfaces where it has threaded itself through small spaces. Like creeping fig, some ivies have mature foliage that is very different from the juvenile leaves. The best bet is to stick to the very smallest cultivars, which have lovely foliage and slightly slower growth habits.

Jasminum polyanthum

Chinese Jasmine Zones 3, 5 and 7

Evergreen flowering, to 20 feet. Shade, part shade, full sun on coast. Tendrils.

This fast grower has lacy foliage that attaches to supports with curling tendrils. The hardiest of evergreen jasmines, its long blooming season begins as early as February and continues into summer. Small, white, star-shaped flowers are intensely fragrant and borne in large clusters on side branches. A good choice for overhead structures, it will develop enough mass to provide limited shading with a bonus of overwhelming fragrance. To control size and shape, prune after flowering.

Lonicera japonica

Japanese Honeysuckle Zones 2 to 7

Evergreen flowering, to 30 feet plus. Sun, part shade. Twining.

Few vines will grow as rampantly as Japanese honeysuckle, and its use should be restricted to very large landscapes. Drought and heat tolerant, there are few places it won't thrive. Its flowers are white, turning yellow as they age, and are legendary for the sweetness of fragrance and nectar. Its vigor is valuable for quickly vegetating slopes as well as very dry or poorly drained areas. Plan on cutting its runners back in fall and spring to prevent accumulation of dead material beneath the actively growing top layer of foliage. Brambles of honeysuckle provide a haven for pests and rodents and may become a fire hazard in dry climates.

Parthenocissus tricuspidata

Boston Ivy Zones 1 to 7
Deciduous, to 20 feet plus. Sun, part shade.
Self-clinging.

This is one of the best self-clinging vines for northern California because it has very few bad habits. Not related to destructive English ivy, it clings with tiny suction cup disks that are safe for masonry or wood surfaces. Although it does not flower, each season offers a different foliage quality. In spring the new growth is a vivid lime green; during summer it darkens to emerald, followed by brilliant scarlet fall color. When leaves drop for winter the underlying surface is visible and the vine is easily cut back to keep in bounds. Boston ivy prefers a northern or eastern exposure although it will grow in full sun. Not fussy about soil, this ivy grows faster with generous watering and mulching to keep roots cool. Requires tying and support until holdfasts develop. *Parthenocissus quinquefolia*, Virginia Creeper, is very similar, more cold tolerant but doesn't cling as well.

JASMINUM POLYANTHEM

Rosa banksiae

Lady Banks' Rose Zones 1 to 7
(protect at highest elevations)
Evergreen, to 20 feet. Full sun. Climbing rose.
Hardy to -10°F.

Banksiae is the only rose in this chapter because it has some special characteristics that make it more like a vine. This fast-growing plant is evergreen or partially deciduous at higher elevations. It is remarkably hardy for such a lush grower, but when temperatures are below 10°F. to 20°F. it should be given some protection from snow and wind along with a root mulch. It is very pest and disease resistant, and the long, arching canes are nearly thornless, making it painless to work with. Once a year, in late spring, it is completely covered with big clusters of miniature fragrant, white or yellow roses. A great choice for covering shade arbors because of its fast growth, this rose doesn't accumulate dead wood like other fast growing vines. It can be easily cut back during winter if the size gets out of hand. Has no means of attachment and must be tied to supports.

PARTHENOCISSUS TRICUSPIDATA FRAMING DOORWAY.

Trachelospermum jasminoides

Star Jasmine Zones 2 to 7
Evergreen to 5 feet. Part shade, full sun on coast.
Twining.

Not a true jasmine, this vine is often used as a groundcover, but the long, twining runners become a

PARTHENOCISSUS TRICUSPIDATA WITHOUT LEAVES.

WISTERIA SINENSIS

maintenance problem when they invade nearby shrubs and perennials. When used as a vine, star jasmine can be trained on wire fences, wrought iron, or lattice, where it will eventually become a dense screen. Twining runners must be threaded through supports, and when coverage is complete, they must be frequently pruned back. Its best quality is the highly fragrant, star-shaped white flowers that are borne over a long blooming season, from April to July. Although tolerant of full sun, its foliage discolors when scorched by reflected heat or very hot western exposures. Looks best when grown with adequate moisture and fertilizer in part shade inland.

Wisteria sinensis

Chinese Wisteria Zones 1 to 7

Deciduous, to 40 feet. Sun, part shade. Twining.

The most popular vine in America, wisteria's pendulous lavender blossoms are always impressive. It is most often trained on porches, arbors, and balconies, where the flowers grow from 6 inches to 12 inches long. A fast, rank grower, it needs strong supports because the runners will eventually become very thick and heavy. Wisteria can cause damage when tendrils pry up wood shingles or siding. Buy only selected, named varieties of wisteria because those raised from seed can take up to fifteen years to bloom. To promote best flower display, prune and thin wisteria after it flowers or when leafless in the winter. Early spring applications of phosphate fertilizer will encourage best flower displays.

GROUNDCOVERS

There have been many false claims made about groundcovers being the "low-maintenance alternative to lawn." This is far from the truth. However, groundcover plants are a valuable solution to erosion problems and slopes where nothing else will grow. Before you consider planting a groundcover, make sure you have done your homework and are prepared to deal with both the good and bad results of your choice.

THE GREAT GROUNDCOVER TRUTHS

There are many factors which have been ignored in favor of the myth that groundcovers are the panacea for all garden problems. This results in a major waste of land, money, and labor.

1. **Groundcovers are not low maintenance.**
   Most people would rather mow a lawn than spend hours on their hands and knees weeding groundcover. Ground-hugging mats such as potentilla or isotoma make the task of pulling invasive grasses especially tedious.
2. **Groundcover plants may not be long lived.**
   The stems and runners of some groundcovers become woody and barren with age, and leaves do not grow as readily from these hardened stems. The resulting exposure of the crown of the plant to direct sun causes it to split apart. In fire-prone areas, this woody, dry accumulation of stems presents a real hazard.
3. **Groundcover areas become havens for pests.**
   Large areas of leafy groundcover can become havens for insect pests and wildlife since there is rarely any foot traffic to disturb nests and young. Gophers, ground squirrels, rats, or mice can all invade groundcover. Accumulations of dead leaves and stems draw earwigs, sow bugs, snails, and slugs.
4. **Groundcovers can be invasive.**
   The best groundcovers are aggressive plants that spread to cover areas quickly and completely, with low water requirements. But these same qualities make groundcovers invasive weeds when they grow where unwanted. Once established they may persist indefinitely.
5. **Groundcovers may die out in patches.**
   Perennial groundcovers tend to die-out in patches for no apparent reason. The California Department of Transportation has eliminated African daisies as freeway right-of-way groundcover for exactly this reason. Over time groundcovers may die-out and require replanting.

CLASSIFYING GROUNDCOVER PLANTS

Plants used as groundcovers grow in two basic forms. Herbaceous plants are set out on regular spacings and spread by either above ground stems or underground roots. Groundcover shrubs are single plants that grow to a large diameter, with vinelike branches covering many square feet.

The spacing for each groundcover species is based on its speed and growth characteristics. The less time it takes for the groundcover to take hold and crowd out weeds, the fewer maintenance problems arise. Planting very close together is expensive, but plants fill in more quickly.

Spreading Groundcover Plants

Spreading groundcovers are almost always herbaceous; that is, they don't have a woody, branching structure. As each plant grows, it creates new plants by either above- or underground stems or roots. Some species, such as vinca, have vinelike runners that become new plants at regular intervals by rooting where they touch the ground. Other types of plants send out strong roots, called stolons, that develop stems and leaves where they break the surface of the soil.

Spreading groundcovers are usually sold in flats, which are shallow trays that contain 50 to 72 plants. Insist that any flat you buy contains all 50 to 72 plants growing vigorously. Don't be persuaded to buy the same plants in 4-inch pots or 1-gallon containers, as the cost of buying a flat of groundcover plants is much more economical.

RULE OF GREEN THUMB

Some spreading groundcovers benefit from occasional renewal by mowing in the early spring. This removes parts of the plants that may have frost damage, sunburn, die-out, or woodiness that no longer produces foliage. It also exposes the soil, to discourage any rodent or insect infestations. The returning new growth is more attractive and vigorous, and in some species it promotes better flowering. If the planting area is accessible by lawn mower, you can mow it at the highest setting and bag the clippings. More difficult areas can be reached with a string trimmer, and cuttings should be raked up and removed. Groundcovers suitable for this treatment are hypericum, periwinkle, dwarf periwinkle, and yarrow.

INSTALLATION OF GROUNDCOVER SHRUBS THROUGH LANDSCAPE FABRIC. *(REEMAY, INC.)*

Creeping Shrubs

Some groundcover plants are woody shrubs or vines that branch outward from a single individual. They are spaced much further apart because one plant at maturity may cover an area from 6 feet to 15 feet in diameter. The key word here is *maturity*, because it could be many months or even years before one of these slower-growing plants fills in the space. In the meantime, heavy mulches or weed fabric will be needed in between plants to control weeds. If a single plant dies later on, a huge area may be left completely barren.

SUCCESS WITH GROUNDCOVERS

It's not difficult to plant groundcover, but there are a few general guidelines that make it easier. Weed control, proper spacing, and decorative mulches are equally important factors which determine how successful your planting will be.

Preplanting Weed Control

If you don't prepare for weeds before you plant, you'll be forced to deal with them later on a much larger scale. The difficulty is with seeds lying dormant in the soil that sprout after you plant. The very worst offenders are bermuda and other runner grasses which sprout from bits of root, then spread rapidly. Refer to the preplanting weed control guidelines for lawn areas in chapter 6.

ARCTOSTAPHYLOS GROUNDCOVER

CAMPANULA POSCHARSKYANA IN BACKGROUND

CERASTIUM TOMENTOSUM

GAZANIA RIGENS LEUCOLAENA

GROUNDCOVER SELECTION GUIDE

S = sun. SH = shade. PS = part sun.
Plants designated as S/PS may require full sun on the coast and partial shade inland.

Name	*Zones*	*Spacing*	*Exposure*
Acacia redolens	3, 5, 7	10 feet	S
Creeping Acacia—flowers yellow. Woody shrub.			
Achillea tomentosa	2 to 7	6 inches	S
Wooly Yarrow—flowers white. Mowable. Herbaceous.			
Ajuga reptans	2 to 7	6 inches	SH/PS
Carpet Bugle—flowers blue. Herbaceous			
***Arctostaphylos* 'Emerald Carpet'**	all	3 feet	S
Creeping Manzanita Hybrid—flowers white, red berries. Shrub			
***Baccharis pilularis* 'Twin Peaks'**	2 to 7	4 feet	S
Baccharis pilularis 'Twin Peaks'—no flowers. Woody shrub.			
Campanula poscharskyana	2 to 7	10 inches	SH/PS
Serbian Bellflower—flowers blue. Herbaceous. Mowable.			
***Ceanothus* 'Carmel Creeper'**	2 to 7	10 feet	S/PS
Ceanothus 'Carmel Creeper'—flowers blue. Woody shrub.			
Cerastium tomentosum	1 to 7	12 inches	S
Snow In Summer—flowers white. Herbaceous.			
***Euonymos fortunei* 'Colorata'**	1 to 7	24 inches	S/PS
Purple Winter Creeper—fall color. Herbaceous.			

Name	*Zones*	*Spacing*	*Exposure*
Fragaria chiloensis	3, 5, 7	12 inches	PS
Wild Strawberry—flowers white, red fruit. Herbaceous. Mowable.			
Gazania rigens leucolaena	3, 5, 7	18 inches	S
Trailing Gazania—flowers yellow. Gray foliage. Herbaceous.			
***Gazania splendens* hybrids**	3,5,7	12 inches	S/PS
Clumping Gazania—flowers many colors. Herbaceous. Nonspreading.			
Hedera helix	3, 5, 7	12 inches to 18 inches	SH/PS
English Ivy—self clinging. Herbaceous. Invasive. Dwarf and Varigated forms: Needlepoint, Hahns, Gold Dust.			
Hypericum calycinum	2 to 7	12 inches	S/PS
Aaron's Beard—flowers yellow. Herbaceous. Mowable.			
Isotoma fluviatilis	3,5,7	6 inches	S/PS
Blue Star Creeper—flowers blue. Herbaceous.			
***Juniperus* spp.**	1 to 7	3 to 10 feet	S
Juniper—No flowers. Woody shrub.			
Lampranthus spectabilis	7	12 inches	S
Trailing Ice Plant—flowers pink. Succulent. Salt Tolerant.			
Lonicera japonica	2 to 7	15 feet	S
Japanese Honeysuckle—flowers yellow. Vine.			
***Mahonia aquifolium* 'Compacta'**	2 to 7	24 inches	SH
Dwarf Oregon Grape—flowers yellow. Herbaceous.			
Pachysandra terminalis	1 to 7	12 inches	SH
Japanese Spurge—flowers white. Herbaceous.			

Gazania splendens hybrid. (*Jack Bodger*)

Gazania splendens mixed hybrids (*Jack Bodger*)

Hedera helix

Hypericum calycinum

ROSMARINUS 'PROSTRATUS' CREEPS OR CASCADES AS SHOWN.

VINCA MINOR ON SLOPING GROUND.

VERBENA. (*JACK BODGER*)

TRACHELOSPERMUM JASMINOIDES

Name	*Zones*	*Spacing*	*Exposure*
Potentilla taberaemontanii (aka P. verna)	1 to 7	12 inches	S/PS
Spring Cinquefoil—flowers yellow. Herbaceous.			
***Rosmarinus* 'Prostratus'**	2 to 7	12 inches	S
Creeping Rosemary—flowers blue. Half-woody herb.			
Trachelospermum jasminoides	3 to 7	24 inches	PS
Star Jasmine—flowers white. Fragrant. Twining plant.			

Name	*Zones*	*Spacing*	*Exposure*
Verbena peruviana	3, 5, 7	12 inches	S
Peruvian Verbena—flowers pink, purple. Short lived.			
Vinca major	1 to 7	18 inches	S/PS
Periwinkle—flowers blue. Herbaceous. Mowable.			
Vinca minor	1 to 7	12 inches	PS/SH
Dwarf Periwinkle—flowers blue. Herbaceous. Mowable.			

Postplanting Weed Control

Mulches and weed barrier fabric used together is a means of reducing the weed contamination of newly planted groundcover. The fabric is laid out first, then the decorative mulch is spread evenly over its surface. To plant, simply move the mulch to the side, make a small hole in the fabric, and plant the groundcover through it. Then replace the mulch around the plant. If mulch is used without fabric, it should be applied at least 2 inches but, preferably 3 inches deep to effectively block weeds.

When using ground bark, remember that large pieces tend to float away in heavy rains and make great toys for Fido and the kids. The best-sized bark is about 1/2 inch to 1 inch in diameter because it packs down enough to allow raking of leaves off the top.

PLANTING GROUNDCOVERS

Each of the groundcovers should be planted at a designated spacing, which dictates how many plants to buy. Measure the size of the area you have and calculate the number of plants you will need by using the following chart.

SPACING GROUNDCOVER PLANTS

Spacing of plants	*Plants per square foot*
8 inches	2.25
10 inches	1.44
12 inches	1.00
14 inches	.73
16 inches	.56
18 inches	.44
24 inches	.25

Groundcover planted too close to shrubs will create competition for water and fertilizer. Do not plant any groundcover plants inside the dripline of shrubs in the same area. You can keep them at bay with a collar of bark mulch. The collar is easy to maintain and also prevents groundcovers from climbing onto the shrub.

LISTS OF GROUNDCOVER "BESTS"

Botanical Name	*Common Name*
Fastest Growing Groundcovers	
Euonymos fortunei 'Colorata'	Wintercreeper
Gazania rigens leucolaena	Trailing Gazania
Hedera helix	English Ivy
Hypericum calycinum	Creeping St. Johnswort
Juniperus conferta	Shore Juniper
Lonicera japonica	Japanese Honeysuckle
Trachelospermum jasminoides	Star Jasmine
Verbena peruviana	Peruvian Verbena
Vinca major	Periwinkle
Vinca minor	Dwarf Periwinkle
Very Low Matlike Groundcovers Under 4 inches Tall	
Ajuga reptans	Carpet Bugle
Armeria maritima	Thrift
Herniaria glabra	Green Carpet
Isotoma fluviatilis (*Laurentia fluviatilis*)	Blue Star Creeper
Potentilla tabernaemontanii (*P. verna*)	Spring Cinquefoil
Drought-Tolerant Groundcovers	
Acacia redolens	Creeping Acacia
Achillea tomentosa	Wooly Yarrow
Arctostaphylos spp. (California native)	Manzanita
Baccharis pilularis 'Twin Peaks' (California native)	Dwarf Coyote Bush
Ceanothus spp. (California native)	California Lilac
Lonicera japonica	Japanese Honeysuckle
Rosmarinus prostratus	Creeping Rosemary
Verbena peruviana	Peruvian Verbena
Vinca major	Periwinkle
Woody Shrub Groundcovers	
Acacia redolens	Creeping Acacia
Arctostaphylos spp.	Manzanita
Ceanothus 'Carmel Creeper'	California Lilac
Juniperus spp.	Juniper
Lonicera japonica	Japanese Honeysuckle

CHAPTER SIX

California Turf Grass

TURF GRASS

In the heat of summer, nothing makes a home look so cool and inviting as a lush green lawn. The climate in northern California is perfect for growing turf grass, and some of the nation's most beautiful golf courses are right next door.

California faces a serious dilemma in the coming years as its population grows larger than the water supply. When drought strikes, lawn is the first part of the landscape to be denied water and it promptly withers and dies. Residents question whether to risk replanting when the rains finally do come, because another dry spell may be just around the corner.

The industry has responded by concentrating its research and development on new strains of deep-rooted, drought-resistant turf grasses, but there are no earth-shaking breakthroughs yet. The best solution is to learn more about how lawn grass grows, how it can be made more drought tolerant, and most importantly, how we can make sure each drop of water is used to its fullest potential.

THE BASICS OF HEALTHY TURF

Golf course turf managers claim they can "make grass grow on concrete with enough water and fertilizer." Although this is an exaggeration, it illustrates just how simple growing turf grass can be. The key is to provide the four basics: sunlight, oxygen, nitrogen, and water. How well these basic materials reach the grass plant is the essence of what caring for a lawn is all about.

• **Water** Lawn grasses have shallow root systems, and water should be applied frequently in warm weather when growth is active and evaporation potential is high. In order to prevent over-wet or over-dry conditions, watering times should be monitored closely and adjusted for seasonal climatic changes.

• **Nitrogen** Nitrogen is the primary ingredient in all fertilizers designed for lawns. Because our weather in California is so mild, lawns should receive more frequent fertilizer applications than in other regions. Fertilizing begins earlier in the spring here, and should be continued much later in the fall to maintain healthy plants and a rich, green color.

• **Oxygen** We all know plants absorb oxygen through their leaves, but the roots must be able to breathe as well. When soils are compacted, or when saturated due to poor drainage, very little oxygen is available to roots. Keeping the soil open and aerated is essential for healthy grass plants.

• **Sunlight** A lawn should receive full sunlight all day long. But as landscapes mature, the canopies of shade trees create more shadow which makes lawns grow sparsely. Lawns weakened by shade become more vulnerable to pests and diseases.

TIPS FOR EFFICIENT WATER USE

When the blades of turf grasses turn grayish-blue, this signals a lack of water in the root zone. The *root zone* of a grass plant is defined as the portion of the soil accessed by its roots. The depth of this zone can vary. Shallow-rooted turf grasses access water from the top few inches of soil. Your goal is to encourage plants to develop a much larger root zone better able to withstand the stress of temporary drought. Here are three ways to increase the root zone of your lawn:

1. Aerate compacted soil.
2. Water less frequently but more deeply.
3. Overseed the lawn with deeper rooted grass species.

How to Deep-Water Slow-Draining Soils

Deep watering can be difficult in clay soils, which absorb water at a very slow rate. Sprinkler water begins to run off long before it can penetrate. A time-consuming but effective method is to turn the sprinklers on until water begins to run off, then shut the system off. Wait ten minutes to a half hour for the water to settle into the soil, then water again. Repeat this process until the sprinklers have been *operating* for a total of fifteen to twenty minutes. Using this method to deep water may take longer, but it need not be done as frequently as surface watering. You can reduce or eliminate the rest periods by aerating the soil whenever it shows signs of compaction.

Automatic and Manually Controlled Sprinkler Systems

Automatic sprinkler systems can be serious water wasters. This is because people are usually asleep, indoors, or aren't at home to notice when the sprinklers are operating. Manually operated sprinkler systems keep you more aware of how the lawn is using water.

Sprinkler systems should function at peak efficiency. Plan to inspect your watering system at least three times a year. Pay attention to each item on the following list to help you cover all the bases.

1. Replace any broken sprinklers with heads of the same type.
2. Raise up any sprinklers that have sunk into the soil to restore coverage.
3. Straighten crooked sprinklers to an upright position.
4. Adjust heads which are out of alignment and overspraying onto surfaces other than lawn.
5. Clean out sprinklers which may be clogged or jammed.
6. Watch for signs of surface silt buildup resulting from underground cracks or breaks in supply lines.
7. Check flow control screws on the top of heads to increase or decrease water output as required.
8. Run the automatic controller through all its stations and watch each valve operate. When you begin to see runoff or if puddles of water form, turn that station off and adjust the timer.

GARDEN HOSE SPRINKLER SYSTEMS

When using garden hose sprinklers, follow these basic guidelines to insure even coverage and efficient water usage.

1. Use oscillating "flip-flop" square pattern sprinklers on square lawn areas.
2. Use impact sprinklers to cover very large areas.
3. Maintain tight connections at all couplers. Replace washers and couplers as needed.
4. Use shut off timer at the hose bib.

Golden State Tips for Greater Irrigation Efficiency

Whether watering with the garden hose or a sprinkler system, these rules of irrigation should apply to everyone.

1. Water early in the morning when neighborhood usage is low and municipal water pressure is high. Your sprinkler system will function better under ideal pressure.
2. Avoid watering during the day. A tremendous amount of water will evaporate between the sprinkler and the ground in hot weather.
3. Mow your grass higher and less often to shade the soil and prevent surface evaporation, especially during hot inland summers.
4. Keep weeds in the lawn under control. They claim soil moisture that should be used by the turf.
5. Although you may sacrifice some of its color, fertilize your lawn less frequently during the summer to reduce growth rate.

FERTILIZERS AND LAWN HEALTH

A lawn consists of hundreds of individual plants growing very close together. Competition for nutrients is fierce and the soil is quickly robbed of its nitrogen. Unless soil nitrogen is replenished, growth rates slow down and plants lose their lush, green color. Lawns must be fertilized more often in California because our growing season is so long. Well-fed, healthy turf grass is better able to resist invasions of insect pests and disease. Only during times of drought should fertilization of lawns be reduced to slow the growth rate and limit the plant's water needs.

Selecting a Lawn Fertilizer

You will purchase more fertilizer for the lawn than for the rest of the landscape combined. When buying in quantity, compare cost and nutrient percentages for the very best price. Name brand lawn fertilizers are more expensive, and often contain the same nutrient percentages as generic brands.

• **Granular fertilizers** Granular fertilizers are the easiest to apply evenly over large areas. A complete lawn fertilizer contains high percentages of nitrogen and small amounts of phosphorus and potassium, with trace elements. Although more expensive, they provide a well rounded diet. Potent, nitrogen-only fertilizers such as ammonium nitrate, ammonium sulfate, and urea are not advisable because the slightest error in application can severely burn the lawn. Liquid concentrate fertilizers are a good alternative for dense, slow-draining soils because they are less likely to burn.

• **Weed while you feed** Some fertilizers contain selective herbicides which kill weeds as you fertilize, but the material is toxic and may not be the best choice where children and pets use the lawn.

• **Organic fertilizers** Organics can be more labor intensive and expensive to buy, but you fertilize less often. A good organic fertilizer created from sewage sludge contains 6 percent nitrogen and is a favorite because it is sold in easy to apply dry granules. Use only composted animal manures free of weed seeds.

Safe Application of Lawn Fertilizers

A lawn is unforgiving and the slightest error in fertilizer application will show up almost immediately. Brown, yellow, very light or dark green spots and stripes indicate fertilizer burn. Use a mechanical drop spreader with an 18-inch to 24-inch long slot next to the axle. For large lawns, a "whirlybird" spreader, which uses a paddle wheel to fling the granules up to 10 feet in each direction, will give quicker coverage.

Each fertilizer label suggests an application rate based in pounds per 1,000 square feet. Although this helps to figure how much fertilizer to buy, knowing exactly how much the spreader is delivering in these terms can be difficult. It's better to apply the fertilizer very lightly at first to see how the lawn responds, then gradually increase the rate of application in small increments.

Always fill and adjust the drop spreader on a paved surface and not on the lawn. Push the spreader over a section of pavement to see how fast the granules come out. If too little fertilizer is applied to the lawn you can

NORTHERN CALIFORNIA TIP

Heavy clay soils and hardpans can be very dense and difficult to feed with a granular fertilizer. Once applied and watered in, the dissolving granules become a very potent solution. If the soil percolates at a slow rate, the solution remains on the top of the soil to burn grass plants. If you have fertilized your lawn and it fails to respond, or becomes more yellow, then try switching to a liquid fertilizer. Liquid fertilizers are weaker, and diluted when they reach the lawn. The plants can also take up liquid nitrogen directly through their leaves since it need not be watered in after an application.

LIGHT AND DARK STRIPES FROM MOWING CLEARLY SEEN HERE. THE DIRECTION OF THE STRIPES GIVES THE ILLUSION OF GREATER SPACE.

RULES OF GREEN THUMB

Every blade of grass has two sides, one smooth and the other slightly fuzzy. Lawn mowers turn the grass blades all one way, which is why baseball fields appear to have light and dark stripes. You can be creative while mowing the lawn and manipulate the striping. Instead of mowing up and down, try making perfectly straight stripes at a diagonal. If you have a freeform lawn, begin at the outside edge, go all the way around and work your way in circles to the center. Your striping will mirror the curves of your lawn and enhance its beauty. The next time do the same thing, but in the opposite direction.

always make another pass, but if too much is used, you'll have to water heavily to dilute the granules enough to prevent burning. Do not apply granular fertilizers to wet lawns because the fertilizer sticks to the blades and burns them on contact. Lawns must be watered thoroughly after fertilizer is applied to insure proper dilution.

MOWING AND LAWN CARE EQUIPMENT

Mowing the lawn can be either a frustrating or rewarding task, depending on how you approach it. Everyone has struggled with a stubborn mower that won't start, clogged debris chutes, or grass that refuses to shear off cleanly. Knowing what causes the problems and how to prevent them is the key to successful mowing and a show quality lawn.

Golden State Rules for Mowing Lawns

1. **Keep the mower clean and well maintained.**
   Dirty mowers don't cut grass well. Clippings build up under the housing, which interferes with the blade and strains the engine.

2. **Avoid mowing when the grass is wet.**
   When the mower cuts wet grass, clippings stick to the housing and accumulate at the bottleneck where they shoot into the catcher. If not cleaned, the opening clogs up completely.

3. **Pay attention to mowing patterns.**
   If you always mow in the same pattern, the grass blades will lean in that direction. To keep the grass upright, mow in an alternate direction each time.

4. **Cut extra tall grass gradually.**
   If you have neglected to mow the lawn, don't try to mow it all at once at the usual height. Instead, set the mower a notch higher and mow the lawn once, then lower it back to normal and mow again.

5. **Keep a sharp mower blade.**
   If your new-mown grass appears to have a white haze over the surface, or if it looks shredded or if blades of grass are left after you mow, the culprit is a dull blade. Many gardeners keep a spare sharpened blade on hand so they can change blades quickly and continue mowing without interruption.

Golden State Rules for Safe Mowing

1. Remove all rocks, sticks, toys, and debris before mowing.
2. Never remove or restrict any safety device on your mower.
3. Refuel the mower only after it has cooled.
4. Do not adjust the mowing height, clean, clear, or repair the mower when it is running.
5. Never operate the mower barefoot or in sandals.

Golden State Rules for Mower Maintenance

1. Check the oil level before each time you use the mower.
2. Avoid using gasoline with methanol or other additives.
3. Thoroughly clean the mower with water after each use.
4. Clean the air filter after each use, especially if dusty.
5. Drain the fuel tank and refill it with fresh gas if the mower hasn't been used for over a month.

RENOVATING FOR HEALTHIER TURF

Golf course turf is renovated on a regular basis by opening up the soil, overseeding to thicken the grass, top-dressing with soil conditioners, and removing the remnants of decaying grass plants. You can do this on a smaller scale to insure a healthy pest- and disease-resistant lawn that utilizes every bit of water and fertilizer you provide.

Aerating a Compacted Lawn

When the soil beneath a lawn becomes compacted, water cannot penetrate quickly enough, nor can it transport fertilizer to the root system. Soil compaction is reduced by the process of aeration, which is done with a specialized machine which extracts plugs of soil a few inches deep at regular intervals over the entire lawn. The resulting cavities speed water and fertilizer past the surface of the soil and directly into the root zone. They also act like sumps to hold water in the root zone until it can gradually seep into the surrounding soil.

Most rental yards have aerating machines. It's a good idea to water and soften the soil a few days before you plan to use the aerator. Run the aerator over the entire surface of the lawn, and it will leave behind cores of soil which should be raked up and removed.

Thatching a Lawn

Thatch is a layer of dead grass, clippings, and other organic materials which build up on the surface of the soil. This moist, decomposing material creates a perfect environment for disease and insects. Excessive use of mulching mowers causes thatch to accumulate into a layer which prevents water, oxygen, and fertilizer from reaching the root zone.

Thatch removal is best done while grasses are actively growing. Use a special rake for small lawns; larger areas requires a de-thatching machine. Rental yards carry these machines, which can also be called vertical power mowers or "verti-cutters." Thatching equipment slices up thatch, which must be raked up and discarded. Avoid adding this material to compost piles if aggressive grasses like bermuda are present.

Renovating the Lawn

Lawn renovation is the renewal of a lawn without removing the existing grass. Renovation begins with thatching, aeration, or both. This is followed by overseeding to thicken the stand of existing grass, or to plant annual grass over a dormant lawn to keep it green in the winter. The final step is to apply a layer of top-dressing material to cover the seed and improve soil quality.

Overseeding in northern California is best done in the fall. This is a good opportunity to incorporate more drought tolerant and endophyte enhanced grass types into your lawn. Use a drop spreader to distribute the new seed at a rate 1 1/2 times that recommended on the label. Then lightly rake the surface of the lawn to help the seed sift down to the level of the soil. To cover the seed and improve the soil, apply a layer of top-dressing material such as composted steer manure, sand, or a prepackaged top-dress mix.

After renovation, keep the lawn evenly moist by watering frequently, but for a short time. Don't be in a hurry to mow as it can damage the newly germinated seedlings. Apply fertilizer at half strength from four to six weeks after overseeding. If not overseeded, you can fertilize the lawn immediately after aeration or thatching to give the damaged plants an immediate boost of nutrients and water.

DIFFERENT WAYS TO PLANT A LAWN

Here in California we can plant lawns by direct seeding, hydroseeding, or by laying sod. This is best done during either the fall or spring while temperatures are cooler. Planting lawns in summer heat places unnecessary stress on the new grass, and winter soil may be too cold and soggy for germination. How you choose to plant your lawn depends on the size of the area, its topography, drainage, your financial budget, maintenance limitations, and time frame.

Which Lawn Planting Method to Use

Method	*Cost*	*Labor*	*Maintenance*	*Timeframe*
Direct Seeding	low	high	high	slow
Hydroseed	med.	low	high	slow
Sodding	high	med.	low	immediate

Preparing the Soil to Seed or Sod a Lawn

Proper soil preparation makes it much easier to establish a new lawn no matter how it is planted. It's best to take more time with the soil preparation in order to remove as many weed seeds as possible before planting.

• **Nonchemical weed seed removal** Weed seeds must sprout before they can be removed from the soil. Watering

RULE OF GREEN THUMB

If a newly aerated lawn is left as is, the holes will gradually collapse and the soil becomes compacted again. To prevent this, top-dress with a thick layer of coarse construction sand. Rake it into the grass so the sand fills the little holes and keeps them open. This is very important for extending the results of aerated turf in heavy clay soils.

USING A DROP SPREADER TO OVERSEED AN EXISTING LAWN. (DOWELANCO)

the lawn area a few weeks before you plan to plant causes those seeds on the surface to sprout. Rototill them under and bring up new seed lying deeper in the soil. Water the area once again until the seeds sprout. Rototill one more time, and repeat the process until most of the weeds have germinated and died.

• **Exceptions requiring chemical controls** Grasses like notorious bermuda can sprout from tiny bits of root. Rototilling actually makes the problem worse by distributing the roots over a much wider area. The realistic solution to controlling bermuda is by using an translocated herbicide with the ability to travel throughout the root system of the plant.

Begin the process by watering the area and wait for the seedlings to appear. But instead of rototilling, apply herbicide according to manufacturer's directions, and wait for up to two weeks for it to take full effect. Only then should you rototill again and wait for new seedlings to appear. The process may be repeated numerous times until only a few seedlings appear after watering.

• **Improve the soil** The next step is to rototill the soil as deeply as possible. Once the soil is broken up, spread a 2-inch deep layer of humus over the entire area, then till it in thoroughly. Coarse sand and manure are excellent for clay soils. Fine compost gives sandy soils greater fertility and water-holding ability. Avoid undecomposed woody materials which will foster fungi and mushrooms. Make sure all soil additives are weed-seed free. To boost soil fertility, add about four pounds of 5-10-5 fertilizer per 1,000 square feet of lawn. Any brand will work if it has a similar nutrient ratio.

• **Finish grading** After working in nutrients, rake the entire area and level it as much as possible, carefully adjusting the grade of low or high spots. While raking, remove larger clods of dirt, rocks, roots, and woody materials so the seed bed is clean and even. You should expect settling over the next two weeks. Lawn rollers are used to reduce this waiting time, but only if there is not danger of compacting clay soil. The surface grade for seeded lawns should be about 2 inches below the top of adjacent pavement. If you are laying sod, the finish grade must be 3 inches below the pavement because sod will be thicker.

• **Check the sprinklers** The final step in preparing the lawn bed is to check the sprinkler system and make sure all the heads are operating properly. Check the angle of each head so there is complete coverage with minimal overspray onto adjacent paved surfaces or planters. *After* seeding or sodding is not time to discover the sprinklers are broken and must be repaired.

How to Direct Seed a New Lawn

Sparsely covered soil is subjected to weed invasions and may wash out without roots to hold it together. When seeded too densely, seedlings grow tall and spindly, weakened by increased competition for light and water. Use a drop spreader to distribute seed evenly. Some garden centers lend drop spreaders to customers who purchase seed, but they are also available at rental yards.

Sow seed at the recommended rate for that variety. Cover the area in two passes, the first in stripes from right to left, and the second from top to bottom. Use the impressions in the soil from the spreader wheels as a means of marking where you've been. After the seed has been set out, top-dress with composted steer manure or a similar humus product. Set the spreader to deliver a layer about 1/8-inch thick, which covers the seed and provides extra nutrients for a good start.

Hydroseeding a New Lawn

Hydroseeding must be done by a landscape contractor with special equipment. Although more costly

NORTHERN CALIFORNIA TIP

Consumers can be ripped off by dishonest hydroseed contractors who buy too little seed and pocket the difference. It's difficult for you to verify whether you are receiving the right application rate when seed is mixed in the slurry. The best way to protect yourself is to seek out the most highly recommended hydroseeder in your area and watch him or her pour the bags of seed into the tank. If you have a sloping lawn, ask the contractor to include a "tackifier" in the mixture. This is a type of organic glue that helps the seed and mulch stick to the soil. It insures the seed stays in place until well rooted and prevents a buildup of seed washed to the bottom of the slope.

ENDOPHYTES—FUTURE FUNGI

Turf grass specialists have discovered unique types of fungi that make grasses less tasty to insects. Turf grass seed is first inoculated with this fungi, called an endophyte. The endophyte goes on to live inside the mature plant in a mutually beneficial relationship. The completely nontoxic endophyte is distasteful to insects, making plants more pest free. When selecting seed for a new lawn, ask for types containing endophytes whenever possible. Our knowledge of the long-term effects of endophytes is still being tested, but experts feel inoculation will become a strong trend for grass as well as many other types of plants in the future.

than hand seeding, you can count on a successful crop of grass. The hydromulch holds the seed in place, and may be the only way to establish a lawn on sloping ground. The fibers absorb a tremendous amount of moisture and hold it around the germinating seeds.

Sodding an Instant Lawn

Sodding is the fastest, but most expensive way of planting. Strips of field-grown sod are laid upon prepared soil where the roots continue to grow downward and anchor the sod in a few weeks time. The industry has recently begun to grow "soil-less turf on plastic," which is sod without soil on the roots. It is light weight, folded rather than rolled, and becomes established much more quickly because the roots aren't severed when harvested. Although slightly more expensive it will soon replace traditional sod.

Coordinate the delivery of your sod so it can be laid out immediately. The inside of rolled sod is vulnerable to rot if left too long, and it can also become overdry on the edges. If you must store the sod for a few days, stack the rolls tightly in the shade and wrap them in sheets of plastic with openings for oxygen. Scatter preplanting fertilizer, formulated for sod, over the surface of the soil at a rate indicated by the manufacturer. Then lay the sod directly on top of it. This fertilizer won't burn the sod roots if used properly, and it helps them to heal more quickly.

The soil should be moist, but not wet, before you begin sodding. Lay out the strips in a staggered pattern, like bricks, with the seams joined together as tightly as possible. Gently press each strip downward to achieve full contact with the soil. Use topsoil or composted steer manure to seal edges from moisture loss. Water the sod lightly right after you're through.

The final step in laying sod is to roll the lawn to prevent air pockets. You may be able to rent one from the garden center where you purchased the sod. Put only a small amount of water inside, or use it empty if you are working on heavy soil. After rolling, keep the lawn squishy wet for ten days, and pay special attention to vulnerable corners and edges.

Watering Newly Planted Lawns

Direct seeded and hydroseeded lawns must be kept evenly moist for the grass to germinate. It's better to water more frequently but for a short time, to prevent washing out the seed. Pay attention to the weather. The chief threats to newly planted lawns are heat and wind. Wind pulls moisture out of the leaves of young seedlings or new sod, and must be compensated for with additional waterings. Gradually extend the time between waterings as the grass becomes established. The goal is to apply water at a rate consistent with the soil type, and water only until there is the first sign of runoff.

If weeds appear, don't be too quick to pull them because you may damage the tender new roots of grass around them. As the lawn thickens, it will naturally choke out some of the weeds, and the others can be pulled by hand after a few months.

Give a seed-grown lawn its first mowing in three to four weeks. Mowing helps the grass grow outward into thick clumps. Each time leaf material is removed, there is more energy given to enlarging the root zone. Don't fertilize the lawn until after the second mowing, and do it carefully. Young plants burn easily and only a very mild fertilizer with a formula similar to 3-1-2 should be used, and at half the recommended rate. It is essential you water heavily after this application to dilute the fertilizer completely. The next month, you can begin using an all-purpose lawn fertilizer, but be conservative with your application rates for a few more months.

COMMON LANDSCAPING MISTAKES

You will at some point encounter advertisements for "miracle" grasses that are extremely durable and drought resistant. What they don't tell you is that the grass is so invasive that once present in your garden it becomes impossible to control. Many species also have a long winter dormancy period when they turn brown. This is the reason why major California turf companies don't sell these "miracle" grasses. Let them be your guide as to what is reliable and proven successful in the northern parts of our state.

AN EXAMPLE OF HOW CALIFORNIA LAWNS SHOULD LOOK IF ADEQUATELY WATERED AND FERTILIZED. THIS SLOPING, MOUNDED LAWN IS EVEN MORE DIFFICULT TO CARE FOR SINCE WATER RUNS OFF THE HIGH POINTS AND COLLECTS AT THE BOTTOM OF THE SLOPES.

THIS UNMOWED TUFT OF TALL FESCUE ILLUSTRATES THE DENSITY OF BLADES AND GENERAL GROWTH HABIT. *(DOWELANCO)*

NEWLY MOWED LAWN PLANTED FROM A BLEND OF TALL FESCUES.

TURF GRASS TYPES FOR NORTHERN CALIFORNIA LAWNS

In northern California, turf grass hybrids are viewed not only for color and beauty, but for practical features as well. Grasses with slow growth help to reduce maintenance and mowing frequency during peak growth times. Water-thrifty grasses are more deeply rooted and withstand dry periods with minimal damage. When planning a new lawn, it's important to choose the right grass type for all factors of your homesite including: climate, exposure, water availability, maintenance, and overall visual quality.

The best turf grasses for northern California lawns consist of bluegrass, ryegrass, or fescue. Bluegrass and fescue are the two most important grasses for our region, and rye is sometimes combined with bluegrass to improve color and make it more durable. There are many suppliers in California offering their own blends of seed under many different trade names. Each is created for a purpose, whether it is drought tolerance, resistance to wear, slower growth, or improved color. Many, but not all are also available as sod.

Tall fescues

Tall fescue is currently northern California's favorite turf grass. This is due to a tolerance of poor soils, and deep root systems better able to withstand drought. This factor, coupled with fescue's natural disease resistance is why it was the first species selected for use with endophytes.

Best use: Lawns in all parts of northern California.
When to plant: Late spring through early fall. Need warm soil to germinate.
How to plant: Seed or sod.
Texture: Coarse.
Shade tolerance: Moderate.
Traffic tolerance: Moderate.
Drought tolerance: Moderate.
Mowing height: 2 to 3 inches year around.

Kentucky bluegrass

Kentucky bluegrass is considered the most high quality turf grass sold today. It is available under many different trade names. Bluegrass is not drought tolerant and requires generous watering in hot, inland areas. Bluegrass will begin to lose its color at 85°F. and may have difficulty with heat over 105°F. For this reason it is often blended with perennial rye grass, which is more tolerant of high temperatures.

Best use: Lawns in humid coastal climates.
When to plant: Spring or fall from seed. Anytime for sod.
How to plant: Seed or sod.
Texture: Fine

Shade tolerance: Poor
Traffic tolerance: Poor
Drought tolerance: Poor
Mowing height: 2 1/2 inches summer, 1 1/2 to 2 inches average.

Perennial ryegrass

Perennial ryegrass is one of the best varieties for foggy coastal areas. It is often combined with bluegrass to create a more heat-, and shade-resistant lawn. Annual ryegrass is very fast to germinate, but not commonly used for lawns in our area. However, it can be overseeded into bermuda grass lawns in the fall to provide winter color during bermuda's dormant season. Annual ryegrass is also often used as a cover crop for other seed mixes because it quickly takes hold and prevents soil erosion until other plants germinate.

Best use: Lawns in cooler areas.
When to plant: Spring or fall.
How to plant: Seed or sod.
Texture: Fine.
Shade tolerance: Moderate
Traffic tolerance: Moderate to poor
Drought tolerance: Low
Mowing height: 2 1/2 inches summer, 1 1/2 to 2 inches average.

BLUEGRASS—SHOWS THE BLUE-ISH CAST OF THE BLADES AND SEED HEADS. *(DOWELANCO)*

A SINGLE PLANTAIN WEED MAY PRODUCE HUNDREDS OF SEEDLINGS WITH JUST ONE FLOWERING. LOW-GROWING, IT OFTEN INVADES LAWNS AND IS DIFFICULT TO REMOVE. *(DOWELANCO)*

WEEDS

There is no exact definition of a weed except that it is an unwanted plant. Vines, grasses, and groundcovers with exceptional vigor have the ability to establish themselves just about anywhere. If it happens to be in your garden, that plant becomes a weed.

UNDERSTANDING HERBICIDES

Herbicides are effective weed control chemicals which are relatively safe if handled properly. There are two

RULE OF GREEN THUMB

During the next spell of wet weather, don't just sit indoors and stare out at your garden. The damp days of winter and fall are prime time for pulling weeds. This is when the soil is soft enough to release even the deepest tap roots without breaking them. The roots of large bunch grasses yield with very little effort. If there's no rain in the forecast, water the area a few days ahead of time to create similar conditions.

TYPICAL EXAMPLE OF AGGRESSIVE PASTURE GRASS INTRODUCED TO THE LAWN THROUGH A TOP-DRESSING OF MANURE. *(DOWELANCO)*

FOXTAIL GRASS *(DOWELANCO)*

QUACKGRASS *(DOWELANCO)*

BARNYARD GRASS *(DOWELANCO)*

DALLISGRASS *(DOWELANCO)*

DANDELION *(DOWELANCO)*

BROADLEAF PLANTAIN *(DOWELANCO)*

main types of herbicide. *Translocated* herbicides travel throughout a plant to kill it right down to the roots, permanently. *Contact* herbicides kill only the parts of the plants they touch, but leaves and stems usually regrow from the remaining living portion. Be sure to use all herbicides strictly according to the manufacturer's directions. Do not use them in windy conditions and wear protective clothing, a respirator, and eye protection.

Translocated herbicides are taken into the plant through pores in the leaf surface. The plant must be actively growing to take in the material. Some gardeners actually water and fertilize their weeds to get them growing rapidly before applying translocated herbicide products.

An ounce of weed prevention is worth a pound of cure. Mulching and cultivation are two regular practices that go a long way to reducing weed populations while improving plant health. But once bermuda grass, nutsedge, morning glory, and other aggressive weeds gain a foothold in your garden, your work effort doubles. Keep a sharp eye on weeds and never allow them to remain in the soil long enough to set seed.

Golden State Rules for Weed Prevention

1. Mulch bare soil heavily in planting areas to prevent seed germination and reduce access to sunlight by weed seedlings.
2. Take steps to reduce the number of weed seeds existing in the soil *before* seeding or sodding a lawn.
3. Keep lawns well aerated and healthy so grass is dense enough to crowd and shade out weed seedlings. Mow slightly higher so grass leaves are long enough to fully shade the soil.
4. Do not allow any weeds to mature and set seed. Many are so prolific that a single plant may produce hundreds of seedlings next year.
5. Never bring manures or other organic materials into your garden unless they are guaranteed weed seed free.

Know the Problem Weeds

It is important to recognize and deal with the following major offenders before they become a serious problem. They are perennial and will persist for many years, gradually enlarging the colony.

• Johnson grass and other perennial bunch grasses These deep-rooted perennial grasses were introduced by agriculture. At first they appear similar to annual grasses, but later mature into very dense clumps with deep roots. These weeds should be removed in a single mass with the root crown intact; if broken, each piece left behind may result in a new plant. If located in planters, kill with a translocated herbicide or dig out the root ball with a shovel. When these grasses appear in lawns, remove them immediately or dig them out later and disfigure the lawn.

• Dandelions and similar tap-rooted weeds Some perennial weeds have tap roots that extend 12 inches or more into the soil. You must remove at least the top 5 inches of tap root to prevent it from growing back. If you break the root into pieces as it comes out of the ground, each one left behind will grow into an entirely new plant. It helps to water the ground a few days before you go after tap-rooted weeds to loosen the soil. Use a weed fork or

Yellow Nutsedge *(DowElanco)*

Bermuda Grass *(DowElanco)*

Musk Thistle *(DowElanco)*

weed popper device to help you reach more deeply in the soil.

• **Nutsedge—the rice grower's nightmare** You can distinguish sedges from grasses by their rough-edged blades. The nutsedge root system produces many small bulblets over a large area, and cultivation can distribute a single plant throughout the garden. The plants also produce a large amount of seed that germinates easily. The key to control is to pounce on sedges immediately after they appear. Use an herbicide designated for this plant or dig out a large rootball and make sure no bulblets remain behind.

• **Bermuda and other aggressive runner grasses** Bermuda, as with other aggressive runner grasses, can spread rapidly, even under the worst conditions. Roots will travel under paving, climb into shrubs, contaminate groundcovers, and create large brown patches in lawns while dormant in winter. Some fertilizers for lawns help to discourage this grass to a limited extent. Controlling bermuda by hand is a formidable task which may take years of diligent pulling and digging, although there is still no guarantee it can be eliminated entirely.

• **Poison oak** This native plant is easily identified by leaves divided into three leaflets that turn scarlet in the fall. It is a deciduous leafy shrub that can grow very tall and climb into the limbs of trees. Each person reacts to a different degree when exposed to the oils present in poison oak leaves, stems, and roots. Never burn poison oak twigs because oils travel in the smoke and are highly toxic to the lungs. The safest way to eradicate this plant is to treat it with herbicide while actively growing in the spring. Attempts at manual removal can result in serious rashes, and for highly allergic people herbicides become the least toxic choice.

• **Star thistle** These seemingly harmless little thistles are one of the greatest threats to California's grassland ecosystems. Introduced only a few decades ago, they have proven to be tenacious and highly invasive. The plants are pale blue with yellow flowers, and sharp spines make handling difficult. Star thistles reseed themselves at an alarming rate and should be removed immediately. Never let even one plant go to seed. There are similar, slightly less invasive thistles which should also be eradicated right away using a translocated herbicide while actively growing.

CHAPTER SEVEN

BULBS AND ROSES

BULBS, CORMS AND TUBERS

Some plants grow from different types of fleshy underground rooting structures. Although storage structures can be called either true bulbs, corms, or tubers, they are similar enough to be lumped together for convenience, and referred to as bulbs.

SPRING- AND SUMMER-FLOWERING BULBS

Bulbs are divided into two main groups: those that flower in the spring, and those that bloom during summer. This distinction is based

FACING PAGE: CREEPING PHLOX AND TULIPS. VICTORIAN HOUSE IN SIERRA NEVADA MINING TOWN, NEVADA CITY. ABOVE: DUTCH IRIS (*NETHERLANDS FLOWER-BULB*)

on flowering time, cold hardiness, and the ability to survive winter in the soil.

• **Spring bulbs** Spring-flowering bulbs are frost hardy, and in California bloom anytime from about December to May. Many require low temperatures to become fully dormant and will even survive in frozen ground. Spring-flowering bulbs are planted from September through December. After they bloom and the foliage has died back, these bulbs can be dug up in the summer to divide the baby bulblets into a new generation of plants. Not all bulbs benefit from digging, such as daffodils, which remain in place for decades. In all but the coldest climates, tulips must be dug and stored in the refrigerator if they are to continue to provide large flowers.

• **Summer bulbs** Summer-flowering bulbs are planted after the weather warms in the spring. Some can be left in the ground throughout the winter if the soil is sufficiently well drained and does not freeze. Once the above-ground portion of the plant dies off with early frosts, the bulbs can be dug up, divided, and stored for the winter. If left undisturbed, the young ones draw growth energy away from the mother plant, which reduces flower size and quantity of blooms. Most summer bulbs do not require exposure to cold.

HOW ARE BULBS, CORMS AND TUBERS DIFFERENT?

Spring- and summer-flowering bulbs grow from either true bulbs, corms, or tubers. All are planted while dormant, without soil, and may resemble either an onion or a potato.

True Bulbs

The storage structure of a true bulb is really a whole plant compressed into a compact unit. It looks like the common kitchen onion, with layers or "scales" surrounding the stems and leaves inside. Some of the most well-known examples are daffodils and tulips. Spring-flowering bulbs are very frost hardy while summer bulbs are more tender.

NORTHERN CALIFORNIA TIP

Our winter temperatures in northern California are much warmer than areas where spring bulbs are grown. When placed on display locally they are exposed to high temperatures, which speeds up growth prematurely. To slow them down, place tulips, hyacinths, and crocus in the refrigerator, *not the freezer*, after you bring them home. Leave them in the crisper drawer in a brown paper bag for 4 to 6 weeks before planting. To help them achieve proper dormancy the following winter, dig them up in the fall and place them in the refrigerator once again, just the same way. It will make your plants more vigorous, producing larger flowers.

Corms

A Corm is a solid, fleshy structure without scales that tends to be much wider than it is tall. On the top is a bud that produces the flowers and leaves, and roots emerge from the bottom. The corm develops new flesh each year and also produces cormels around its base which can be separated to become new corms. The most well-known member of this group is gladiolus, but anemone and crocus are also corms.

Tubers

The most commonly known tuber is the potato. A tuber can sprout from buds or "eyes" scattered over its surface, or from a single crown or neck, depending on the type. They can be much larger than true bulbs or corms. Dahlias and canna lilies are all loosely called tubers. Bearded iris has a root similar to a tuber, but it's called a rhizome because it sits just beneath the surface of the soil and is the primary root.

PLANTING AND GROWING TIPS FOR BULBS

Bulbs are easy to plant and grow, even for beginners. The first year most will bloom well, but obtaining equally as beautiful flowers in the following years is more difficult. Since this group of plants is so large and diverse, count on a few exceptions to every rule.

Planting Bulbs

One or two bulbs blooming in a landscape are easily overlooked, but ten or twenty make a stunning display. This is the key to success with all flowering plants, a factor which novice gardeners underestimate. Set out your bulbs in generous groups and be sure to plant the taller and brighter flowering varieties to the rear, with shorter and softer colors in front.

The most important rule is that bulbs must have well-drained soil or they will rot in the ground. Most require full sun, preferably a southern exposure to prevent over-wet conditions. The proper depth for planting bulbs varies with each species. In general, a bulb should be planted at a depth three times the diameter of the bulb.

Soil preparation can be done on a large scale for massed plantings. Cultivate to a depth of 12 inches and incorporate compost and bonemeal or special bulb fertilizer for rapid root development. *Do not use manure.* If you are reworking a bed that has already been planted in bulbs, enrich the soil every other year.

It's best to use a bulb-planting tool which digs a

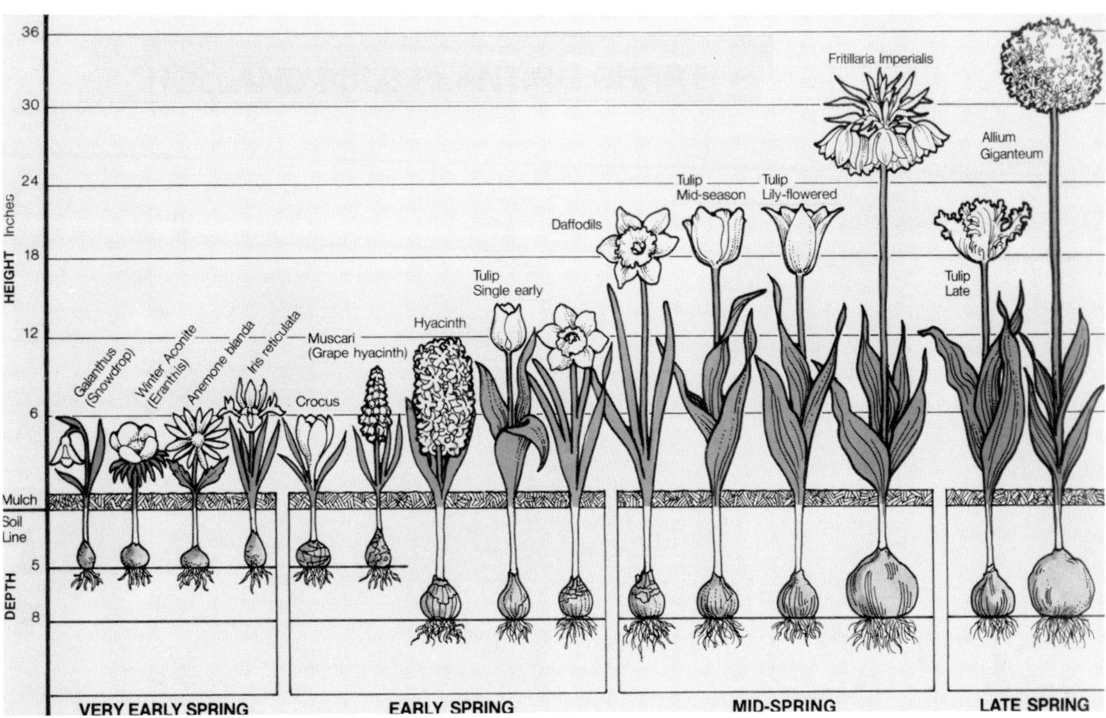

(*NETHERLANDS FLOWER-BULB INSTITUTE*)

single hole for each individual bulb. For larger scale projects, a long-handled form of the same tool or an auger attachment for a cordless drill is worth the price. Use the bulb planter to make a cone-shaped hole in the soil at the proper depth. Rough up the soil at the bottom of the hole and add a small amount of bonemeal. Since the bulb will rest directly upon this soil, avoid using general-purpose fertilizers because they are too strong. Also, improve the soil that was extracted from the hole.

Place bulbs firmly in the soil with the pointed end up. When planting in masses, don't crowd the bulbs and keep spacing consistent for sufficient rooting area and even distribution of color. The final step is to cover the bulbs with soil, lightly pressing it downward as you go to prevent air pockets. In heavy soils, don't over-compact the soil because this may create drainage problems. Cover newly planted areas with a mulch, particularly if you are experiencing an unusually dry fall or winter. The mulch also helps to keep the bulbs insulated from unseasonal temperature changes.

Caring for bulbs

When the first shoots appear, sprinkle the soil around each bulb with a mild bulb fertilizer. This food helps the plants develop during the growing season. If you encounter unusually warm, dry, or windy weather, check to make sure the soil is still moist.

Bulb plants produce both a flower stalk and foliage. Cut the flowers if you wish, while they are in full bloom. If you'd like them to remain in the garden, wait until each one fades and cut it off without damaging the foliage. The remaining leaves may live for many months as they convert sunlight into growth energy stored in the bulb.

When the foliage has died back or turned brown on its own, the plant is dormant. Gently dig up the bulb and try not to nick or gouge it. This kind of damage creates an avenue for fungus diseases to invade bulbs while in storage. Set the bulbs out in a single layer in a shady place to dry, then remove all the remaining soil. Dust the bulbs

BULB POISON HAZARDS FOR CHILDREN AND DOGS

The bulbs of tulips, amaryllis, iris, crocus, and most of the daffodil clan are poisonous to both humans and pets. The fact that gophers won't eat daffodils proves this isn't limited to domestic pets. Unless your dog is an avid digger and unearths your bulbs, the only time when poisoning is likely to occur is during the process of digging them up and storing. Be cautious where you dry the bulbs. Make sure they are stored well out of the reach of children and dogs likely to see them as handy playthings or chew toys. Avoid planting them close to dog runs.

with a powdered fungicide and store in a brown paper bag, nest of wood shavings, or open cardboard box. Keep them cool, ideally around 50°F. until it's time to plant in either fall or spring.

Golden State Rules for Success with Bulbs

1. Never plant bulbs in poorly drained soil.
2. Never use strong fertilizer or manure for soil improvement.
3. Dig bulbs only after foliage dies back on its own. When cutting flowers, leave all foliage undisturbed.
4. Do not allow seed pods to form after flowers fade.
5. After digging, dry bulbs in the shade and prevent them from exposure to direct sunlight. Do not store in an airtight container.

SPRING AND SUMMER BULBS FOR NORTHERN CALIFORNIA GARDENS

Most climate zones in northern California are perfect for growing bulbs because the soil rarely freezes except in the high country. Summer bulbs should be planted after the last frost and dug before winter in all but the warmest climate areas.

BULB SELECTION CHART

Note: Planting and bloom times may vary slightly in each climate zone. Bloom height may vary among hybrids.

Name	*Planting time*	*Bloom height (inches)*	*Bloom time*
Allium	Sept–Dec	10	Mar–Sept
Anemone	Aug–April	8	Feb–Aug
Canna	Jan–Mar	24 to 70	May–Sept
Crocus	Sept–Jan	5	Feb–April
Dahlia	Jan–May	36	May–Oct
Daffodils	Sept–Feb	10 to 18	Feb–April
Freesia	Sept–Nov	12	Feb–Mar
Gladiolus	Dec–June	34	Mar–Sept
Hyacinth	Sept–Feb	12	April
Bearded Iris	Aug–Dec	24	May–Aug
Dutch Iris	Sept–Dec	22	May–June
Ixia	Sept–Jan	12	April–May
Lily	Oct–April	48	June–Sept
Narcissus	Sept–Jan	12	Dec–April
Ranunculus	Aug–April	10	Feb–Aug
Sparaxis	Sept–Dec	12	Feb–Mar
Tulip	Sept–Jan	16 to 30	Mar–April
Watsonia	Sept–Jan	36 to 40	April–May

ALLIUM GIGANTEUM (NETHERLANDS FLOWER BULB INFORMATION CENTER)

Allium

Ornamental Onion

Spring bulbs True bulb Full sun

Ornamental allium bulbs can be found in a wide assortment of hybrids which are as easy to grow as the edible onion. Planting depth and spacing vary according

NORTHERN CALIFORNIA TIP

Abandoned farm sites are often marked by large populations of naturalized narcissus undisturbed by gophers. This attests to the old wives' tales about using barriers of bulbs to protect other, more vulnerable plantings. Narcissus, garlic, and scilla or squill bulbs are the most effective choices for barriers. Plant them close together in dense rings around masses of other bulbs or plants. Even the roots of these special bulbs are distasteful, and gophers won't pass beneath them to get to the more edible bulbs.

to the size of each variety. Most bloom with large, ball-shaped flowers on tops of tall stalks. Avoid planting too close together. Most alliums bloom late in the season, between late April and June. Dig and divide bulblets into new plants during early summer. Keep plants evenly moist for best results. Flowers are suitable for drying.

ANEMONE 'ST. BRIGID' (*NETHERLANDS FLOWER BULB INFORMATION CENTER*)

Anemone coronaria

Poppy Anemone

Summer bulbs Tuberlike corms Full sun or part shade

Anemones are very easy bulbs to grow and are often coupled with ranunculus because they are of similar size. Flowers are brightly colored with black centers. Soak corms for 12 hours in warm water before planting. Plant about 4 inches deep and spaced 8 inches apart. May be left in place year around in milder locations. Good choice for shady areas or use as an edging plant.

Canna x *generalis*

Canna Lily

Summer bulbs Tuber Full sun

Cannas love water and sun, although they will survive late summer dryness very well. Very heat tolerant. These plants are unusually exotic, with broad, succulent leaves and rapid growth to over 6 feet tall. Dwarf varieties are available. Distinctly tropical appearance. Flowers resemble orchids with brilliant, hot colors. Plant 18 inches apart after last frost of spring, and dig once foliage has died back in the fall. May remain in place year around in all climates except zone 1. Tubers may become very large and invasive if not dug and divided every few years.

CANNA HYBRID (*NETHERLANDS FLOWER BULB INFORMATION CENTER*)

Crocus

Crocus

Spring bulbs Corm Full sun or part shade

There are many different varieties of crocus, but all are very small plants only a few inches tall. They are usually the first flowers of spring and will bloom even in the snow. During Victorian times, they were planted in the lawn, and many original plants are still in place today. Avoid mowing lawns for four weeks after plants bloom to give foliage a chance to nutrify the corm. Crocus prefer a light sandy soil. A good choice for shallow soils, crocus need not be dug nor divided and naturalize well.

CROCUS (*NETHERLANDS FLOWER BULB INFORMATION CENTER*)

Daffodil, Narcissus

Spring bulbs True bulb Full sun, part shade

You'll find the many hybrids of the genus *Narcissus* called daffodil, jonquil, or just narcissus. All have the characteristic trumpet-shaped flowers, and many are quite fragrant. In the north state, these bulbs can be planted in uncultivated areas and left in the ground permanently to naturalize into large colonies. These bulbs are rarely dug

Above: Trumpet narcissus (*Netherlands Flower Bulb Information Center*)
Left: Narcissus (*Netherlands Flower Bulb Information Center*)

Gladiolus 'Sans Souci' (*Netherlands Flower Bulb Information Center*)

Orange Cactus Dahlia Hybrid (*Netherlands Flower Bulb Information Center*)

Bearded Iris

Field-grown dahlias staked for exhibition blooms.

Dutch Iris 'Yellow Queen' (*Netherlands Flower Bulb Information Center*)

up except to divide new bulblets into new plants. Rarely bothered by gophers, they may be the only bulbs to survive in rural gardens. Planting in a tight ring around new trees and shrubs helps to discourage gophers and moles. Colors range from white to yellow with occasional dark orange accents. Less expensive when ordered in large quantities from bulb catalogs, and mixtures of different varieties are available.

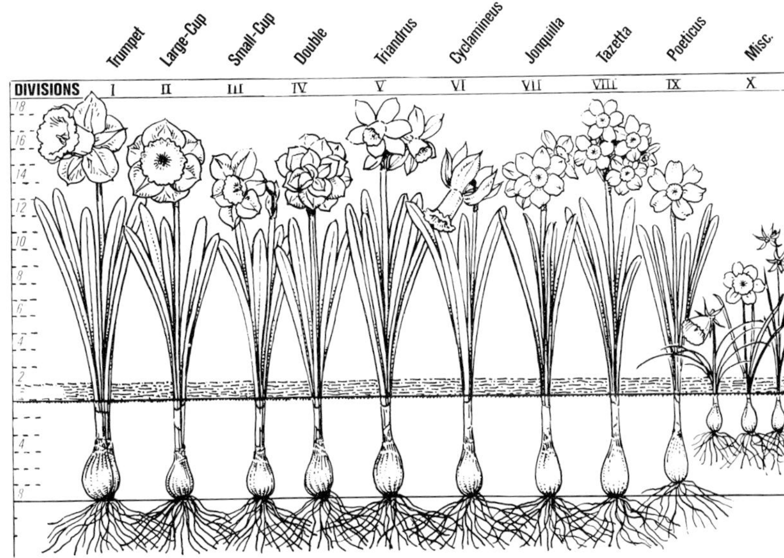

DAFFODILS (NARCISSUS) (*NETHERLANDS FLOWER BULB INFORMATION CENTER*)

Dahlia

Summer bulbs

Tuber Full sun

Few plants have as many hybrid forms as the dahlia. A rainbow of color choices and flower shapes, with plants ranging in size from 12 inches to 6 feet tall. All grow from a sweet-potato-shaped tuber which sprouts only on the end indicated by the slightly swollen red eyes. Dahlias are not frost hardy. They should be planted after the spring frost danger is past and dug just after the first frost of fall. On the coast, mild temperatures allow dahlia bulbs to remain in the soil permanently and are only dug every few years to divide tubers into new plants. Dahlias are heavy feeders, and require plentiful moisture during the hot inland summer. They can be burned by intense afternoon sun and tall varieties should be staked for support.

Gladiolus

Gladiolus

Summer bulb Corm Full sun

Even a rank beginner gardener can count on showy blooms for very little effort from this old favorite. Plants are tall, up to 4 feet, with stalks of large showy flowers in a rainbow of colors. Gladiolus need a sunny spot and should be staked for support or their top-heavy flowers will make plants fall over. Cut flower stalks while still in bud and watch them open indoors. Plant in spring for welcome late summer color. Water and fertilize generously for best results. Dig corms in fall, after foliage has died back on its own. Separate off the cormlets and store all until spring.

Bearded Iris

Iris, Flags

Summer bulb Tuberous rhizome Full sun

Northern California is bearded iris country. They naturalize anywhere there is plenty of sunlight and sufficient drainage. The fleshy rhizomes of this iris grow horizontally, just under the surface of the soil. They develop into dense networks which are dug every other year and divided into new plants. Few flowers can boast a similar range and diversity of color: from royal purple and deep maroon to almost black, as well as faint blush apricot and pure white. Enemies of iris are wet, soggy soils and dense shade. Keep dried up leaves cut away from plants and avoid damaging the rhizomes when working nearby. Plant about 12 inches apart.

Bulbous Iris

Dutch Iris

Spring bulb True bulb Full sun

There are many different types of bulb iris called Dutch because they were first hybridized in Holland. Distinctly different from their bearded cousins, these plants require better soil and far more moisture. Like other true bulbs, plants bloom in spring and the foliage dies back in summer. Bulbs should not be stored more than two months out of the soil, and in most parts of northern California they can be left in the ground indefinitely. Dutch iris are frequently used around water gardens to provide color while blending in with other reed-like foliage plants.

Ixia

African Corn Lily

Summer bulb Corm Full sun

This is one member of a group of similar plants which originate in southern Africa where the climate is very similar to that of California. The foliage is narrow and grasslike, with flowers brightly colored in various warm hues. *Ixias* available today are hybrids of the native species and are some of the very best bulbs for drought-tolerant gardens. Their intrinsic ability to withstand the very dry winters of Africa make these lesser-known bulbs

Darwin Hybrid Striped Tulip (Netherlands Flower Bulb Information Center)

Watsonia hybrid

ideal for the west coast. See *Sparaxis* and *Watsonia* for other dryland bulbs to combine with *Ixia*.

Ranunculus asiaticus
Persian Buttercup
Spring bulbs Tubers Full sun

Some people think the brightly colored, double flowers of ranunculus resemble those of the many petaled cabbage rose. They make excellent cut flowers in a wide variety of clear colors and can be combined with anemone for spectacular bedding displays. Ranunculus is simple to grow, but will flower much better in the coastal mountain ranges than it does in drier locations inland. Tubers are small, and benefit from a good soaking in warm water to soften before planting. Avoid over-watering after planting because winter rains will be sufficient. Keep moist in the spring and cut off faded flowers to encourage late blooms.

Sparaxis tricolor
Harlequin Flower
Summer bulb Corm Full sun

Another native from southern Africa, *Sparaxis* is a natural for California. Papery, dry flowers rise in abundance from reedy foliage to bloom in late spring or summer. The flower is usually red, with a yellow throat accented by splashes of other colors for highlights. Plant in the fall on the coast, but inland wait until spring to avoid problems with frost and soggy soil. *Sparaxis* may have a longer blooming period if spent flowers are regularly clipped off. Closely related to *Ixia*, they are often planted together in dry rock gardens where drainage is assured. An excellent source of color for drought-tolerant gardens.

Tulipa hybrids
Tulips
Spring bulbs True bulbs Full sun

No other flower is so widely known and loved than the tulip. But gardeners also struggle to coax flowers from the bulbs after a few years' time because California temperatures are so much warmer than the growing ground. Buy tulips as soon as they are set out at the garden center, because even a few days of exposure to temperatures over 70°F can cut flower size in half. Tulip bulbs must be exposed to near freezing temperatures for many days each year if they are to thrive. When in doubt, keep bulbs in the refrigerator indefinitely. Tulips cannot tolerate extreme heat, and if planted too late they may be exposed to very hot, false spring conditions typical here in northern California. Tulip bulbs should be dug up as soon as foliage dies back, then stored in the refrigerator immediately to hasten the dormant state.

Watsonia
Watsonia
Summer bulb Corm Full sun

Watsonia, like *Ixia* and *Sparaxis*, are native to southern Africa. This plant is the largest of the three, with foliage as long as 3 feet and tall flower spikes of tubular blooms. *Watsonia* may be difficult to find, but they're perfect for California dry gardens. Once established, they quickly spread into large clumps that become very showy; but if growing too densely they can be dug and divided in winter. There are many species and all make excellent garden plants with a bonus of exotic cutting flowers. An excellent northern California bulb and well worth a special order.

RAMBLING ROSE—THIS OLD SPECIMEN HAS ENGULFED AN ENTIRE TREE.

ROSES

Roses have been an important plant in California since the Spanish first imported musk roses from Europe to plant at the missions. Early residents discovered our warm, dry climate was perfect for these robust and colorful plants. Since that time, the popularity of the rose in California has grown into a major horticultural industry.

In the beginning, all cultivated roses, like those at the missions, were wild species native to the Middle East. Most bloomed only once a year with simple, yet highly fragrant flowers. These were distributed throughout Europe by the Romans, who held them in highest esteem. Eventually, early species were crossed to create the first hybrids, which were then bred into many varieties loosely called "old roses." During the nineteenth century, a new strain was found in China and designated Tea roses. Although of lesser fragrance, these new plants bloomed continually throughout the warm months and offered a much wider selection of flower colors. Plant breeders were quick to cross their old varieties with the Tea roses, which resulted in today's Hybrid Teas. Although they were superior to the old varieties in many ways, some Hybrid Teas were weakened, as breeders crossed and recrossed strains to obtain new flower colors.

ENGULFED IN BLOOM, A FORGOTTEN OLD RAMBLER SURVIVING ON NATURAL RAINFALL ALONG THE NORTH COAST.

Gardeners across America are rediscovering old roses because they have become disillusioned with some Hybrid Teas. Old rose varieties offer intense fragrance, more versatile landscape plants, and a general improvement in disease and pest resistance. For example, the family of *rugosas* are so frost tolerant they can survive the winter at Lake Tahoe with bright red hips that stand out in the snow. Whether you are growing old varieties or Hybrid Tea roses, the cultural requirements are the same. Only the pruning time and techniques are slightly different.

HOW TO SELECT AND BUY ROSES

Almost all roses sold today are grafted plants. This means the variety of plant you select (scion) has been grafted onto a more vigorous rootstock. This allows grow-

'SPARRIESHOOP,' SHRUB ROSE, REMONTANT.

Climbing roses in the Sierra Foothills garden at the Empire Mine State Historic Park.

Home-dried, miniature rose buds and flowers ready for use.

ers to create many more plants from a single parent plant because only a small amount of scion wood is needed for the grafting process. The graft union, that bulge in the stem of your rose, is where the scion and rootstock meet.

With the old varieties back in cultivation again, there is a new trend to grow roses on their own roots, without grafting. Many feel the graft union is vulnerable to disease, and omitting the grafting process results in healthier plants. Only the strongest roses can be grown on their own roots and many newer hybrids simply won't survive unless grafted. But the oldest species of roses have retained their vigor and are good candidates for nongrafted plants.

The Many Forms Roses Can Take

The form of a rose is its growth habit and overall size at maturity. This form dictates how and where it is used in a garden.

• **Shrub roses** Shrub roses can be used just like any other kind of shrub in a landscape. They are upright growers with plenty of foliage and flowers on extremely large, robust plants. They can be called Polyantha, Floribunda, or Grandiflora, and most are Hybrid Teas, although some old varieties can be included as well.

• **Ramblers** This loose term refers to roses that grow with a wider, more spreading habit. The most important fact about ramblers is that they need lots of space. They are some of the best for rural gardens where plants can sprawl uninhibited. Some species roses can develop into mounding plants up to 20 feet in diameter.

• **Climbers** Many varieties sold as shrubs are available in climbing forms. Climbers have very long canes which are trained onto fences, arbors, or the walls of buildings. Most climbing roses are grafted.

• **Tree roses** Tree roses are created from the most vigorous and popular Hybrid Tea varieties. The scion wood is grafted directly into the top of a stem, which later develops into a rounded mass of foliage and flowers resembling a small tree. Tree roses can be weak and require more care and attention.

• **Miniatures** These tiny rose plants have equally tiny flowers. They are very popular with urban gardeners who must contend with limited space, or apartment dwellers who grow roses in containers. Growing miniature roses well is a specialty and is a popular source of arts and crafts material.

What to Look for When Selecting a Rose Variety

Most people select roses strictly by the flower color shown in a catalog or advertisement. But roses are plants with many qualities which contribute to success and long-term satisfaction. Make sure you have considered all these factors before you make the final choice.

• **Climate** Rose varieties differ in their ability to

tolerate extremes of winter frost and summer heat. Zone 1 is limited to only the hardiest roses such as Rugosas. Hybrid Teas are definitely out. Roses in the coastal zone 7 may be prone to mildew because of the mild, wet winters. Plants grown inland must survive very hot summer afternoons, and tender varieties may burn or simply go dormant when the mercury rises above 90°F.

• **Flower color** Flower color in old varieties is limited to white through a range of pinks to red. Occasionally you may come across a yellow briar, but in general, colors are limited. Hybrid teas on the other hand offer an incredible spectrum of colors. Some varieties have two-toned flowers, or more than one color on the bush at the same time. Be aware of color and make sure you select shades in keeping with the general character of your garden. Avoid combining many different colors together haphazardly, as the stronger shades overwhelm the more subtle ones.

• **Form** The various growth habits of rose plants are described above. When choosing a rose, make sure its size and shape are suitable for the space provided. Roses require generous air circulation and should not be crowded together or set too close to any other plant, fence, or building.

• **Remontant roses** A rose that blooms repeatedly throughout the growing season is remontant. Most hybrid tea roses sold today are remontant. Old roses are not often remontant and flower only once a year. However, this flowering time may be as short as a week or may extend to as much as two months depending on the variety. Be sure to read a thorough description of all old-rose varieties to determine how they flower before you buy.

• **Hips** After a rose has flowered, the petals drop, leaving behind a fertilized ovary, called the hip, which becomes the seed capsule. Rose hips contain an incredible amount of vitamin C. Most hips turn red as they mature and are good color sources in winter. The size and shape of hips changes with variety.

• **Fragrance** Not all roses are fragrant, and many Hybrid Teas are nearly devoid of scent as a result of breeding. The oldest species roses have the most potent scents and are the source of rose oil. But early old-rose hybrids are nearly as fragrant and some even have scented foliage.

'White Wings,' shrub rose, very large blooms (5 inches wide), with unique red stamens.

'Cécile Brünner,' the "Sweetheart Rose," climbing or shrub forms. Very small, but perfect, blooms on standard-sized plant, easier to grow for crafts than miniature hybrids.

Ways to Buy Roses

Almost all roses sold in California today have been field grown and are shipped bare-root to retail nurseries or directly to the consumer. Not all bare-root roses are the same size, so a system of grading plants was developed.

The very best are labeled *select heavy #1*. These are large, healthy plants that produce well their first and second seasons. This grade sells out quickly unless your order is placed in advance. A bit smaller, the *standard #1* rose will require more time to become established, but

THE HIPS OF *R. EGLANTERA.*

AFTER THE END OF BARE-ROOT SEASON, THESE 'AUSTRIAN COPPER' OLD-FASHIONED ROSES HAVE BEEN POTTED UP FOR SALE IN 5-GALLON POTS.

'ALCHEMIST,' OLD CLIMBING ROSE. NOT REMONTANT.

eventually catches up with the others. The smallest grade is *common store rose,* which is usually the cheapest.

It is important to buy your roses from reputable companies. Poorly grown plants, sloppy grafting, and dried out roots can all reduce growth rates after planting. Diseased roses introduce big problems into your garden. You may have paid a lower price, but it's not a bargain. It's a better value to spend a few more dollars per plant to get a big rose that blooms well the first season.

• **Mail order bare-root roses** One of the best mail-order plant values is in bare-root roses, which may be the only way to obtain old and rare rose varieties. Mail order allows you to shop for roses at home with colorful catalogs bearing photos and generous descriptions of each plant. You need not worry about getting to the nursery before supplies run out because you reserve your plants months in advance. They will be shipped bare-root at the proper time for your area.

• **Garden center** All northern California garden centers begin stocking bare-root roses in December, and the season extends until the end of February. However, the longer a rose remains in our warm climate, the less dormant it becomes. When roses with their roots packaged in plastic wrappers are displayed in the sun, by the end of February the buds have burst into foliage. It is essential you get to the nursery at the earliest date possible in order to get your bare-roots in the ground *before* they break dormancy.

Container roses At the end of bare-root season, garden centers may have plants left over. These have been picked through and are not of the best quality. The plants are potted up in 5-gallon containers to be sold while in bloom during the spring and summer. Rose plants grown for bare-root stock have thick, long roots which are weakened when forced into a pot. But if you are too late for bare-root season, containers allow you to see the rose in bloom before you buy.

RULE OF GREEN THUMB

Roses should not be planted in lawns, yet gardeners persist in this practice. Sprinkler water is not good for rose foliage. Roses are starved when grasses on the soil surface gobble up water and fertilizer before it can reach the roots. Lawns require high nitrogen fertilizers, and roses in or adjacent to lawns may grow lots of stems and leaves, but very few flowers. Devote a separate planting area to your roses where they may flourish without competition from other plants.

HOW TO CORRECTLY PLANT A ROSE

Successfully growing roses begins with selecting the right place. Secondly, roses should be planted properly to get them off to a good start. These are the two most important factors influencing whether or not a rose will perform in your garden.

Where to Plant a Rose

Rose plants require full sun, but may tolerate afternoon shade in hot inland climates. When a rose is shaded in the morning, dew on its leaves becomes a breeding ground for fungus diseases like mildew. If it is shaded most of the time it may not flower well. Remember that although the coast may be moist, it receives plenty of sun and roses will accept full exposure there.

But northern California's inland heat becomes a problem, as it forces roses into temporary dormancy. Unusually hot spots are created by reflected heat from walls and nearby paving. Although the thermometer says it's 80° F, the place where the roses are growing may be much closer to 100°F due to accumulation of reflected heat.

Roses must have plenty of air circulation around all parts of the plant. Nonclimbing roses planted against fences, walls or a background of dense foliage may not receive much air movement and become subject to disease.

Roses are heavy feeders that prefer fertile, deep clay or clay-loam soil. Compensate for low fertility of sandy soils by providing more water and fertilizer than normal. Most difficult are shallow soils on top of bedrock or hardpan layers which refuse to drain and restrict rooting space. In this situation, it's best to select a new site if possible or try a more shallowly rooted plant.

How to Plant a Rose

The majority of roses sold in California are bare-root. They have been shipped in moist packing material and should be planted immediately. If you can't get them in the ground right away, bury them in moist garden soil, compost, or sand to keep the roots from drying out. This practice is called heeling-in. You can also place them in the refrigerator for a few days as long as roots remain wrapped in plastic to retain moisture.

Before you plant, set the plants in a bucket and fill it with water to just above the graft unions. You can add some B_1 or Superthrive to the water to reduce transplant shock. The water helps to get the roots really wet before they go into the ground.

Bare-root roses are planted just like any other bare-root plant. Dig a generous hole large enough to contain the roots without bending. Don't cut them shorter if they don't fit—dig a bigger hole. Enrich the pile of soil you excavated with plenty of humus and work 1/2 cup of bonemeal into the bottom of the hole. Then fashion a cone of soil in the center of the hole to support the plant so the graft union will be about 2 inches above the level of the surrounding area. Then place the plant on the cone with the roots arranged evenly and begin to backfill the hole. Do this in layers about 6 inches thick.

'Ulrich Brunner Fils,' old Rambler hybrid.

On top of the first layer, place four fertilizer planting tablets evenly around the edge of the hole. Then tamp the layer down firmly. Continue to fill the hole layer by layer, and use the leftover soil to create a watering basin when you're through. This basin insures water is concentrated over the root zone and fully saturates the planting area. Fill the basin with water, wait until it completely soaks into the soil, then water once again. Since bare roots are planted in the winter, they are dormant and don't have many hair roots to absorb water. The goal is to keep plants evenly moist but not saturated until spring when visible growth begins.

TAKING CARE OF YOUR ROSES

There are two things everyone wants from their roses: bigger plants and more flowers. This goal is not nearly as difficult as it appears, and there are only five things you must do to produce winning roses in California. If any one of these is neglected, plants will cease to grow and bloom.

Golden State Rules for Successful Roses

1. **Cultivate the soil.**
   Unless you cultivate the soil beneath your roses, water and fertilizer may not penetrate into the root

zone. Open compacted soils so root development is encouraged and water moves more freely downward. Deeply rooted plants are less vulnerable to dry spells and take maximum advantage of fertilizer.

For award-winning plants, you must cultivate in two ways. Once a month, cultivate the soil to a depth of three inches to prevent surface crusting. Twice a year, in spring and fall, work up the entire bed with a spading fork as deeply as you can. This biannual spading is the best time to work humus and mulches into the soil. Organic matter helps to keep the soil opened up and prevents it from compacting back together when moistened.

2. **Water your plants.**
A vigorously growing rose plant produces flowers constantly, and all that activity requires a large amount of water. Roses will tolerate summer heat waves much better if their roots are sufficiently moist. Water is also the vehicle for fertilizer movement. Keep a basin around each plant and fill it without wetting the foliage. This allows the soil to become deeply saturated, and encourages more adventurous rooting. Fertilizer can also be contained in the basin for maximum nutrient availability.

Sprinkler systems can do more damage than good as far as roses are concerned. Many rose diseases result from wet foliage, and repeated sprayings make them difficult to eradicate. Water on the leaves in direct sunlight will burn them severely. If you must use sprinklers to water the roses, try bubbler heads or a drip system, both of which don't spray.

3. **Fertilize regularly.**
Roses in California grow and bloom for many more months than in cooler regions. Plants require fertilizer applications both earlier and later in the season, with peak feedings during the summer. You can use any general purpose fertilizer on roses as long as it doesn't have an unusually high nitrogen content. Formulas like 12-12-12 are fine for roses and most other garden plants. You can buy fertilizers especially designed for roses, but they are more expensive.

Healthy plants are better able to resist pests and diseases. Keep nutrient levels consistantly high by feeding on a regular schedule. During the peak growing season, a mature rose plant can use a cup of 12-12-12 every 30 to 60 days. Application rates should be lighter in early spring and gradually increase until summer. In fall, taper off in the same way until the weather cools off.

It's a good practice to water roses before and after you fertilize. Distribute the granules around the dripline of the plant or within the watering basin, then lightly cultivate them into the soil. Water generously two or three times after applying fertilizer so the granules dissolve. When using liquid fertilizers, water lightly, then pour on the mixture. You can give them a second watering afterwards as long as there is no runoff.

4. **Prune flowers off.**
The best part about growing roses is that you must cut the flowers if you want more buds to form. Flowers left on the plant rob the growth energy needed to form seeds. Flowering wood has a tendancy to become thin and frail, producing small blooms. When cutting flowers, you prune out thin wood so thick, healthy wood can form. Please refer to the section on pruning roses following for proper pruning techniques.

5. **Inspect plants closely.**
Difficulties with insect pests and diseases are easily controlled when treated early. If you wait until mildew has covered much of the plant, the problem can be almost incurable, even with liberal use of fungicides. Growing tips with a few aphids may be cleaned off by hand or with a strong jet of water, but an infestation may require more drastic measures. These examples illustrate why it is essential you inspect your rose plants frequently. Many gardeners do this as they cut flowers every few days. Be sure to look at the backs of the leaves as well as the fronts because many sucking insects hide there. Never forget that small problems are simple to resolve, but the bigger ones can become overwhelming.

ROSE PRUNING—NOT AS HARD AS YOU THINK

Pruning is one aspect of horticulture which is difficult to learn from a book. That's because each plant presents a new set of circumstances that influence where cuts are to be made. But don't let that discourage you because roses are forgiving and grow fast enough to compensate for our errors in a very short time. Relax, because it's practically impossible to kill a rose with incorrect pruning.

In order to learn how to prune roses the right way, you must understand a few terms. The branches of a rose are called *canes.* Canes are classified as either *framework* wood or *flowering* wood depending on their location and purpose. Framework wood is comprised of the thick support canes that bear smaller flowering wood. When you winter-prune a rose, you are trying to keep the framework wood young and productive so it can more abundantly sprout flowering wood. The smaller, supple stems of flowering wood produce blooms. When you cut flowers from roses to encourage new buds, you are controlling the size and location of flowering wood.

No matter what kind of pruning you do, the same basic rules apply.

• **Clippers** Avoid using anvil-type clippers because they crush the cane. Your clippers must be kept very sharp, and cuts should be as clean as possible, without damage to remaining tissue. Damaged tissue will die back and create a haven for pests and disease.

• **Die-back** When you cut both large and small canes, moisture escapes through the wound. As a result, the cane will die back and that area will turn brown. If you have cut to a certain bud, make sure to leave some extra length so the die-back won't kill the bud.

• **Painting wounds** When thick canes are cut, there is a sizeable wound where diseases and insect pests can very easily enter the plant. The cane will also suffer from moisture loss and die-back. Because our plants in California aren't completely dormant during winter pruning, it is most important you seal the end of each cane after it is cut. Instead of black tree seal, use interior latex paint without fungicides. Try a light color that won't absorb heat and blends in with the plant.

• **Remove broken, diseased, dead, or conflicting wood** As with all other types of plants, canes which are broken, diseased, or dead should be promptly pruned out at any time of year before they create problems. If two canes touch or grow into one another, remove the less vigorous one before a wound is created.

A CLIMBING ROSE WITH THE CANES PROPERLY ARRANGED TO ALLOW EACH THE MAXIMUM AMOUNT OF LIGHT AND AIR.

How to Prune Flowering Wood

Each time flowering wood branches off, the new shoot will always be thinner, so try to keep all wood no smaller than the diameter of your little finger. As you cut flowers, you are shaping the plant. The goal is to produce a vase-shaped plant with an open center by always pruning to an outside facing bud. Sometimes these are hard to spot, so look closely. The open-centered plant allows more light and air circulation to reach all the foliage equally and prevent disease.

When you have identified a cane bearing flowers, trace it back to where it branches off the framework wood. Count three buds up from that junction, and if the bud faces outward, cut just above it. If the bud faces inward, to the side, or if it conflicts with other canes, you can cut at the next closest bud facing in the right direction. "Spare the clippers, spoil the rose" applies here. When flowering wood is cut too long, flowers will be small on spindly stems. Big blooms always come from big wood. In summary, here are the four rules of pruning flowering wood:

1. Cut flowering wood frequently during the growing season.
2. Cut off all flowering wood with a diameter smaller than your little finger.
3. Strive for a vase-shaped plant and cut to outside facing buds.
4. Always cut back to three buds above the framework wood.

Pruning Framework Wood

In northern California, roses retain some of their leaves right through the winter. It's not a good practice to winter-prune roses short because this may shock the half-dormant plants. Winter pruning of framework wood should leave behind a few sizeable canes to support next year's flowering wood. Plan on winter pruning your roses with the new year in January.

Big, fat, basal canes which are young and green make the best framework wood. One reason you feed and water roses heavily is to produce new basal canes from just above the graft union. If a cane begins at a point below the graft union it is rootstock and you should cut it off immediately. The existing framework canes age and eventually become woody, supporting less and less flowering wood each year. When you winter prune, the idea is to replace each old, less productive cane if a suitable new one grew the summer before.

The other goal in winter pruning is to remove all the flowering wood. It will not be as productive its second year. Vigorously growing roses replace all their lost flowering wood early in the season, but if the wood is left on the plant growth rates and flower production will be more conservative. When the flowering wood is gone, you can prune back the tips of the big canes to an outward facing bud, then paint the open end to seal it. This may seem complicated, but if you watch how the plant grows after you prune a certain way, that will tell you whether you cut too much or too little. In summary, use these four rules for winter pruning of flowering wood:

1. Winter prune roses in January.
2. Remove all the flowering wood of the previous season.
3. Replace any old woody canes with new vigorous ones.
4. Use paint to seal the newly cut end of each cane.

Pruning Climbing Roses

The unique canes of climbing roses can reach 15 feet in length and are trained in a near horizontal position. There flowering wood grows out of each upward-facing bud, and a single cane may have ten or more stems of flowering wood which together create bowers of dense color. In order to prune this flowering wood to encourage more blooms, simply cut back each flowering cane to the third bud above the long framework support cane. The bud should face outward from the fence or wall.

To winter-prune a climbing rose, first remove all the flowering wood. There is no need to prune framework canes unless they are to be replaced with new basal canes of sufficient size and length to be trained properly. When new basal canes appear during the growing season, they will have flowers at the end. If you cut off the tip with the flowers, the cane grows no longer. When encouraging basal canes, you should train them in a near horizontal position while fresh and supple. If you wait until the end of the season they may prove too stiff.

Pruning Old Roses that Flower Once a Year

Since there are so many different growth habits in this group of roses, it's difficult to apply clear-cut rules. Observe your plants to see how they are inclined to grow before pruning. Most old roses bloom for a single period in early spring on wood which grew the summer before. They should not be pruned in the winter except when thinning over-dense plants. Prune these roses very lightly, but only *after they finish blooming.*

Although the rangy species of roses don't require any pruning, plants may be thinned and shaped if they grow too large. Remove any old, unproductive canes so new ones may grow in their place. With smaller ramblers, you can cut back the over-long canes by one-third and nip the ends of other canes to encourage lateral branching. The more lateral branches the plant produces, the more flowers you get next year.

PESTS AND DISEASES OF ROSES

Although there are many diseases which afflict roses, we must only contend with a few here in California. Refer to the appendix of this book for more information on controlling pests and diseases in plants.

Common Diseases of Roses

Rose varieties differ in their ability to resist diseases. The three most common rose diseases are all fungi, which thrive in moist conditions and on plants weakened by poor care. Diseases will vary from year to year according to weather conditions. Garden fungicides for rose diseases are the only means of control, but if the condition is allowed to spread unchecked, it can be nearly impossible to stop.

• **Blackspot** This disease appears as black, circular patches on the leaves, and eventually they fall off the plant. Most roses will have a few black patches on their lower leaves. Hand-pick the leaves with spots off the plant and gather up those which have fallen and dispose of them off site.

• **Mildew** Mildew looks like a sprinkling of talcum powder on the leaves, and eventually causes them to crinkle and become distorted. Mildew grows rapidly when days are hot and nights are cool and moist. It can be *very difficult* to control and plants should be treated with a fungicide immediately after mildew appears.

• **Rust** This fungus, like blackspot, rarely causes serious damage. It is easy to identify by pin-head sized, rust-colored spots on the backs of the leaves, which may disappear as weather warms up.

Common Insect Pests of Roses

There are only a few insects that can damage roses, and regular inspection of your plants will reveal their presence while still in small numbers. Before you consider insecticides, follow the least toxic controls detailed in the appendix.

• **Aphids** Aphids congregate and feed on the tender, growing tips of rose plants and are very easy to see. They also hide on the undersides of leaves. The presence of ants on your rose bushes is a good indicator that aphids are nearby. Simply brush them off with your hand or use the garden hose now and then to decrease their numbers.

• **Red spider mites** These tiny red-colored spiders are much smaller than a pin head and live on the undersides of the leaves. They cause a silvering of the leaf and you may see specks and very fine webbing on the back side. Spider mites prefer dust and a clean plant should not develop a problem.

• **Roving grasshoppers** During the middle and late summer, grasshoppers can do some damage to the buds and new leaves of roses. The damage is easily identified by the clean edges of wounds where they have fed. Grasshoppers are long gone by the time you notice the damage, and control is impossible. It's best to let the insect have his meal, and only turn to more drastic measures if you feel as though your roses are falling to the proverbial plague of locusts.

• **Rose midge larvae** The adult midge is actually a tiny fly that lays its eggs in the soft stem tips of rose bushes. The egg hatches into a ravenous larvae which proceeds to tunnel down into the cane. The sure sign of this problem is the sudden wilt and drooping of the end of a rose cane. If you cut the tip of the cane back carefully you may encounter the maggot or its tunnel. Once the maggot is removed, the cane will regrow and be healthy. The best control is to cut off the end of the cane just as soon as it wilts and dispose of it off-site.

CHAPTER EIGHT

ANNUALS FOR EVERYONE

Annuals are bedding plants that grow for one season, then go to seed and die as winter approaches. This limited growing period makes them quick to flower, and they continue blooming for a long time if conditions are right. In the mildest parts of northern California, frost-tolerant annuals bloom throughout the winter months. Most plants are very easy to grow and widely available in a variety of sizes from small seedlings to mature, flowering adults.

ABOVE: *ESCHSCHOLZIA CALIFORNICA* (NATIONAL GARDEN BUREAU)

Annuals can be divided into two main groups, hardy annuals and tender annuals. Hardy annuals such as poppies require cool soil temperatures to germinate, and are best sown directly into the ground during the fall or winter. These plants flower earlier in the spring and some species do not transplant well. Tender annuals are sown in late spring when the soil has been thoroughly warmed. To prolong the blooming season, plants can be started indoors and transplanted to the garden after the last frost.

THE BENEFITS OF PLANTING ANNUALS

Annual bedding plants can be a continually changing part of the permanent landscape. Annuals are perfectly suited to hanging baskets and pots because their root systems fit easily into small spaces. The key is to select the right plants, provide plenty of water, and apply fertilizer on a regular basis to keep them healthy and vigorously blooming.

INSTANT COLOR

Annuals bring instant flowers into a garden. Young plants can be purchased already blooming to dress up the yard for a party the same night. A quick infusion of annual color improves curb appeal for homes on sale. Annuals are a good way to fill in gaps between plants in newly installed landscapes. In short, if it is color the gardener seeks, the most direct means of obtaining it is with annual bedding plants.

CUTTING FLOWERS

Many annuals have both tall and short hybrids of the same flowers. The taller ones are used by florists for the longer stems. These tall plants can become rangy as they age, and while still producing excellent cutting flowers they will require staking for support. The shorter dwarf hybrids, with their more compact form, are best for mass planting in landscapes or pots. Some gardeners grow cutting flowers separately in vegetable plots or utility areas where they can age gracefully without spoiling a landscape.

COMMON GARDENING MISTAKES

One of the keys to eye-popping annual color is to plant enough of it to make a big splash. Massing single colors makes them stand out boldly, and certain combinations are very dramatic. Inexperienced gardeners plant a few seedlings here and there, which is fine for tiny gardens, but in most cases they go unnoticed. A strong hand with color in larger landscapes is essential for the time and effort of planting to really pay off. Rather than three pink petunias, plant three six-packs full. Don't just edge part of a planter with dwarf marigolds, ring the entire lawn with them. Observe other gardens and see how they have used large masses to create a strong color statement. Don't be afraid to experiment with annual color, and if you feel hesitant, ask yourself if you have ever seen a flower garden that wasn't beautiful? The answer is always no.

WHERE TO BUY ANNUAL BEDDING PLANTS

Bedding annuals are sold in more places than any other kind of landscape plant. The key is knowing how to purchase the best plant for the lowest price.

GARDEN CENTER

What we used to call a nursery is now termed garden center because most no longer propagate their own plants. Plants are bought from specialty and huge commercial growers to be sold retail through garden centers. Here is where you'll find unusual annuals for more creative gardening. The owner is a reliable source of information on plants and their care, but the sales employees may not be as highly skilled. If you have a problem with your plants, the garden center professional will be there to help. Bedding plants sold at garden centers are a bit more expensive than other sources, but they usually receive better care.

HOME IMPROVEMENT CENTER

Shopping for hardware and plants at the same time is a great convenience for busy gardeners. Large chain stores purchase plants from the growers in such quantities that the prices are lower than garden centers. Unfortunately, the sales people aren't experts, and plant stock doesn't receive the kind of care necessary to keep annuals in top form. The key is to find out when the growers make deliveries and only buy plants out of the fresh stock.

SUPERMARKET

During spring and summer, many supermarkets offer bedding plants. Prices are competitive but slightly higher than home improvement stores. This is a great place to pick up a few annual plants, but stock is usually insufficient for larger plantings. Markets don't have the ability to provide special care, and plants may linger on the display for months. Here too, it's wise to wait until a new delivery is made before buying plants.

OTHER SOURCES

Universities and community colleges have plant sales at the end of the school year. These are plants grown by horticulture students and the money is frequently used for a good cause. Botanical gardens also offer plant sales to raise money and here you may find some real bargains. Both are good sources for unusual and rare plants such as California natives as well as less common varieties of annuals.

WHAT SIZE TO BUY

All bedding plants are sold and priced according to the size of their planting container. The larger the container, the older and more expensive the plant. Before spending a penny, make sure you are buying the most economical size for your intended use.

GROWING ANNUALS FROM SEED

Anyone who has looked through a full-color seed catalog will attest to the incredible number of species and hybrids offered. This selection is far better than any retail source, and you are guaranteed the exact color and hybrid desired. Growing from seed is the least expensive way of obtaining annuals, but it can be the most time consuming.

SIX-PACK CONTAINERS

A six-pack is a plastic container that has six plants growing in separate compartments. Since annuals are usually planted in quantity, buying six at a time is more efficient. There are two sizes of six-packs; the small ones are sometimes called "pony packs" and the larger ones "color packs."

Pony packs are the smallest plants and the least expensive to buy. These are the ones to look for if you have lots of time and a tight budget. Plants should flower in 4 to 6 weeks, depending on the species. Since they are not blooming, there is no way to know what flower color you have unless each plant is well labeled.

Color packs are getting downright expensive these days, but the plants may already have buds and even blossoms. This is a good size for color pots or hanging baskets. The seedlings are better equipped to survive very hot weather and even a little neglect. The actual size and age of the plants in these containers varies depending on when they were potted up from pony packs.

FOUR-INCH POTS OR LINERS

Annual plants are also sold in small square containers called 4-inch pots because they are about 4 inches square, and sometimes the term "liner" is used for the same thing. This is the size to buy for instant effect, as plants are well established, budded up, and actively blooming. Because there is only one plant in the pot, the price is much steeper than six-packs, and its easy to run up quite a bill.

THE DO'S AND DON'TS OF BUYING ANNUAL PLANTS

With many different sources for bedding plants, it pays to know how to pick out the very best ones. Just like buying produce at the supermarket, avoid those that aren't in top condition or you may be disappointed later on. Try not to feel sorry for the "poor doer" and attempt to nurse it back to health because you will pay the same amount for this one as for a young vigorous plant. In most cases, no amount of nursing will make a weak plant perform any better.

PICK OUT THE BEST PLANTS

It is your right to buy only large and healthy plants. Don't worry about ruining a display by sorting through it as you closely inspect each individual for scars, broken stems, or dead flower buds. Pick up the pot and gently shake it while watching for white flies, which are a common nursery problem. If shaking causes a few buds to fall off, the plant may have been stressed from heat or lack of water. Leaves are a good barometer of plant health. Trouble signs are yellowing of the lower leaves or an unusual amount of fallen leaves beneath the plant. Look for sucking insects that hide on the undersides where we least expect them.

Because there are so many different hybrids available to California gardeners, labeling is very important. Young plants of the same species look similar, but may have very different flower colors, sizes, and growth habits. Sloppy plant sellers often lose the labels and you should not have to bear the consequences.

ROOTS TELL THE STORY

The only way to tell if a plant has overgrown its container is to inspect the roots. Gently lift up the corner of the soil in a six-pack, or turn larger pots over carefully and tap the plant part way out while supporting it with your hand. If you see plenty of dark soil, the plant is fresh and healthy. Plants that show a mass of of yellow roots should be passed up. Other bad signs are roots coming out of the drain holes, or if they are visible on the top of the soil.

HOW TO PLANT ANNUALS

Annuals do a lot of work before the end of their short life span. They must reach adult size very quickly and begin blooming in just a few weeks, a mammoth task which takes plenty of fertilizer and water. Thorough preparation of soil in the planting area is the best insurance that annuals will grow well and bloom for the entire season.

SOIL PREPARATION

There are two reasons for improving soil: to open it up and enhance fertility. When organic matter or humus is added to the soil, it helps to prevent compaction. The more humus and the deeper it is worked into the soil, the better growth rates will result. Since annuals are heavy feeders, an all-purpose fertilizer can also be added in very small amounts to boost levels of N-P-K. Use a spading fork or rotary tiller to work up the ground as deeply as possible, then add humus and fertilizer and till it again until the materials are evenly worked in.

PLANTING ANNUALS FROM CONTAINERS. SHOWS CORRECT CONDITION OF ROOTS FOR HEALTHY BEDDING PLANTS. (*NATIONAL GARDEN BUREAU*)

NORTHERN CALIFORNIA TIP

Growing annuals or any other plant from seed is an inexpensive way to create a colorful garden. Our arid climate makes it more difficult to start seed because both soil and new seedlings dry out very quickly. Easy-to-use seed starter kits are sold at most home improvement stores or garden centers for a very reasonable price. They consist of a plastic tray, empty six-packs, seed-growing medium, and a plastic covering. The tray has ridges to keep the six-packs up out of the water that collects in the bottom. The plastic covering retains moisture and the whole unit can even be left for a day or two without watering. For anyone serious about growing plants from seed, a starter kit guarantees success.

PLANTING FROM CONTAINERS

The best time of day to plant is in the evening, to give the seedlings a whole night to adjust to their new location before the hot sun rises. Before planting begins, gather up all the tools and materials you'll need so the work can be done rapidly, with the least amount of stress on the plants.

It's best to arrange the plants in the bed while still in their containers. Adjusting the spacing is much easier to do while they are in the pots than after half the bed is planted. If you are working with six-packs, cut them up with scissors or a knife into individual little pots. It's a good idea to use a triangular spacing or offset-row arrangement to avoid an obvious grid pattern.

Start planting at the back of the bed and work your way to the front so there's no danger of stepping on plants already in the ground. Make sure the soil is packed firmly around the root ball and avoid pinching the base of the stem with your fingers. Rough handling will crush the tender stems and make it difficult for the plant to transport moisture from roots to leaves. Once everything is planted, water in thoroughly to prevent air pockets from drying out the roots.

PLANTING FROM SEED

Both hardy annuals and tender plants that germinate easily can be sown directly into the soil. Soil must be free of dirt clods, rocks, roots, and other debris. Soil should be finely worked in order for seeds to remain at proper planting depths. Scatter the seed thinly, but evenly. If planted too densely, they become leggy and difficult to thin out later. Don't rake the seed, but cover it with a layer of peat moss and sand or fine topsoil at the proper thickness for that species.

THINNING OF HARDY ANNUAL SEEDLINGS SOWN DIRECTLY INTO GARDEN SOIL. (*NATIONAL GARDEN BUREAU*)

Watering seed can be tricky because soft soil washes away so easily. Use a misting nozzle for your hose that emits water in a fine, even spray. Water twice a day if necessary to keep the soil evenly moist. If it dries out just once at a critical point in the germination process, the new roots may die or have a setback. As the seedlings emerge, thin them out to the proper spacing while young, before they influence each other's growth pattern.

To start annuals indoors, use any container that is shallow and well drained. Save the empty containers from six-packs and reuse them for starting your own seeds. Milk cartons, coated paper cups, and styrofoam cups all work well. Ask at your local garden center for leftover six-packs that would otherwise be thrown away. Purchase a bag of seed-growing soil that is light and contains lots of finely ground peat. It's worth the cost and insures a perfect growing medium for healthy plants.

Your seed trays will need a sunny window to keep the soil warm enough for germination. If you aren't using a starter kit, cover the containers loosely with plastic food wrap to hold in moisture. Poke a few small holes in the plastic for oxygen. Seedlings don't need fertilizer at this early stage because seeds contain enough nutrients to get them started. Use a weak solution a few weeks after sprouting, and again when they are potted up to larger containers or straight out into the garden.

RULE OF GREEN THUMB

When sowing very small seeds like poppies directly into garden soil it's easy to overdo it. If seedlings are too densely planted, the process of thinning can be time consuming and threatens the root systems of the seedlings that remain. To avoid overseeding, mix the seed into some clean sand to insure thinner, and more even seed distribution with less waste. Don't use beach sand because it contains salt, and avoid sand that may have weed seeds mixed in.

GOLDEN STATE RULES FOR ANNUAL PLANT CARE

Anyone can be successful with annual bedding plants as long as sufficient care and attention is provided. Stick to these five basic rules and you can't go wrong.

1. **Buy quality plants and thoroughly prepare the soil.**
   Even the best plants will fail if planted in poor soil. Efforts to improve the soil with fertilizer and amendments are the key to a strong root system. Healthy plants grow larger, bloom better, and are more able to resist pests and disease.

2. **Watch closely for pests.**
   There are pests that want to eat your flowers even before the buds open. The most common are a huge group of caterpillars that eat the petals and leave behind tiny BBs the color of the flowers they have consumed. Keep a sharp eye out for missing pieces of petal or leaf. Watch for discoloration of leaves or withering that is not consistent with other plants nearby. Of course, shiny snail trails are a sure sign of nocturnal visits. The sooner a problem is identified, the easier it is to eliminate.

TRANSPLANTING SEEDLINGS FROM THE FLAT TO A 6-PACK CONTAINER. (*NATIONAL GARDEN BUREAU*)

3. **Fertilize plants frequently.**
We know that annual plants require lots of food to do a good job. In general, most balanced commercial fertilizers will work fine and should be applied frequently, but in low concentrations to avoid burning. Granular fertilizers can be hard on fragile seedlings because they must be worked into the soil and dissolved with lots of water. Liquid-based types or water soluble crystals are easier to use and won't burn foliage. They can be applied with a watering can or hose-end sprayer. Since liquid fertilizers are already dissolved, the liquid goes directly to the roots for more immediate results.

4. **Cultivate, cultivate, cultivate.**
Most soils develop a dry crust on the top that prevents water and fertilizer from moving downward. Clay soils can compact and become as hard as concrete, causing irrigation water to run off before it has a chance to penetrate. To reduce water consumption and help oxygen reach the root system, cultivate the ground frequently. If you are using mulch to retain soil moisture, cultivate less often and be sure to renew the mulch afterwards.

5. **Pick off the dead flowers.**
This single activity is the real key to successful annuals. When a bloom withers, the plant immediately begins developing a seed capsule. With marigolds this seems to happen overnight! The maturing seed capsule signals the plant that the season is drawing to an end and it has fulfilled its sole purpose in life, to reproduce. But if the remnant of each flower is picked off as soon as the petals fade, there is no signal to stop and bloom production continues indefinitely.

If the flowers are picked off every day or two, the task becomes an opportunity to inspect each plant up close and catch pests or disease long before they become a problem. This is the secret of great gardeners whose plants seem to bloom much longer and more profusely than anyone else's.

CONTROLLING DISEASE AND PEST DAMAGE

A few bugs are no reason to drench a plant in insecticide. But infested plants can be threatened by insects to such a degree that drastic measures are needed. The very best way to avoid infestation is to keep healthy plants, because if you watch closely, you'll see that insects tend to attack the weakest plants first.

WATCHING OUT FOR INSECT PESTS

The biggest threat to annual plants in northern California are caterpillars. These voracious feeders are the larvae of many moths and insects. As mentioned earlier, their presence will be signaled by missing sections of leaves and blooms, and tiny BBs scattered about on the plant. Many species only come out at night to feed, then return to the ground during the daytime, making control very difficult.

Chewing insects like earwigs and sowbugs feed primarily on dead or decaying organic matter, but they also eat flower parts and feed at night. Earwigs are long, flat brown bugs identified by the prominent pinchers at the ends of their tails. Pill bugs or sowbugs are easy to identify when they roll up into little gray balls. Slugs and snails, with their characteristic silvery trails, can ruin a whole plant overnight and may be very difficult to control. It is thought that too much manure in the soil attracts them and provides a perfect environment for breeding. Occasional roving grasshoppers can also consume large portions of tender growing tips and flowers, only to move on their way before you know it.

Aphids and spider mites are sucking insects that cluster on the undersides of leaves. Spider mites are tiny and cause the front of the leaf to take on a silvery sheen, and the underside to carry tiny red or black flecks.

When annuals are planted where conditions are too moist or when weather conditions are right, diseases such as powdery mildew may appear. It looks like its name, similar to a light coating of talcum powder that disfigures the leaves. Rust is another fungus that lives on the leaves and is easy to recognize because of its fuzzy, rust-colored patches.

CHECKLIST: TEN STEPS TO GUARANTEED SUCCESSFUL ANNUAL COLOR

1. Buy healthy, well-labeled plants and quality seed.
2. Select plants suitable for the designated exposure.
3. Plant in masses for a bolder color display.
4. Thoroughly prepare soil before planting.
5. Sow seed thinly and at the proper depth.
6. Keep a sharp eye out for early signs of pests and disease.
7. Apply fertilizer on a regular basis.
8. Cultivate the soil often.
9. Frequently pick off spent blooms.
10. Water deeply, especially during hot weather.

WILDFLOWERS FOR LANDSCAPING

A FIELD OF NATIVE CALIFORNIA POPPIES. (*NATIONAL GARDEN BUREAU*)

Wildflowers such as California poppies and lupine are a common sight in our mild climate. Most wildflowers aren't fussy about soil fertility as they will bloom profusely in the dry gravel along roadsides. Many species inhabit crevices between boulders on steep, rocky south-facing hillsides where they grow in a few tablespoons of soil in nature's own rock garden.

Growing large masses of wildflowers is more successful when hydroseeded because germination rates are significantly higher, with less waste. They can also be hand sown, with slightly lower germination rates. Seed mixes are formulated for coastal, valley, foothill, and mountain conditions.

PROBLEM SOLVING WITH WILDFLOWERS

Wildflowers are often the only plant that will grow under extreme conditions of heat and drought. Hydroseeded mixes do very well in sandy, desert soils and help to bind them together to prevent wind erosion. Quick germination allows them to mature and flower during the brief desert spring and reseed themselves before the heat of summer arrives.

Throughout the state, wildflower mixes have been given a strong role in revegetating cut slopes. Here they are combined with grasses to hold steep hillsides through the first winter rains. As time goes by the wildflowers will naturalize or die-out if conditions are not perfect for reseeding. In many cases they are simply added to beautify new subdivisions until other plants mature.

In rocky areas where rotory tillers fear to tread, wildflowers may be the only plants tolerant of shallow, infertile soils. Many will take hold and create colonies that expand with each winter's rains. The degree of success with wildflowers in natural areas varies with the temperatures and rainfall for that individual year. In the wild, the size of wildflower populations changes with weather patterns, degrees of frost and length of the rainy season.

NATIVE CALIFORNIA LUPINE, *LUPINUS PERENNIS* (*JACK BODGER*)

WILDFLOWER PLANTING TIPS

Just because they are called wildflowers doesn't mean the seed can be thrown out upon the ground and expected to grow. Rodents, birds, and wind do away with a large portion of the seed before it has a chance to sprout. Of course, hydroseeding is the ideal method for application to large areas, but for small sites, spots of wild color must be hand sown.

Aggressive grasses and weeds prevent successful wildflower germination, and highly fertile soils can also inhibit a good stand. Before sowing, repeatedly water and

ANNUAL BEDDING PLANT SELECTION GUIDE

	Unusual Foliage	California Native	Drought-Tolerant	Poor Soil	Edging Plants	Cutting Flowers	Fragrance	Massing
Antirrhinum majus—Snapdragon					•	•		
Begonia semperflorens—Wax Begonia	•				•			•
Calendula officinalis—Pot Marigold				•		•		•
Catharanthus roseus—Madagasgar Periwinkle				•	•			•
Consolida ambigua—Annual Larkspur				•		•		
Cosmos bipinnatus—Cosmos			•	•				
Dahlia pinnata—Bedding Dahlia					•			•
Eschscholzia californica—California Poppy		•	•	•				•
Helichrysum bracteatum—Strawflower			•	•		•		
Impatiens wallerana—Impatiens								•
Lathyrus odoratus—Sweet Pea	•					•	•	
Lobelia erinus—Lobelia					•			•
Lobularia maritima—Sweet Alyssum			•	•	•		•	•
Papaver nudicaule—Iceland Poppy								•
Pelargonium hortorum—Zonal Geranium	•		•		•			•
Pelargonium peltatum—Ivy Geranium			•	•				•
Petunia hybrids—Petunia				•	•			•
Portulaca grandiflora—Moss Rose	•		•		•			•
Primula malacoides—Fairy Primrose					•			•
Salvia splendens—Scarlet Sage			•	•		•		•
Senecio cineraria—Dusty Miller	•		•	•				
Tagetes erecta—African Marigold				•		•	•	
Tagetes patula—French Marigold				•	•			•
Tropaeolum majus—Nasturtium	•		•	•	•			•
Verbena hybrida—Verbena			•	•			•	•
Viola cornuta—Viola					•			•
Viola tricolor—Johnny-Jump-Up					•			•
Viola wittrockiana—Pansy					•			•
Zinnia elegans—Zinnia			•	•		•		•

cultivate or use an herbicide to reduce the number of weed seeds and viable grass rootlets present in the soil. Wildflowers can take from two to four weeks to germinate, and sowing of unirrigated plots should be timed just prior to winter rains.

To hand-seed large sites, it is important to scar the surface of the soil before planting. This can be done by pulling a drag board studded with nails along the ground. Tie a rope to each end of the board to make a tow line that may be pulled by hand or behind a tractor or riding lawn mower. Drag the entire area thoroughly to rough up the surface and make it ready for planting. If your wildflower seed is very small, mix it with sand to avoid overseeding and broadcast evenly over the entire area. Then seed is sown, turn the board over and drag the flat side to smooth out the soil and lightly cover seed.

SOUTHWESTERN WILDFLOWERS (*ENVIRONMENTAL SEED PRODUCERS*)

CHECKLIST: SEVEN STEPS TO SUCCESS WITH HAND-SEEDED WILDFLOWERS

1. Select wildflower species that suit your climate and needs.
2. Buy high-quality, weed-free seed.
3. Plant before winter or spring rains.
4. Work up or scar the surface of the soil to accept seed.
5. Combine seeds with sand for more even distribution.
6. Sow seed at the recommended density.
7. Be sure seeds are adequately covered.

A SELECTION OF THE BEST ANNUAL BEDDING PLANTS

DWARF SNAPDRAGON

Antirrhinum majus

Snapdragon

Exposure: Sun, part shade. Size: 3 feet tall, 12 inches wide. Colors: White, yellow, rose, and pink. Flowers: Winter, spring. Hardy annual.

Snapdragons have long been the favorite of children, with flowers having miniature "jaws" that can be manipulated by small fingers. These showy flowers bloom on the ends of tall stalks that often need staking for support. After the first flower clusters are cut, the plant will branch out to produce numerous smaller blooms. Like pansies they too are a winter flower in California and should be planted from seedlings in the fall. Occasional pinching of young plants will yield much bushier adults with stronger stems. Excellent drainage is essential. Many dwarf varieties are suitable for massing and stay conveniently short.

Begonia semperflorens

Begonia semperflorens

Wax Begonia, Fibrous Begonia

Shade, part shade. Size: 8 inches tall, 8 inches wide. Colors: pink, red. Bloom: Late spring, summer, and fall.

Dwarf begonias have a fibrous root system and prefer a light, evenly moist soil. Their low, dense growth habit makes them suitable for massing or as a border in shade gardens. They are especially effective in color pots located under trellises and arbors. Some hybrids are considered sun tolerant in coastal areas, but shade is advisable inland. Foliage is rich green with bright, shiny leaves. Flowers are born on colored stems in various shades of pink, red, or white. Blooming period extends from early summer to late fall. May winter over in mild areas, or plants can be potted up and stored in a sheltered place until spring.

Calendula officinalis

Pot Marigold

Full sun. Hardy Annual. Size: to 30 inches tall, 18 inches wide. Colors: Orange, yellow. Bloom: Fall, winter, and spring.

This should be considered the winter marigold because it will grow and bloom in cold weather. The flowers are large, daisylike disks with lots of petals. Historically it is edible, and was used during the Civil War to dress wounds. Calendulas are rugged plants, grow quickly, and bloom off and on through three seasons if spring temperatures aren't too warm. This tall variety is an excellent source of cutting flowers when few other plants are blooming. The hybrid dwarf strain blooms with the same flower size and color, but plants stay low, about 12 inches tall. As young plants, the full size and dwarf calendula are nearly identical, so proper labeling is a must.

Catharanthus roseus (aka *Vinca rosea*)

Madagascar Periwinkle. Full sun coastal, part shade inland. Size: 12 inches tall, 6 inches wide. Colors: white, rose pink. Bloom: All seasons.

There is always confusion between this annual plant which was formerly called *Vinca rosea,* and the vinca groundcovers because they also share the common name periwinkle. This periwinkle is a very common flowering annual that is perennial in coastal and protected inland areas. Its flowers are not showy, with just five petals about an inch or so across. It makes a great bedding plant for massing or as edging or borders because it can bloom all year around with a neat form and dark green foliage. Although periwinkle prefers a shaded location, it is surprisingly tolerant of hot, dry conditions.

Consolida ambigua (aka *Delphinium ajacis*)

Annual Larkspur

Exposure: Full sun, part shade. Size: to 4 feet tall, width varies. Color: shades of blue most common, white, lavender, pink, and red. Blooms: Spring and early summer. Hardy annual.

Do not confuse this plant with the perennial delphinium, which also blooms predominately in blue. Larkspur is a fine cutting flower, a hardy annual grown directly from seed. It is sewn into well-drained garden soil during late fall or winter and does not germinate well in hot weather. Does not transplant well. It has a casual, cottage-garden character with a spindly form that grows sometimes to 3 feet tall. Flowers occur in large spires on top of plants that may need staking. Great for the back of a flower border, in cutting gardens or sown with wildflower mixes.

Madagascar Periwinkle
(*All America Selections*)

Annual Larkspur (*Jack Bodger*)

Cosmos bipinnatus

Cosmos

Exposure: Full sun. Size: to 5 feet plus tall, 3 feet wide. Colors: pink, red, or white. Bloom: Late summer and fall.

One of the easiest annuals to grow from seed, cosmos is delightfully heat and drought tolerant. It grows rapidly into an open, airy plant that blooms during the dog days of late summer. Flowers are daisylike with broad petals and a bright yellow center. Colors are predominately rose pink but hybrids with white or red flowers are available. To appreciate its rangy nature, cosmos should be given lots of space and isn't suited for small, compact gardens. It is not particular about soil fertility except that it should be well drained. A good informal addition to rural or country style gardens with an old fashioned theme.

Dahlia pinnata

Annual Bedding Dahlia

Exposure: Sun coastal, part shade inland. 18 inches tall, 12 inches wide. Colors: Many. Bloom: Summer and fall

Dahlias can be separated into two groups, those considered perennials, which are grown from tubers, and the annual bedding dahlia, grown from seed each year. Bedding dahlias are sold in six-packs and are smaller, more suited for annual color splashes. Flowers can be single or fully double in an incredible array of colors from deepest reds to brilliant yellow. Dahlias prefer morning sun and do poorly when exposed to direct sun or afternoon heat. Plants may be plagued with mildew if air circulation and morning sun are inadequate. Pinch back the tips of young plants to promote bushier growth habit and more blooms. For best results soil should have plenty of humus and regular watering. Frequent, but light applications of balanced fertilizer stimulates stronger growth.

Eschscholzia californica

California Poppy

Exposure: Full sun. Size: 12 inches tall, 10 inches wide. Colors: Orange or yellow. Blooms: Summer and fall. California state flower, native wildflower. Hardy annual.

California poppies cannot be purchased as seedlings because, like most wildflowers, they do not transplant well. Poppies are directly seeded into the soil before winter rains, and once established, develop self-seeding colonies. Older plants become perennial where winters are exceptionally mild. Excellent drainage is critical as their natural habitat is on nonirrigated rocky or grassy south-facing hillsides. Like most California natives, plants are sensitive to irrigation in summer, which is their normal resting period. Although a separate genus, it is related to the Asian poppy and California Native Americans used the root to reduce the pain of toothache. A frequent addition to wildflower mixes.

Cosmos bipinnatus

ESCHSCHOLZIA CALIFORNICA

IMPATIENS HYBRIDS

Helichrysum bracteatum

Strawflower

Exposure: Full sun. Size: 24 inches tall, 12 inches wide. Colors: Yellow, orange, pink, red, and white. Bloom: Late summer, fall.

Strawflowers are usually grown as an everlasting because their rich, sunset-colored flowers hold their form and color when dried. Plants tend to be leggy with lots of brown leaves toward the bottom of each stalk and are best grown in a cutting garden rather than as bedding plants. A good annual for dry gardens, it requires only moderate watering and grows well even in poor soils. Sow seed directly into garden soil or start early indoors.

Impatiens wallerana

Impatiens

Exposure: Shade, part shade. Size: 14 inches tall, 16 inches wide. Colors: Many shades of red, pink and white. Blooms: All summer.

In very mild coastal areas impatiens will become perennial if adequately protected, and they thrive in moisture and foggy conditions. An outstanding addition to any shade garden, impatiens bloom profusely over many months. If grown in heavy shade, plants may become leggy and will benefit from regular pinching back or pruning to encourage more compact new growth. Flowering is enhanced by frequent but mild applications of liquid fertilizer. Many hybrids offer a good selection of flower colors, even striped petals, and double-flowering varieties are especially attractive. Good for massing, as accent color or in pots.

Lathyrus odoratus

Sweet Pea

Exposure: Full sun. Size: Vine to 6 feet plus. Colors: Many. Hardy annual. Bloom: Spring, early summer.

Sweet peas are a favorite old-fashioned garden flower. They grow in vines that climb by tendrils, which require a trellis of wire or string like edible peas. *All parts* of this plant are toxic, including the small pods. Flowers come in many different colors and are sweetly fragrant. Plant seed directly into garden soil in fall or winter for spring bloom. Seeds are very hard and germinate better if soaked in warm water for about two hours before planting. Flowering may slow down as hot weather approaches inland. To prolong blooming season, apply a thick mulch with lots of water and keep spent flowers and pods picked off. Many hybrids available.

Lobelia erinus

Lobelia

Exposure: Full sun coastal, part shade inland. Size: Cascading plants to 6 inches tall. Colors: Many shades of blue. Bloom: Spring, summer, and fall.

Lobelia is a very common annual plant that is one of the very best for hanging baskets. Its beautiful trailing form may spill as much as 6 inches to 10 inches below a moss basket, and works well in rock gardens or hillside pockets. Flowers profusely with dozens of small blooms in many hues, from iridescent midnight blue to pale azure. Older plants may be cut back to tighten clumps of foliage and encourage flowering. Excellent for borders and as edging. Prefers cool, moist coastal conditions. Beware of reflected heat from building walls and pavement. Best buy in small six-packs.

LOBELIA ERINUS

Lobularia maritima

Sweet Alyssum

Exposure: Full sun, part shade. Size: 6 inches tall, 10 inches wide. Colors: White, purple. Blooms: Spring and summer.

Many seasoned gardeners lament that once sweet alyssum begins to reseed itself, it sprouts up everywhere like a weed. This common hardy annual can become perennial where winters are mild, and a fall shearing of the foliage renews it for yet another season. Popular in pots and hanging baskets, where it cascades, or planted out to fill in empty garden areas where rapid spreading color is needed. Neat mounding habit is suitable for massing or borders of single color. May be grown from seed sown directly into garden soil. Fast growth makes it suitable for planting from the smallest six-packs. Frequently added to wildflower seed mixes.

SWEET ALYSSUM (WHITE)

Papaver nudicaule

Iceland Poppy

Exposure: Full sun. Size: 18 inches tall, 12 inches wide. Colors: Shades of yellow, orange, pink, and white. Blooms: Early spring. Hardy annual.

Iceland poppies are the most delicate member of the poppy family. They grow into neat little tufts of foliage, and flowers rise to over 18 inches high on wiry stems. Blooms are vividly colored, paper-thin cups of crinkled petals with bright yellow centers. Their breezy, almost feminine nature is easily swallowed up by more robust flowers. Plant in large clusters or masses for full effect. All annual poppies grow best in the early spring, before hot summer weather arrives. They tend to have much better stands of flowers in coastal areas. Iceland poppies require cool soil temperatures to germinate and like most hardy annuals should be directly seeded into garden soil in the fall. Poppies are sensitive to transplanting, but Iceland

PAPAVER NUDICAULE

Zonal Geranium

poppies are an exception and are abundantly available in six-packs. For best results buy very young plants because they transplant much better than mature adults. Iceland poppy is actually a perennial, but in California it's treated as an annual.

Pelargonium

Bedding geraniums are members of the genus *Pelargonium,* not genus *Geranium,* which creates lots of confusion. During the 1940s and 50s, geraniums were one of the most popular plants in California and other temperate states. They have been extensively hybridized into dozens of colors. In the mildest areas along the coast and sheltered valley locations, some geraniums will winter over, barring unexpected freezes. They root easily from cuttings and may be spread throughout the garden. This ease of propagation is why avid fans of geraniums have been known to steal cuttings off of plants wherever they go. Two main bedding varieties are loosely called zonal uprights and ivy trailing geraniums. Other types have been a part of herb gardens for centuries, grown for their uniquely scented leaves.

Pelargonium hortorum

Zonal Geranium

Exposure: Full sun coastal, part shade inland. Size: 3 feet tall, 2 feet plus wide. Bloom: Spring and summer. Colors: Many shades of red, pink, and white.

Zonal geraniums are very succulent plants that can survive under dry conditions, but regular watering promotes more attractive foliage and larger blooms. Plants are upright and may begin to sprawl if not regularly cut back. In areas where they winter over, stems become tough and woody unless severely cut back in fall to promote new, succulent growth the following spring. Zonal geranium's round fuzzy green leaves have reddish circular accents that are very attractive in their own right, and some hybrids have more deeply lobed foliage. Flower heads offer brilliant colors, with particularly delicious coral pinks and deep magenta, for most of the spring and summer. Keep spent flowers picked off to promote longer blooming season and pinch back young plants to encourage compact growth and more flowers.

Pelargonium peltatum

Ivy Geranium

Exposure: Full sun, part shade. Size: 12 inches tall, trailing to 3 feet. Colors: Many shades of red, pink, lavender, and white. Bloom: Spring and summer.

Ivy geraniums are highly versatile because they spread like groundcovers and hang gracefully like vines. They are always popular for hanging baskets or at the tops of walls and slopes, where their green tresses can become a huge mass of trailing blooms. Foliage is glossy green but some varieties offer variegation, with leaves evenly spaced on long tendrils that drape but do not climb. Very easy to propagate from cuttings. Plant as an annual except in mildest coastal climates, where they may survive the winter. Cut back to promote fuller branching and new growth if plants develop too many stems and not enough leaves. For best results keep soil moist and avoid intense reflected heat from walls and pavement.

Petunia hybrida

Garden Petunia

Exposure: Full sun, part shade. Size: 10 inches to 18 inches tall, 9 inches wide. Colors: Many! Bloom: Spring and summer.

Petunias are one of the easiest annuals to grow and can make a beginner gardener look like an expert with their profusion of brightly colored flowers. They tolerate

Hanging basket of ivy geraniums.

both heat and dry soils, although sufficient water and regular feeding speeds growth and encourages more prolific flowering. Petunias can be divided into two sorts: trailing and bush type. Trailing petunias are great for hanging baskets, taller pots, and cascading down walls or slopes. Bush types are only slightly more upright and suitable for injecting into bare spots of the garden for instant color or planting in low, wide pots and for massing.

Zillions of hybrids offer colors from deepest purples to vivid blue, red, and purest white. Some even have petals that are striped, ruffled, or fully double. Petunias are plagued by voracious caterpillars, but BT is a nontoxic and very effective defense. Pinch back plants that grow leggy at the end of summer for a bonus of fall flowers. Fast growth makes them a "best bet" for buying in six-packs. Insist on well-labeled plants to insure proper growth habits and flower color.

PETUNIA 'POLO BURGUNDY STAR' (*ALL AMERICA SELECTIONS*)

Portulaca grandiflora

Rose Moss, Portulaca

Exposure: Full sun. Size: 6 inches tall, 18 inches wide. Colors: Bright shades of red, pink, orange, yellow, and white. Blooms: Summer and fall.

One look at the intensely vivid flowers of portulaca is enough to snare anyone. This heat-tolerant succulent plant shares the same vigor of its weedy relative purslane, and has long been a part of older California gardens. It is a low grower which creeps into dense mats or cascades off walls and the edges of pots. A very popular plant in coastal gardens for its tolerance of salt air and sandy soils. A good choice for dry, neglected parts of the garden or around landscape boulders, where it is not bothered by the reflected heat. Very tiny seed may be sewn directly into fine garden soil, but portulaca is better planted midspring from nursery-grown seedlings.

Primula malacoides

Fairy Primrose

Exposure: Shade, part shade. Size: 12 inches tall, 6 inches wide. Colors: Red, pink, lavender, and white. Bloom: Winter, early spring.

Most primroses are perennials except these two which are usually planted as annuals because they have difficulty surviving our long hot summers. The pastel flower spires of fairy primroses are most dainty and provide welcome color to shady areas beneath tree canopies. In mild coastal areas they grow well during the winter, but, where hard frosts are common, it's best to wait until early spring to set out seedlings. Like all forest floor plants, they do best with plenty of moisture and soils rich in organic matter. Fairy primroses create a softer woodland effect than the perennial English primrose.

Salvia splendens

Scarlet Sage

Exposure: Full sun, part shade. Size: To 24 inches tall, 12 inches wide. Color: Shades of hot red. Blooms: Summer.

Scarlet sage is grown strictly for its flowers and is not used as a culinary herb. Plants grow tall and narrow, ending in large spikes of red flowers in many different shades. Very showy addition to partially shaded gardens, but many prefer the closely related but more sedate blue-flowering sage. Best to plant out from nursery seedlings in midspring for full summer color. Vertical growth habit

PRIMULA MALACOIDES

SALVIA SPLENDENS (JACK BODGER)

SALVIA, BLUE HYBRID (JACK BODGER)

SENECIO CINERARIA

makes it great for divider strips, back of borders, or as miniature hedges. So commonly planted in early twentieth century California gardens, scarlet sage became a sign of poor taste, with flowers so garish "the color is heard before it is seen."

Senecio cineraria

Dusty Miller

Exposure: Full sun, part shade. Size: To 24 inches tall, 18 inches wide. Colors: Silvery gray foliage, yellow flowers. Blooms: Spring, summer.

Dusty miller is grown primarily as an accent plant for its silvery gray foliage. It is one of the best choices for night gardens because the leaves reflect moonlight with such perfection that the entire plant appears to glow. Flowers are small, yellow or cream colored, rising just above the foliage and are really insignificant. Dusty miller can grow quite large and bushy, but occasional shearing will renew the leaves and tighten its form. When planted in a row to outline mass plantings or as a small hedge, this annual can really spice up a landscape. It also brings the illusion of light into partially shaded settings that need a shot in the arm. Easy to grow, it's an unusual but rewarding selection for beginners.

Tagetes
Marigold

Without a doubt, marigolds hold the honor of being California's favorite bedding plant. They are reliable, rugged, and grow well even when conditions are less than perfect. Marigolds are purely American flowers once cultivated in the gardens of the Aztecs and later sent back to Spain and North Africa. Today many Mexican farmers still grow them as fodder for their livestock. Marigolds are divided into two main groups although many other species exist. Those plants that ended up in North African gardens were eventually named African marigolds. Those brought to England from Spain by the French are called French marigolds.

Marigolds serve many uses in the garden besides just providing beautiful flowers. They are known to discourage nematodes, a soil-borne disease that infects plant root systems. Their pungent scent repels certain insects, and many find it offensive while other folks love it. For both these qualities it is frequently planted in vegetable gardens. Be aware that no part of either African or French marigolds is edible.

Dwarf French Marigolds

Tagetes erecta
African Marigold

Exposure: Full sun. Size: To 36 inches tall, 18 inches wide. Colors: Yellow, orange. Blooms: Spring through fall.

African marigolds are best suited to the cutting garden. Their flowers are large, dense pom-poms of petals that when wet become so heavy they threaten to tear the plant apart. Often scoffed at by more sophisticated gardeners, these plants are so easy to grow and the flowers so satisfying that beginners are guaranteed success. As plants age, they become leggy and will need staking to support the flowers.

Tagetes patula
French Marigold

Exposure: Full sun. Size: 6 inches to 14 inches tall, 10 inches wide. Colors: Yellow, orange, brick red, and combinations of all three.

French marigolds are often called dwarfs, but are actually full-sized plants. Their dense, compact growth habit makes them a favorite for edgings and large masses where uniformity of size is important. Marigolds develop seed pods so rapidly after the flower fades that it is quite a chore to keep them all picked off. It's worth the effort though, because they will continue blooming for many months from spring through summer and into the fall if kept from going to seed. French marigolds are the backbone plant of most California annual plantings because they tolerate the heat of our long summers. Hybrids provide flowers that range from single to fully double miniature pom-poms. Colors are predominately yellow and orange with hybrids bearing some red accents. Those with red petals highlighted by yellow edges are particularly striking.

Tropaeolum majus
Nasturtium

Exposure: Full sun, part shade. Size: 12 inches to 18 inches high, runners up to 6 feet long. Colors: Red, orange and yellow. Blooms: Spring, summer, and fall.

Nasturtiums are technically annual vines that have limited climbing ability. The plants also work well as a temporary groundcover. The peppery tasting yellow and orange flower petals add festive color to salads. Its green, unripe seed pods were once pickled and used as a substitute for capers. Nasturtium leaves are round and regularly spaced along runners that may climb up trellises or twine themselves through picket fences. They grow best in sandy soil with low fertility and minimal watering. They do very

Nasturtium

VERBENA (*JACK BODGER*)

VIOLA CORNUTA

JOHNNY-JUMP-UP

well in coastal gardens and tolerate salt spray. Cut flowers often to stimulate bloom. Sow seed directly into garden soil in early spring.

Verbena hybrida
Garden Verbena
Exposure: Full sun. Size: 12 inches tall, 36 inches wide. Colors: White, pink, red, purple, and blue. Blooms: Summer, fall.

There are many different species of verbena, but this one is probably the fastest grower. It is often used by landscape contractors to quickly fill in spaces between young shrubs in newly planted gardens. Garden verbena grows like a groundcover, in low, dense mats that can become a brilliant sea of color for many months. Foliage is dark green and aromatic. It can be mowed to renew growth in areas where winter frosts are mild enough for it to become perennial for a few years. Best buy is in flats.

Viola
There is always confusion over the differences among violas, pansies, and violets. All three are members of the genus *viola*, but only true violas and pansies are commonly used as bedding plants today. An old saying makes it easier to remember: "While all pansies are violas, not all violas are pansies." In the nineteenth century, violas were extensively hybridized into over 400 different large and colorful pansies, and these became one of the most valued flowers in Victorian gardens.

Viola cornuta
Viola, Tufted Pansy
Exposure: Sun, part shade. Size: 6 inches tall, 8 inches wide. Colors: Many. Blooms: Fall, winter, and spring.

This viola is smaller than a pansy and the flower petals are of a single color. Plants with clear Dutch blue and bright yellow flowers were favorites in old-fashioned gardens. Good plant for winter color in mild areas, and is particularly attractive when planted with bearded iris. Plants will tolerate considerable frost and keep blooming. Flowers decrease as hot weather approaches but start up again when temperatures drop in the fall. Sow directly into garden soil or plant out from 6-packs in fall or spring.

Viola tricolor
Johnny-Jump-Up
Exposure: Sun coastal, part shade inland.
Size: 6 inches tall, 12 inches wide.
Color: Yellow and purple on same flower.
Bloom: Fall, winter, and spring.

The small but powerful Johnny-Jump-Ups are the oldest of the pansy clan and were around in their present form during medieval times. The easiest viola to grow, they were not overbred and retain their original flower color and disease resistance. These plants are more casual and tend to creep along like groundcover, with a profusion of tiny flowers. They cascade gracefully from hanging baskets or down the edges of walls and pots. A great companion for lobelia and sweet alyssum. Regular pinching of growing tips makes plants more compact with higher density of blooms. When old and leggy, cut them back gently for renewal.

MIXED PANSIES (*NATIONAL GARDEN BUREAU*)

Viola wittrockiana
Hybrid Pansy
Exposure: Full sun, part shade. Size: 10 inches tall, 12 inches wide. Colors: Many. Blooms: Fall, winter, and spring.

It's hard to beat the mammoth flowers and broad spectrum of colors provided by today's hybrid pansies. These never fail to provide lots of color during California's colder months, when few other plants are blooming. Pansies are neat, low-growing plants that are best used in masses and in single or double rows as borders. Good as groundcover over early spring bulbs like tulips and daffodils. Set out pansies in fall for winter flowering and are a best buy in six-packs. Keep spent blooms picked off for long flowering season from winter through late spring. Avoid overhead watering if possible because droplets weight down petals and cause rot where flowers contact the soil.

ZINNIA 'SCARLET SPLENDOR' (*ALL AMERICA SELECTIONS*)

Zinnia elegans
Zinnia
Exposure: Full sun. Size: To 40 inches tall, 24 inches wide. Colors: Brilliant red, orange, yellow, pink, purple, and white.
Bloom: Summer, fall.

Zinnias are real sun lovers and thrive in more heat and drier conditions than most annual flowers. Flower heads are daisylike with many variations of petal shape and size, from small pom-poms to giants nearly 5 inches across. Colors are neon shades so bright they tend to overwhelm other flowers. Good for combining with Mexican sunflower and African marigolds, or may be planted to provide late summer color in drought-tolerant and native plant gardens. Seed germinates readily and may be sown directly into warm garden soil or set out from nursery-grown seedlings in very late spring. Water deeply but not from overhead, and fertilize often for maximum flower production. Very large flowers make zinnias a rewarding annual for beginning gardeners.

CHAPTER NINE

PERSISTENT PERENNIALS

Northern California is one of the best regions for growing perennial plants, with more well-defined seasons than in the south. A perennial is an herbaceous plant that flowers year after year and does not die at the end of the growing season like an annual. Perennials are showiest in their second or third years, after plants become fully established. As a bonus, many types develop large clumps that can be divided into new plantlets and spread throughout the garden. A perennial can provide just as much color as an annual plant, but flowering occurs for a much shorter period of time.

FACING PAGE: TALL FOXGLOVE, WHITE SNOW-IN-SUMMER, AND VARIGATED SHRUBS AT GATEWAY.

A vast assortment of plants are loosely called perennials in California, ranging from evergreen lilies to rather short-lived semiwoody native shrublets, and some annuals. Annual plants may become perennial in the mildest coastal regions where they winter over and continue to flower through a second year. The foliage of most perennials will freeze to the ground while roots remain alive and sprout new stems and leaves the following spring. Surprisingly enough, the most difficult task facing perennial plants in northern California is surviving the hot, dry summers. Except for high elevation mountain zones, the beginning gardener can be assured a wealth of color from most perennials with very little effort, or special attention.

HOW PERENNIALS DIFFER FROM ANNUALS

A perennial plant can be expected to grow for many years while annuals typically live for only one. Some perennials are more expensive to buy than annuals because propagation can be difficult and time consuming. Although the purchase price is higher, the longevity of perennials makes them more economical, and when not in bloom they make better landscape plants.

With the passing of each season, plants will grow into slightly larger clumps and provide more flowers. Since they are to remain where originally planted, mainline perennials fare much better when mulched and regularly fertilized. This does not apply to all perennials because some California natives and aromatic herbs tolerate drought and considerable neglect. This diversity makes it more difficult to apply general rules to perennials than annuals.

RULE OF GREEN THUMB

Before attempting to grow perennials from seed, it is essential to understand the special requirements that must be met before they will sprout. Some types of seed must be refrigerated or soaked in warm water for twenty-four hours before planting, and others should be scratched with sandpaper or nicked with a knife. The mantilija poppy, a California native perennial, requires exposure to fire before it germinates and this is why it is always in short supply.

Under the umbrella of perennials are many different types of plants. The members of the evergreen lily group, including daylily, lily of the nile, and red hot poker, have fleshy roots that are very easy to divide. On the other hand, lavender cotton, sage, and California fuchsia look more like miniature shrubs than true perennials, and do not tolerate disturbance. From this broad group comes a variety of foliage and flower accents that are an integral part of that special character found only in the gardens of California.

Some of the very best cutting flowers are perennial. These are regal members of the flower garden and their spires of color can be awe inspiring. Among them is hollyhock for country gardens, delphinium for sophisticated growers, and foxglove, the reigning queen of the shade plants. The golden heads of tall yarrow, all members of the vast clan of chrysanthemums, and valerian, a very ancient flower, are all guaranteed to keep every vase full and a permanent pair of flower shears in the kitchen.

WHERE TO PLANT PERENNIALS

When planted in clusters, perennials attract attention to different parts of the landscape as they flower with the changing seasons. The most common are strap-leafed plants because their foliage provides a needed contrast to the rigidity of shrubs. They are very easy to grow and require no special care. Sometimes their thin leaves suggest reeds and lend the cooling illusion of nearby water.

Perennial Borders

We have inherited the perennial border from the English, who plant long strips from 4 feet to 10 feet wide with flowering plants. It is densely filled with perennials arranged so the tallest are at the rear and the smallest to the front. Avid enthusiasts take great care in organizing plants according to flower color and season of bloom. The goal is to have the perennial border in flower for as many months as possible.

Potted Perennials

Gardening in containers is really the domain of annuals, although perennials are sometimes used to provide more long-lasting foliage. In some cases perennials are planted by themselves to reduce the need for seasonal replanting or for special conditions where annuals aren't suitable. English primroses are one of the most frequently used perennials for container growing because they bloom during the winter months with vivid colors on very small plants. Another perennial for pots is the kaffir lily because it blooms similarly to amaryllis but tolerates some of the deepest shade. The perennial basket-of-gold alyssum, with its bright yellow flowers, cascades beautifully down the sides of large pots and can be drought tolerant.

HOW AND WHERE TO BUY PERENNIALS

Buying perennial bedding plants is much more expensive than buying annuals, but the additonal cost is offset by the greater longevity. Some perennials are difficult to propagate and growers pass the cost on to consumers. In many cases a perennial may have been potted up to progressively larger containers many times before it is finally ready for sale.

BUYING PERENNIALS IN CONTAINERS

Like all other nursery-grown plants, perennials are priced according to their container size. The smaller the container, the lower the cost. Some perennials are offered in large six-packs for the same price as annuals, and you'll get more for your money by choosing the perennial. Very young plants like these may not bloom the first year, although a few small flowers may appear late in the season. Hardy perennials or those in coastal climates can be planted in the fall instead of the spring to give them a head start.

Many perennials are sold in 4-inch pots or "liners" which contain plants that are well on their way to maturity. It can be difficult to find this size because growers know they can pot each liner up to a 1-gallon container and make a higher profit margin on each one. Look for the best deal on liners at college or high school plant sales and botanical gardens.

A good nursery or garden center is the best place to find a wide selection of perennials. But they won't be cheap and containers tend to be strictly 1 gallon. Because of the higher prices, it pays to be extra picky when selecting perennials. These plants must be strong enough to survive not just one season but many years of growth. A poorly growing perennial isn't worth the price under any circumstances.

ABOUT MAIL ORDER PERENNIALS

The market is flooded with color catalogs offering perennials for sale. Keep in mind that these cater to gardeners who live where it is too cold for nurseries to sell perennials during winter months. Here in California it doesn't pay to send away for plants when such a broad selection is available at home. Rather than order from the catalog, use it to point out what you want to a knowledgeable garden center sales person and ask if it can be special ordered. It may take awhile to find, but the perennial that comes in will be much less expensive, larger, and more successful than mail-order stock.

COMMON GARDEN QUESTION

"What kind of stakes should I use to support tall perennial flowers, and where is the most economical place to buy them?"

Most garden centers and even less expensive home improvement stores carry both redwood and bamboo stakes. Redwood stakes are about 3/4 inches square and 3 feet long, but this is not a very strong wood and stakes may break if pushed too hard. Bamboo stakes are usually painted green and may be as small as 1/4 inches in diameter and 24 inches long, up to huge timber bamboo tree stakes. In the fall, look for neat bundles of sticks out on the curb for garbage collection, as these are a free source of plant stakes. Another option is using straight prunings from your own trees, particularly water sprouts and suckers of fruit trees.

HOW TO CARE FOR PERENNIALS

A perennial will remain in one place for many years and should be planted with the same care as a shrub. It is important to dig a large hole and backfill with earth rich in humus if your soil is poor. Well-prepared soil allows plants to root deeply, which makes them more tolerant of late summer heat.

Perennials can be planted in the fall when temperatures are cooler, or in early spring. In fall the warm soil encourages young plants to root more aggressively. Cold, wet soil in spring discourages growth and plants may sit dormant in the ground until temperatures warm up.

SOIL MAINTENANCE

The soil around each perennial should be cultivated and improved in the early spring to open it up to air and fertilizer. During the middle and late summer months, perennials sensitive to heat will suffer if hard, dry soil prevents water penetration. It is very helpful to use a thick mulch of compost, well-rotted manure, ground bark, or other organic materials to keep roots cool and prevent moisture from evaporating from the soil surface. Later in the fall this mulch can be cultivated into the soil as an amendment.

WATERING, FERTILIZING, AND STAKING

Watering is also critical to helping perennials survive the summer. A deep flooding with the garden hose is

PERENNIAL SELECTION GUIDE

	Tall Spike Flowers	Cutting Garden Flowers	Unusual Foliage	California Native	Drought Tolerant	Poor Soil	Edging Plants	Shade Plant	Aromatic or Herb
Acanthus mollis: Bear's Breech	•	•	•			•		•	
Achillea filipendulina: Fernleaf Yarrow	•	•			•	•			•
Achillea millefolium: Common Yarrow		•			•	•	•		•
Agapanthus africanus: Lily of the Nile			•		•	•			
Agapanthus africanus 'Peter Pan': Dwarf Lily of the Nile			•		•	•	•		
Althaea rosea: Hollyhock	•				•	•			
Alyssum saxatile: Basket-of-Gold Alyssum						•	•		
Aquilegia hybrids: Columbine		•				•		•	
Armeria maritima: Thrift			•				•		
Bergenia crassifolia: Leather Leaf Bergenia			•			•	•	•	
Centranthus ruber: Red Valerian	•	•			•	•			
Chrysanthemum morifolium: Chrysanthemum		•							
Chrysanthemum maximum: Shasta Daisy		•			•	•			
Clivia miniata: Kaffir Lily			•					•	
Coreopsis grandiflora: Coreopsis		•			•		•		
Delphinium 'Pacific Strain': Perennial Larkspur	•	•				•			
Dianthus barbatus: Sweet William		•							
Dianthus chinensis: Chinese Pink						•	•		
Dicentra Spectabilis: Bleeding Heart								•	
Dietes vegeta: Fortnight Lily			•		•	•			
Digitalis purpurea: Foxglove	•	•				•		•	
Echium fastuosum: Pride of Madeira	•				•	•			
Fuchsia hybrids: Hybrid Fuchsia								•	
Gaillardia grandiflora: Blanketflower		•							
Hemerocallis hybrids: Daylily		•	•			•			
Heuchera sanguinea: Coral Bells		•					•	•	
Iberis sempervirens: Candytuft							•		
Kniphofia uvaria: Red Hot Poker		•	•		•	•			

PERENNIAL SELECTION GUIDE

	Tall Spike Flowers	Cutting Garden Flowers	Unusual Foliage	California Native	Drought Tolerant	Poor Soil	Edging Plants	Shade Plant	Aromatic or Herb
Lantana montevidensis hybrids: Lantana					•	•			•
Lupinus 'Russell Hybrids': Russell Lupines	•	•							
Oenothera berlandieri: Mexican Evening Primrose					•	•			
Papaver orientale: Oriental Poppy									
Penstemon gloxinioides: Garden Penstemon	•	•			•				
Penstemon heterophyllus purdyi: Blue Bedder Penstemon				•		•			
Primula polyantha: English Primrose							•	•	
Romneya coulteri: Matilija Poppy				•	•	•			
Rudbeckia hirta: Black-Eyed Susan		•			•	•			
Salvia greggii: Autumn Sage					•	•			•
Salvia leucantha: Mexican Bush Sage					•	•			•
Salvia officinalis: Garden Sage	•				•	•			•
Santolina chamaecyparissus: Lavender-cotton			•		•	•	•		•
Zauschneria californica: California Fuchsia				•	•	•			

best. Water applied overhead by sprinklers can cause sensitive plants to discolor, develop fungus diseases, and become sunburned. Flower heads and tall plants can be weighted down by water and break or damage the stalks, not to mention ruin the bloom.

The best time to fertilize perennials is after they finish blooming because this is when the plant stores up energy to grow flowers the following year. Well-fed plants are the key to spectacular flower production, but it does take some foresight and planning. After the spring rush of garden chores, we don't often think about fertilizing perennial plants at the end of the summer when everything else is going to seed. A well-balanced granular or liquid fertilizer is sufficient for most plants.

The only exceptions to this rule of watering and fertilizing are California natives, which have their dormant season during the summer. Plants may need some moisture their first season or two, but roots will suffer if watered when well established. Penstemon and California fuchsia are the two most common native perennials that can be expected to survive much of the summer with limited watering. All other native plants growing wild in the vicinity should receive no water in summer because unseasonal moisture is deadly.

Tall plants like delphinium, foxglove, and even hollyhocks may need to be supported by stakes and loosely tied up. Take care when inserting the stakes into the soil because damage to the root system can result. It is best to install a short stake when the perennial is first transplanted into the garden. Mark the spot each year so a fresh stake can be forced into the same hole.

BEST PERENNIAL PLANTS FOR NORTHERN CALIFORNIA GARDENS

Notes: Plants noted as "hardy perennials" can be expected to survive the winter in the soil where they grew the previous year. This is based on climatic conditions in zones 2 to 7. The high mountain regions of zone 1 are an exception where roots are threatened by soils subjected to heaving from repeated freezes and thaws. There, roots of dormant perennials can be protected by mulching *after* the soil has frozen, but survival rates will vary.

Acanthus mollis

Bear's Breech

Exposure: Shade, part shade. Size: 24 inches tall, 3 feet wide. Color: White and lavender spires. Blooms: Summer.

Acanthus is a very old plant cultivated since Roman times, and its unique flower shape was the inspiration for the Corinthian column. Winter frost makes it die back to the ground in all but the most sheltered locations, but it will rapidly grow back in the spring. Its leaves are very large like those of the tropical elephant ear, and acanthus makes a great frost tolerant substitute. Flower spikes grow to nearly 5 feet tall and are excellent for cutting. Plant acanthus where it will be protected from hot afternoon sun and its underground roots will quickly spread deep green foliage throughout a planter. When plants become too crowded their roots may be dug and divided during winter months.

Acanthus mollis

Achillea filipendulina (Jack Bodger)

Achillea filipendulina

Fernleaf Yarrow

Exposure: Full sun. Size: To 3 feet plus tall, 18 inches wide. Color: Golden yellow. Blooms: Summer, fall. Hardy: Zones 2 to 7

Yarrow is an aromatic plant that is a reliable source of color for drought-tolerant gardens. Where water is plentiful, yarrow tends to grow more foliage and fewer flowers. Plant yarrow behind more attractive foliage plants or where its flowers can be appreciated from a distance. Fernleaf yarrow is the largest of this genus, rising to flat topped clusters of brilliant yellow flowers that can be dried and still keep their color. A smaller variety, *Achillea millefolium,* has white flowers and is much lower growing. This yarrow has been used successfully for erosion control and offers a bonus of being moderately fire retardant.

Agapanthus africanus

Lily of the Nile

Exposure: Full sun, part shade. Size: 3 feet wide, 3 feet tall. Colors: Blue, white. Blooms: Early summer. Zones 3, 5, and 7.

Agapanthus is the most common perennial plant in California gardens because it seems to survive the worst frosts and drought conditions of valley and coastal areas. It is a member of the strap leafed clan with its long, flat,

Achillea millefolium (Jack Bodger)

Agapanthus africanus

lilylike leaves and thick, fleshy roots. Blue flower clusters occur in perfect spheres at the end of thin, 3-foot stems that rise above the foliage. Great filler plants that never outgrow their space, providing contrast and cover for bare lower branches of rigid woody shrubs. Older plants may be lifted and divided during winter months. Dried leaves will accumulate at the base of the plant and should be removed in spring. A separate species, *Agapanthus orientalis* flowers in white, but in all other respects is virtually identical. The dwarf *Agapanthus*, 'Peter Pan' is much smaller and makes an excellent edging plant. It is very useful in gardens with limited space.

Althaea rosea

Hollyhock

Exposure: Full sun, part shade. Size: To 6 feet tall, 18 inches wide. Colors: Many. Blooms: Summer.

No other flower provides such a down-home country character as hollyhock. It appreciates plenty of sunshine and drier conditions, with overhead clearance to stretch to its full height. It is biennial, but size and number of flowers decrease during second and third years. Rust, a fungus of the same color, attacks the lower leaves of older hollyhock plants, making them less attractive late in the season. Best results when planted in fall for spring bloom either from nursery-grown seedlings or seeds sown directly into garden soil. Hollyhock blooms in many different colors and flowers grow larger when provided with ample water and fertilizer. Each flower quickly produces seed which will self sow if conditions are right.

Althaea rosea, Hollyhock

ALYSSUM SAXATILE (JACK BODGER)

Alyssum saxatile (aka *Aurinia saxatilis*)

Basket-of-Gold

Exposure: Full sun, part shade. Size: 10 inches tall, 18 inches wide. Color: Golden yellow. Blooms: Late spring, early summer. Hardy perennial. Cascading.

Although this creeping perennial was once listed under genus *Alyssum*, it has recently been reclassified into its own genus, *Aurinia*. Its gray foliage and nearly iridescent golden flowers can be seen in the charming perennial gardens of the north coast and in the lower Sierra foothills. Tolerant of dry conditions, basket-of-gold prefers well-drained sandy slopes or rock gardens, where its cascading growth is not bothered by reflected heat. Flowers create a low carpet of color made more beautiful when combined with dainty coral bells, which bloom at the same time. A reliable and versatile perennial that can be renewed by cutting back about 30 percent after blooms fade.

Aquilegia hybrids

Columbine

Exposure: Sun coastal, part shade inland. Size: 18 inches tall, 14 inches wide. Colors: Many. Blooms: Spring, summer. Hardy perennial.

Few perennials can rival columbine for graceful foliage, airy habit, and unusual flowers. Some species are native to California, but cultivated plants are usually the hybrid McKana Giants strain, which offers larger flowers and a wider choice of colors. Columbine grows in the partial shade of the woodland garden where soils are on the acid side and rich with humus, but it will mildew and grow poorly in soggy ground. Difficult to germinate, it is best purchased as a nursery-grown seedling and set out in the fall for prolific spring bloom. This is not a long-lived perennial and is often considered a biennial, lasting for only two seasons, occasionally three. A second flowering can be stimulated by cutting back gently after spring blooms fade. Attracts hummingbirds.

Armeria maritima

Thrift

Exposure: Full sun. Size: 6 inches wide, 12 inches tall. Colors: Pink. Blooms: Summer.

Thrift is also listed in the groundcover chapter of this book, but it is best used as a perennial. Foliage is a low, ground-hugging mat of tiny leaves that prefers the rapid drainage of mounds or rock gardens. Works well to make landscape boulders appear more natural when planted around the bases. Shooter-marble-sized, fuzzy round flowers rise on thin stalks to 12 inches with larger varieties, and only 6 inches for the smaller ones. Surprisingly drought tolerant, it is a good alternative to Irish moss and works surprisingly well with ornamental grasses.

Bergenia crassifolia

Leather Leaf Bergenia, Winter-Blooming Bergenia

Exposure: Shade, part shade. Size: 14 inches tall, 12 inches wide. Color: Pink, lavender. Blooms: Winter, early spring.

Bergenia is an old-fashioned garden perennial that will always be associated with the California bungalow. Plants are valued for their large, flat, succulent leaves that grow densely on short, thick stalks. Most often planted close together as an edging or exotic low hedge around water features or bordering walkways. Flowers rise on deep pink stalks into little clusters that bloom in late winter. Over time plants may become drought tolerant, but lack of water dulls the sheen and browns the edges of the leaves, reducing the impact of its best asset. Tolerant of poor soil but attractive to slugs and snails.

AQUILEGIA HYBRIDS

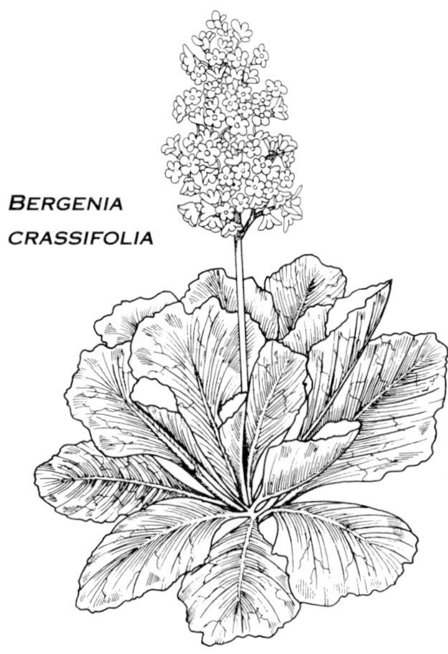

CHRYSANTHEMUM MAXIMUM

Centranthus ruber

Red Valerian

Exposure: Full sun. Size: To 3 feet tall, 12 inches wide. Colors: Red, pink, and white. Blooms: Spring, summer.

This plant is very difficult to find in today's market, which is a shame because it's perfectly suited to California gardens. In south-state beach towns, valerian grows on cliffs and in sandy soil under limited rainfall. A staple and important member of England's famous cottage gardens. Plants are relaxed and bloom in terminal clusters of flowers in every shade of pink. Excellent for natural gardens and slope planting where it will self sow. Cut plants back after blooming to encourage new buds and more dense foliage. Perhaps if enough gardeners request this plant, growers will be encouraged to make it more widely available.

CENTRANTHUS RUBER

Chrysanthemum morifolium

Florist's Chrysanthemum

Exposure: Full sun. Size: Varies. Colors: Many. Hardy Perennial. Blooms: Fall.

Florist's chrysanthemums have been bred into dozens of varieties with widely different flower forms and colors. Many of the exhibition hybrids require constant attention with copious amounts of water, fertilizer, and pinching back to produce the kind of blossoms florists use. Mums root quickly where stems contact the soil, and are easy to propagate. They may also be grown from cuttings taken in the late fall. Keep plants well fed with a balanced fertilizer, water frequently, and stake plants if they threaten to lie down on the job. When not in bloom, mums are unattractive and should be restricted to a cutting garden where they won't clutter up a landscape.

Chrysanthemum maximum

Shasta Daisy

Exposure: Full sun, part shade. Size: 24 inches tall, 18 inches wide. Color: White. Blooms: Spring, summer, fall.

Shasta daisy is a tough perennial that will perform well with very little effort. Although there are newer hybrids, all have the same large white flower with a yellow center. They do especially well in mountain and foothill areas where soils are marginally fertile and evenings cooler. Shasta daisy is prone to overexposure in hot, dry valley locations. Plants grow easily from seed, but an investment in a few "mother plants" can be easily divided and spread throughout the garden. A great neutral background plant or for naturalizing in meadow gardens.

CLIVIA MINIATA

COREOPSIS GRANDIFLORA

Clivia miniata

Kaffir Lily
Exposure: Shade. Size: 16 inches tall, 14 inches wide. Color: Orange with yellow accent. Blooms: Early spring.

This strap-leaved perennial is a bit too tender for most parts of northern California, but it can be grown successfully on the coast or under cover inland. Consider it similar to amaryllis lily in foliage and flower, but the blooms of clivia are smaller and clustered at the end of a single stalk. This little plant is a lifesaver for those dark shady areas where few other plants will grow, much less flower. Feed clivia with light doses of fertilizer suitable for acid plants, and mulch roots during the cold weather. The dark green leaves and bright flowers make great accents for fern and moss gardens, giving a hint of the tropics.

Coreopsis grandiflora

Coreopsis
Exposure: Full sun, part shade. Size: 24 inches tall, 30 inches wide. Color: Yellow.
Blooms: Summer. Hardy Perennial.

Here is an easy-to-grow perennial that will thrive in almost any soil, fertile or otherwise. Coreopsis is perfect for California gardens because of its tolerance to occasional dry spells and late summer heat when established. It is reliably pest resistant and flowers profusely with yellow tufts of petals atop thin stems that rise above the foliage. Cutting flowers as soon as they fade will prolong bloom season. Coreopsis has compact foliage that is attractive even when the plant is not flowering. This little plant is suitable for beginners because it is forgiving of neglect, but performs beautifully with regular water and light feedings.

Delphinium elatum 'Pacific Hybrids'

Perennial Larkspur
Exposure: Full sun coastal, part shade inland.
Size: To 7 feet tall, 12 inches wide.
Colors: Many shades of blue. Blooms: Late spring, early summer. Hardy perennial.

There is no other perennial that blooms as magnificently as delphinium, with its sophisticated blue spires. This is the perennial sort, not to be confused with annual larkspur. Delphinium is an expert gardener's flower, requiring special care to encourage the huge spires we see at garden shows. They do not grow well in California's inland heat, performing far better in cool, moist coastal gardens. Plants should be located in fast-draining soil to prevent rotting during the winter months. Keep soil cultivated and well mulched with compost, and water frequently. Begin staking long before plants need it to keep stalks growing straight. Cut stalks off at the base immediately after flowering is complete to encourage a second, smaller blooming in the fall. Plant in large clusters from six-packs for best results.

DELPHINIUM HYBRIDS

Dianthus

This large genus of perennials includes carnations and nearly 300 other plants, most only suitable for experienced gardeners. The two most commonly available and easy to grow in California gardens are China pinks and sweet William. Both are actually biennial and may die out at the end of the second or third year. They have been in cultivation for centuries and are important plants for old-fashioned cottage gardens. Seed sprouts readily, and plants may self sow if conditions are right.

DIANTHUS 'IDEAL VIOLET' (ALL AMERICA SELECTIONS)

Dianthus chinensis

China Pink

Exposure: Full sun, part shade. Size: 10 inches tall, 10 inches wide. Colors: Many shades of lilac, pink, red, white, and bicolored flowers. Blooms: Summer, fall.

China pinks grow in neat little clumps with narrow blue-gray leaves that will be covered with nickel-sized flowers from midsummer to fall. They are very dense and make good edging plants, remaining small enough for the front of a perennial border. Diligently cutting off spent flowers promotes a much longer bloom season, and grass shears do make a faster job of it while keeping foliage from becoming lanky. Pinks quickly rot in wet, poorly drained soils and will tolerate slightly drier conditions than most perennials. Inquire about hybrids with fringed petals; they are certainly worth hunting for.

DIANTHUS 'STAR PICOTEE' (ALL AMERICA SELECTIONS)

Dianthus barbatus

Sweet William

Exposure: Full sun. Size: 14 inches tall, 6 inches wide. Colors: Shades of red, pink, lilac, and bicolored flowers. Bloom: June.

This old-time favorite is loved for its fragrant flower heads clustered on top of sturdy stems. Unfortunately, it too is really a biennial and plants may not survive beyond a second year. Many gardeners keep a bed just for sweet William and add new plants each year as others die out or become weak. Use them for edging, in masses, or cluster in the perennial border. Plants are unattractive when not in bloom and for this reason they are often treated as annuals.

Dicentra spectabilis

Bleeding Heart

Exposure: Shade, part shade. Size: 18 inches plus tall, 12 inches wide. Color: Pink and white. Blooms: Late spring. Hardy perennial.

One look at the pendulous heart-shaped flowers of this woodland plant will make anyone a lifelong fan of bleeding heart. Its fernlike foliage is beautiful, and thin stems rise above the leaves bearing sometimes ten flowers each. Bleeding heart grows from thick, fleshy roots in the mulch of the forest floor, where it provides welcome color.

DICENTRA SPECTABILIS

DIGITALIS PURPUREA

Foliage dies back when cold weather hits, but quickly regrows in the spring. Plants may be purchased at any time of year in containers, but it is more economical to seek out or preorder bare-roots during the winter. An excellent old-fashioned plant for gardens beneath coastal redwoods or in the forests of the Sierra Nevada and other California mountain ranges.

Dietes vegeta

Fortnight Lily

Exposure: Sun, part shade. Size: 36 inches tall, 24 inches wide. Color: White with yellow and blue accents. Blooms: Summer.

The fortnight lily is second only to lily-of-the-Nile in landscape value, and can be found growing in almost every California garden. It is a sharp tipped, strap-leaved plant with a white flower that closely resembles Japanese iris. Fortnight lily is free flowering and will bloom repeatedly all summer if the spent flowers are cut off. Very durable and tolerant of occasional frosts, these plants are at home in Oriental gardens. The reedlike foliage looks great near garden pools and can also imply the presence of water in dry stream beds. Under extreme drought or very hard freezes, foliage will become dry and brown. Remove it as soon as possible and new blades will grow back. A second species, *Dietes bicolor,* has a simpler, five-petaled flower the color of glow-in-the-dark plastic, with exotic red blotches near the center. Bicolor is especially attractive with large foliage plants in subtropical gardens.

Digitalis purpurea

Foxglove

Exposure: Shade, part shade. Size: 5 feet tall, 18 inches wide. Colors: Purple, pink, and mauve. Blooms: Spring.

Foxglove is one of the showiest flowers of the shade garden, with its tall spires covered in tubular flowers with spotted throats. It is an old garden plant dating back to medieval times and is the source of the heart medication digitalis. It is said that witches included it in their "flying potions," which were poison concoctions that caused them to hallucinate with visions of actually flying. **All parts of Foxglove plants are poisonous.** Excessive handling of crushed leaves may cause absorption through the skin and it is best to keep it away from children and pets. Despite its drawbacks, foxglove is easy to grow and will naturalize in moist coastal gardens.

Buy nursery-grown seedlings or sow seed in fall or winter for spring bloom. Although considered a perennial, foxglove plants may produce for only two years and new seedlings should be planted each spring. Keep well mulched and avoid overwet soils. Stake blooms if they begin to fall over and cut back immediately after flowers fade to encourage a second, multiple flowering.

ECHIUM FASTUOSUM

Echium wildpretti

Fuchsia hybrid

Fuchsia hybrid

Echium fastuosum

Pride of Madeira

Exposure: Full sun, part shade. Size: 6 feet tall, 5 feet wide. Color: Purple. Blooms: Late spring.

This is a very large, shrubby perennial that grows profusely along the coast, but will not tolerate frosts inland. Echium has become naturalized along most of the California coast, attesting to its ability to tolerate salts and arid conditions. In many cases it is used to stabilize sandy palisades with its fibrous root system and indifference to soils. When not in bloom the plant is rather leggy, with thick, woody stems and insignificant foliage. But the blooms of echium are something to behold, candles sometimes 12 inches long of iridescent blue-purple flowers are unrivaled by any other drought-tolerant plant. Cut off faded flower spikes and occasionallly head back branches to encourage more compact growth.

A cousin, *Echium wildpretti,* called tower-of-jewels, is a horticultural oddity that can be found growing in Victorian towns along the north coast. During the second year its tuft of foliage bolts into a single massive flower spire reaching 6 feet to 10 feet tall, shrouded in purple-red blossoms. After blooming, it sets seed and dies entirely. Seeds germinate readily and produce many new plants.

Fuchsia hybrids

Fuchsia

Exposure: Shade, part shade. Size: varies. Colors: Many. Bloom: Summer, fall.

Who can resist the little ballerina-shaped pendulous flowers of any fuchsia? This special world is populated by hundreds of different hybrids that range in size from hanging baskets to huge landscape shrubs. In all except the mild coastal zone, plants are grown in hanging pots which can be brought indoors during winter or stored in a dark, dry place. In spring cut back one third of last year's growth and bring back into the garden. Water and feed frequently to encourage fast growth and very large flowers. Regular feeding and frequent generous wa-

GAILLARDIA

tering keeps flowers coming all summer. Lanky growth should be pinched back to make branches strong enough to bear the heavy flowers. Hot inland summers may reduce the vigor of some fuchsias and they should be grown in the coolest part of the garden. Attracts hummingbirds.

Throughout the north coast, despite occasional frost, old species fuchsias can be found growing wild on natural rainfall to immense proportions. Clearly these are unnamed seedlings of species escaped from early gardens before extensive hybridization occurred, and they have retained their vigor and disease resistance. These plants are more upright than the hybrids, lending themselves to being espaliered to walls or draped over fences or arbors. These have very small but plentiful white, pink, or red flowers that may cover the entire plant during the early summer.

Gaillardia grandiflora

Blanketflower

Exposure: Full sun. Size 40 inches tall, 18 inches wide. Color: Crimson red with yellow margins. Blooms: Summer, fall. Hardy perennial.

Here is another great perennial for arid California gardens. The bright Halloween-colored daisies of blanketflowers are numerous, blooming continually from June until frost. Plants flower the second year with long stems suitable for cutting and they keep well. Good drainage is more important than soil fertility, making them a good choice for sandy coastal or desert soils. Heat- and drought-tolerant, blanketflower is a good source of color in fall gardens blooming right along with chrysanthemums. If old plants fail to produce flowers, dig them during the winter and divide roots into new plants. May be difficult to find plants for sale, but seed germinates easily in only 5 to 8 days.

Hemerocallis hybrids

Daylily

Exposure: Full sun, part shade. Size: 4 feet tall, 3 feet wide. Colors: Red, pink, yellow, orange. Blooms: Summer.

Daylily is a strap-leaved plant which grows into large clumps of lime green foliage no taller than about 18 inches. Clusters of 3 or 4 large, trumpet-shaped flowers rise another 2 feet on thin stalks that are perfect for cutting. Daylily is northern California's most dramatic, easily grown perennial and is commonly sold in 1-gallon containers. Nursery supplies are usually limited to yellow and orange, but many other colors are available from well-illustrated mail order catalogs. The salmon and a new lavender hybrid are the most beautiful. Daylilies will die back to the ground inland, tolerating surprisingly hard freezes without protection except in the high mountain elevations. When clumps become too large, plants may be lifted in winter and divided. This is an excellent companion plant for lily-of-the-Nile because they both bloom at about the same time with flowers borne at similar heights.

DAYLILY 'LEEBEA ORANGE CRUSH'
(DAYLILY DISCOUNTERS)

DAYLILY 'LAVENDER WHISPER'
(DAYLILY DISCOUNTERS)

Daylily 'Red Volunteer' (Daylily Discounters)

Coral Bells

Heuchera sanguinea
Coral Bells
Exposure: Sun coastal, part shade inland.
Size: 14 inches tall, 6 inches wide.
Color: Shades of coral red. Blooms: Late spring, summer.

Dainty is the best word to describe little coral bells. The plants are very small, just a rosette of geraniumlike leaves no taller than 6 inches at the most. But from them rises slender deep red stems topped with clusters of tiny bell shaped flowers. They grow almost anywhere that is well drained, and are best suited to rock gardens or as an edging coupled with basket-of-gold alyssum and Serbian bellflower. Plants refuse to perform well in clay and best results can be expected from humus-rich sandy soils. When clumps become too large they can be lifted during late fall and divided. Make sure they are not overwhelmed by larger plants or those with strongly colored flowers.

Iberis sempervirens (Jack Bodger)

Iberis sempervirens
Candytuft
Exposure: Full sun coast, part shade inland.
Size: 12 inches tall, 18 inches wide. Color: White.
Bloom: Late spring. Hardy perennial.

Candytuft's compact form and charming pure white flowers have made it an old-time favorite. When not in bloom, its foliage is still attractive and remains evergreen throughout the winter if frosts aren't too severe. Its low, spreading habit is perfect for edging or in rock gardens where it will cascade like a white bridal veil between boulders or off low walls. Candytuft requires well drained soil and will tolerate some dryness, but plenty of moisture will help it through our hot inland summers. Because this is such a small plant, it's wise to purchase seedlings in six-packs and plant them together to create a mass large enough to be seen from a distance. If plants become rangy, carefully cut them back after blooms fade to encourage more compact growth.

Kniphofia uvaria
Red Hot Poker
Exposure: Full sun. Size: To 4 feet tall, 3 feet wide. Color: Red, orange, and yellow in one flower. Bloom: Spring, summer.

The flowers of this strap-leaved plant look like a cluster of the yellow-and-orange candy corn that is so popular during Halloween. These unusual blooms rise 2 feet above the clump of foliage on thin stems, and mature plants may have as many as five or six at one time. Red hot poker makes a passable substitute for torch ginger and

LANTANA

LUPINE 'RUSSELL HYBRIDS'

OENOTHERA (JACK BODGER)

other tropical plants that will not grow in our cool climate. This plant is so drought tolerant that it can be found growing wild at the sites of long abandoned farm houses surviving strictly on natural rainfall. It's frost hardy enough to tolerate the occasional frost inland, and under deep freezes the foliage dies back but soon returns with warmer weather.

Lantana montevidensis hybrids

Garden Lantana
Exposure: Full sun. Size: 4 feet tall, 3 feet wide.
Colors: Many. Blooms: Spring, summer, fall.

Lantana is a very rewarding perennial because it is disease resistant, grows rapidly, and flowers so profusely the entire plant seems to be always covered with blooms. It is tolerant of salt air, sandy soils, and does particularly well along the coast where frosts are light. But inland it may not survive the winter or suffers frost damage and die-back. Fortunately, the dead branches can be pruned off and foliage grows back quickly to flower yet another year. Lantana has many hybrids with dozens of vivid flower colors from white to electric orange and even deep purple. This plant is incredibly heat tolerant and is often the only alternative for dry, rocky sites where it seems to flower the best. Use it to fill in and provide color to new landscapes.

Lupinus 'Russell Hybrids'

Russell Lupines
Exposure: Full sun. Size: 3 feet tall, 18 inches wide. Colors: Many. Blooms: Late spring. Hardy perennial.

The Russell hybrid lupines are related to our blue native species, but these magnificent plants are available in a wide variety of colors. In California, cultivation is limited to the middle and high elevations of our mountain ranges where summers are cool and short. Lupine seems to need this mild weather and consistent moisture to flower properly. Plants grow best from seed sown directly into garden soil because their deep tap roots defy transplanting. Lupine grows surprisingly well in the poor rocky soils. Mulch roots in winter after soil has frozen to prevent damage from freeze-thaw heaving.

Oenothera berlandieri

Mexican Evening Primrose
Exposure: Full sun. Size: 2 feet tall, 30 inches wide. Color: Pink. Blooms: Summer.

A few years ago, this plant was a rare sight, but California's drought conditions have encouraged growers and it can now be found blooming cheerfully in many flower beds. But the Mexican evening primrose is far more important because it will survive and even thrive in conditions too hot and dry for other perennials. It is a low-spreading plant that flowers with large, pink cups of paper-thin petals that seem too delicate for such a durable plant. In some cases it can become invasive but this characteristic is what makes it so valuable, covering large areas with new seedlings. Plant oenothera near driveways and paving where reflected heat is a problem. Introduce it to slopes and rocky embankments where water runs off too quickly for most other plants. It blends well with natives to provide a reliable source of color in late summer.

PAPAVER ORIENTALE

Papaver orientale

Oriental Poppy
Exposure: Full sun. Size: 3 feet tall, 2 feet wide. Blooms: Spring. Colors: Shades of red, pink, and white. Hardy perennial.

Like the Russell lupines, the perennial oriental poppy has difficulty with the hot inland summers of northern California, which will shorten its lifespan. This plant grows far better on the coast and at higher mountain elevations. Oriental poppies leaf out and bloom in late spring, die-back with the heat of summer, and begin growing again in the fall. Where temperatures remain too hot, this fall growth may not occur, as the plant gradually loses vigor. Growing oriental poppies is rewarding when they mature into large clumps that produce large vividly colored flowers. Since they have a short blooming period and are not attractive the rest of the year, use them as accent plants that will be covered up by more vigorous summer-flowering plants. All poppies are sensitive to transplanting and it's best to buy them as bare-roots from mail order catalogs with a large selection of colors to choose from.

PENSTEMON GLOXINIOIDES

Penstemon gloxinioides

Garden Penstemon, Beard Tongue
Exposure: Full sun coastal, part shade inland. Size: 3 feet tall, 12 inches wide. Colors: All except yellow. Blooms: Summer, fall.

Penstemon is well suited to northern California gardens because it prefers warm, dry weather, even in the winter. It also demands light, well-drained soils and won't tolerate wet feet, which makes it perfect for slopes and rock gardens. Penstemon blooms on the ends of tall plants in showy flowers similar to foxglove. If flowers are cut off after they fade, side branches develop with a second crop of blooms. Plants often require staking because they tend to lie down if too top heavy, and this casual habit is better for informal, natural gardens. For best flowers and healthy plants, water frequently, feed lightly, and mulch roots in winter. Buy plants as nursery grown seedlings or grow from seed, which germinates easily.

BLUE BEDDER PENSTEMON (*JACK BODGER*)

Penstemon heterophyllus purdyi

Blue Bedder Penstemon
Exposure: Full sun. Size: 3 feet tall, 2 feet wide. Color: Lavender, blue. Blooms: Late spring, early summer. California native.

There are over forty different species of penstemon native to California and most of the genus is native to the western United States. These plants are rangy little perennials that bloom with small tubular flowers on tall spikes that rise above the foliage. This is one of the more frequently propagated species, but in general it is rare to find any native penstemons for sale at garden centers. Like all natives they do not grow well in containers and even when planted out are sensitive to watering during the summer while dormant. For hillside gardens in foothill and mountain regions and even on the sandy bluffs near the coast, penstemon can be planted and will grow well under natural rainfall. For gardens in valley locations, it's best to plant in raised planters with perfect drainage and sandy soil. Occasionally plants benefit from a deep watering in unusually dry winters. Many gardeners grow them from seed sown directly into garden soil. Seed is available for this and many other species of penstemon from wildflower seed distributors.

PRIMULA POLYANTHA

Primula polyantha

English Primrose
Exposure: Sun coastal, part shade inland. Colors: Many. Size: 8 inches tall, 6 inches wide. Blooms: Winter, spring.

Early in the spring when occasional frosts prevent all but the hardiest of flowers, English primroses are in their glory. In northern California they are treated like annuals, but are actually perennial and will bloom for many seasons. In the hot summer these little plants tend to die-back while the roots remain very much alive. Too often they are accidently dug up or dry out and die before the cool days of fall arrive. It pays off to heavily mulch garden primroses with compost for the summer to keep soil around them evenly moist and roots cool. Since primroses are so small, they are easily lost in larger plantings. Most effective massed in pots as annual color which can later be planted out into the garden after they cease to bloom. Low, neat plants make excellent edging in mixed or single colors. Best buy is in large six-packs or 4-inch pots.

Romneya coulteri

Matilija Poppy
Exposure: Full sun. Size: 6 feet tall, 4 feet plus wide. Color: White. California native. Blooms: Early summer.

This native perennial is sometimes called the fried egg plant because its large, white-petaled flowers have yolk-sized, bright yellow centers. It can be a frustrating experience to grow matilija poppies because they are sensitive to root disturbance, drainage and summer watering. Most growers don't stock this difficult to propagate plant and small container sizes are a rarity. But the rewards of a successful mature plant are inspiring as it grows into a 5-foot tall clump that spreads by underground stems. A good site for the matilija poppy is on warm, low land or coastal slopes with loose, fast draining sandy soil combined with other sensitive native perennials. Cut back stems after flowering when the plant is going dormant for the summer to encourage new growth in the fall.

ROMNEYA COULTERI

Rudbeckia hirta

Black-Eyed Susan

Exposure: Full sun. Size: 18 inches to 4 feet tall, 24 inches wide. Colors: Yellow, yellow with brown or maroon accents. Blooms: Summer, fall.

In the gardens of the higher Sierra Nevada foothills, rudbeckia seems to grow better than most garden flowers. They perform in the thin, infertile mountain soils and even tolerate the cold, dry winters. These old-fashioned perennials create bright masses of yellow deep into the fall and grow large enough to temporarily screen off unsightly areas. Their casual, upright nature is a must for the cottage garden character. After the first summer flowering, cut plants back to encourage another crop of blooms. When plants become too thick, dig the roots up the following spring, and divide them into new seedlings. Rudbeckia is often added to wildflower mixes because it self sows and sprouts readily in garden soil. Plants are also available in six-packs, which should be used in masses to the rear of planting areas with more compact bedding plants in front.

RUDBECKIA HIRTA

SALVIA

Drought conditions have brought many species of salvia to garden centers throughout California. Although most plants are basically perennial, colder winters in many parts of the north state force them to be treated like annuals. On the coast where frosts are exceptionally mild, gardens are full of the tender sages with their rangy shapes and bright flowers. Most red-flowering sages will attract hummingbirds. Although only three sages are covered here, there are many others perfectly suited to northern California gardens.

Salvia greggii

Autumn Sage

Exposure: Full sun, part shade. Size: 4 feet tall, 2 feet wide. Color: Pink, salmon, red.

Blooms: Late summer.

This sage has become more popular with profes-

SALVIA LEUCANTHA

sional landscapers as a mounding, shrublike perennial that will tolerate considerable heat and dry conditions. More important, it will take salty soils within reason, which is critical to many newer subdivisions where irrigation has caused salinity problems. Plant autumn sage in both natural rock gardens and manicured borders. It will send up very showy flower spikes with tubular red flowers that may continue through the fall. In zones 2 to 7 plants may die-back with frost but will regrow in spring.

Salvia leucantha

Mexican Sage

Exposure: Full sun, part shade. Size: 3 feet tall, 3 feet wide. Color: Purple, lavender.

Blooms: Spring, summer, and fall.

Mexican sage is the showiest and most tender member of this group, but like all the others it is considerably drought tolerant. It can be found growing only in the mildest coastal areas, attesting to its tolerance of sandy and low-fertility soils. There, Mexican sage develops into sizeable clumps of soft, fuzzy leaves which are attractive in their own right. But when the warmer months come, the ends of the stems send out lengthy flower spikes that rarely stand straight up, but lie at about a 45-degree angle toward the sunlight. The violet-purple velvet flowers accented in white cover each stem and are great for cutting. Plants can be renewed by cutting to the ground, or divide and replant stems with a bit of root attached.

Salvia officinalis

Garden Sage

Exposure: Full sun, part shade. Size: 24 inches tall, 18 inches wide. Color: Blue.

Blooms: Summer.

This plant is the sage of herb gardens which also double-times as a perennial flower. In early summer it sends up spikes of blue flowers that are very attractive to bees. Like all sages, it is not particular about soil, but plenty of humus and good care makes for larger plants. Fertilize in spring to encourage new growth to support summer flowers. Lanky plants can be made to produce more compact growth and more numerous flower spikes by pinching back the tips of each stem during early spring growth. When all flowers have faded, cut back to reduce the amount of foliage subjected to frost in cold areas. Mulch for winter protection.

Santolina chamaecyparissus

Lavender Cotton

Exposure: Full sun, part shade. Size: 16 inches tall, 12 inches wide. Color: Yellow.

Blooms: Summer.

The petite santolina never fails to satisfy with its drought-tolerant, disease-resistant nature. Its gray foliage is frequently used in knot gardens as a dividing hedge and makes a perfect edging material for walkways. Santolina retains its small, mounding form, but in time it may require an occasional shaping to prevent woodiness that tends to die out in patches. This perennial flowers with

SANTOLINA

little yellow daisies that rise on short stems, which should be cut off immediately after fading.

Beware of overwatering inland where soils are heavy and rich. Excellent with other drought-tolerant plants in rock gardens, slopes or traditional perennial borders.

Zauschneria californica

California Fuchsia

Exposure: Full sun, part shade. Size: To 24 inches tall, 18 inches wide. Color: Bright red. California native. Blooms: Summer.

Few of the California native perennials take to the cultivated garden as well as this one does. Foliage is grayish, borne on stiff stems that will grow upwards when young, but tend to lie down with age. Flowers are fiery red and draw hummingbirds like flies. Plant in perfect drainage and withhold summer water. Cut back after flowering to stimulate new upright stems during the winter growth period. Many consider it a shrub but short lifespan is more consistent with a perennial. Another species, *Zauschineria cana,* is just as beautiful but much larger. Availability of established plants for sale is spotty. For the best drought-tolerant perennial border, plant with *Salvia greggii* and the native penstemons.

The tubular blossoms of California fuchsia.

CHAPTER TEN

ENTERTAINING EXOTICS

EXOTICS, PALMS, FERNS, AND ORNAMENTAL GRASSES

Just because northern California experiences various degrees of winter frost doesn't mean that planting a tropical garden paradise is impossible. There are many plants which tolerate cold and still lend an exotic character. Occasional extreme conditions like the 1990 freeze tested these hardy exotics to their limits and most came through successfully.

HOW FROST IMPACTS PLANT GROWTH

Cold winter temperatures are influenced by the lay of the land. Cooler air always drops to the lowest point,

FACING PAGE: STUCCO WALL AND GATEWAY WITH EXOTIC, TROPICAL CHARACTER.

and it is here that frost will be more frequent and temperatures lower than surrounding high spots. Some ridges in the coastal and Sierra foothills experience what is locally called the "banana belt" microclimate. At night, warm air that accumulated during the day in sheltered valleys rises to rest upon the ridges as cold air rushes in to fill the void below. This cold air sits overnight, causing frost pockets which may not heat up until late the next morning.

In the central valley, tule fog also contributes to the frequency and degree of frost. Some years this ground fog lingers day after day without clearing, and gradually the ambient daytime temperature drops down into the low 40s. A single night of severe frost will damage plants, but they recover quickly. It is long-term low temperatures which pose the most severe threat and often kill plants outright.

Frost is also influenced by the presence of tree canopies or structures that shelter plants. This is because frost is created as warm air travels upward at night, but a covering reduces this movement and temperatures remain higher. Radiant heat from buildings is also released at night, furthering the ability to partially modify climate on a smaller scale. Wind helps to warm an area by forcing cold air up and out of the low spots, but conversely, the wind chill factor can also serve to make sunny areas colder.

Garden plants can be protected in a similar way by creating an overhead barrier. A popular practice is to drape bedsheets or sheets of plastic over the plants. This method traps the warm daytime air under the barrier and prevents cold air from settling around the plant.

REPAIRING FROST DAMAGE

How badly a plant is burned by the cold dictates how it should be cared for. Do not be in a hurry to trim back frost-damaged plants because they may surprise you and leaf out again where least expected. If there is more cold weather to come, the plant uses the damaged parts to protect whatever living portions remain. If trimmed off too quickly additional damage could result.

THE FIVE DEGREES OF FROST DAMAGE

First Degree—Tip Die-back

The mildest damage is limited to tip die-back, which is the burning of the tender growing ends of stems and branches.

Action: Trim off dead tips.

Second Degree—Defoliation

Lower temperatures may burn all the foliage, and leaves turn brown and drop off within a week or two.

Action: Wait for regrowth of foliage.

Third Degree—Branch Die-back

More severe temperature drops will kill the top and side branches of woody plants. The water present in the cambium layer just below the bark expands as it freezes and separates the bark from its vascular system.

Action: Wait for new growth to define limits of die-back, then prune off dead portions.

Fourth Degree—Above-Ground Die-back

The worst damage a plant can experience and still survive kills all above ground portions including branches and trunk. The roots remain alive and will resprout with multiple suckers.

Action: Cut back dead trunk and branches to assist new growth. If suckering heavily, prune out all except one or two main trunks.

Fifth Degree—Total Loss

The worst case scenario is that even the roots die either from soil freezing or as a result of complete above-ground die-back.

Action: Total replacement of the plant.

EXOTIC PLANTS FOR NORTHERN CALIFORNIA GARDENS

Asparagus densiflorus 'Sprengeri'

Sprenger's Asparagus

Exposure: Shade, part shade. Size: 18 inches tall, 30 inches plus wide. Zones: 2 to 7. Foliage plant, red berries.

Asparagus ferns are a common site in houseplant stores, but they also grow very well outdoors. Branches have fine foliage on frondlike stems, and the entire plant

ASPARAGUS 'SPRENGERI'

takes on a unique airy character. Most often grown in pots or hanging baskets interplanted with seasonal color. Roots are dense with fleshy tubers that become pot-bound very quickly. Tolerant of some direct sun, dryness, and poor soils. Frost-tolerant to 24°F. A close relative, *Asparagus* 'Meyers' is less frost hardy but very attractive, with rigid, cigar-shaped fronds that stand up vertically.

Aspidistra elatior

Cast Iron Plant

Exposure: Shade, part shade. Size: 24 inches tall, 18 inches wide. Zones: 2 to 7. Foliage plant.

The cast iron plant is aptly named because it will survive the most serious neglect. It looks more like a houseplant, and lends a tropical appearance with its wide, bladelike foliage. One of the most shade-tolerant plants available today, it is often planted under patio covers, in niches, between buildings, and other dark places where no other plant will survive. Less common but far more interesting is the variegated form with lighter colored foliage to brighten shady areas.

Canna x *generalis*

Canna Lily

Exposure: Full Sun. Size: To 6 feet tall, 24 inches wide. Zones 1 to 7. Blooms: Summer.

Flower color: Shades of red, orange, and yellow.

Cannas have been around California gardens forever and we often take their easy manner for granted. But these tall, narrow plants with wide leaves and hotly colored flowers resemble orchids. Plants die to the ground with the early frosts but roots sprout up again in the spring. Cannas grow from a fleshy tuberous root which is planted in early spring. The best prices and color choices are from mail order nurseries that sell them as bare-roots. Besides the standard red, orange, and yellow there are many exquisite shades of pink and coral, some with bright gold margins or exotic spotted petals. Cannas are water lovers and grow very well in hot climates.

CANNA 'TROPICAL ROSE' (*ALL AMERICA SELECTIONS*)

Cordyline australis

Dracaena

Exposure: Full sun. Size: To 30 feet tall, 5 feet wide. Zones 2 to 7. Foliage Plant.

When mature, this dracaena looks more like a yucca sitting on top of a very tall, sinuous trunk. Plants reach a considerable height over time. Very frost tolerant; damage occurs at about 15°F. Its long, thick tap root makes this dracaena very heat and drought tolerant. Although it grows in poor soil, deep fertile earth gives it more stability. Plants are deceiving when young as they are a benign clump of long, narrow, sharply pointed leaves. To keep them low and bushy, cut back new growth each spring. Flowers in spring with clusters of small but fragrant white flowers which are particularly beautiful at night.

CORDYLINE AUSTRALIS

Cycas revoluta

Cycas revoluta

Sago Palm

Exposure: Shade, part shade. Size: 30 inches tall, 36 inches wide. Zones: 3, 5, and 7. Foliage plant.

The age of cycads and dinosaurs occurred millions of years ago, and the earth was covered in great forests of giant cycads. This primitive plant has fronds which radiate out from the center like a palm, but it reproduces by cones like a conifer. Cycads as a rule are very slow growing, but ask only for sufficient shade and moisture. The sago palm has long been used in Oriental gardens and looks best when planted around rocks or with other exotics. A bit more expensive than other plants sold in the same container size. Popular for low-light conditions, and its controlled growth is perfect for limited space of atriums and courtyards.

Equisetum hyemale

Equisetum hyemale

Common Horsetail

Exposure: Full sun coast, part shade inland. Zones: 1 to 7. Size: 24 inches tall, 12 inches wide (spreads underground). Foliage plant.

Horsetail can be found growing wild in boggy areas from Nevada to the Pacific coast. It quickly spreads by underground runners to invade large areas where there is persistent moisture. Its long, thin, tubular reeds are segmented like bamboo. Considered an invasive wayside plant, horsetail is not commonly planted in gardens, but should be. Appears most natural near ponds and fountains, but striking when grown in exotic ceramic containers which can be moved around as desired. Not often found in nurseries. Sometimes the best source is to dig up a few roots out in the countryside and bring them home.

Fatsia japonica

Japanese Aralia

Exposure: Shade, part shade. Size: 6 feet tall, 5 feet wide. Zones 3, 5, and 7. Foliage plant.

Old specimens of this outdoor aralia can be found in the gardens of Victorian homes, planted because they

Opuntia hedge

OPUNTIA

PHORMIUM TENAX

were exotic and newly introduced during that era. Here is a remarkably frost-tolerant, shade-loving foliage plant with large, flat, light green leaves. Aralia can become leggy as it matures, dropping lower leaves as new foliage is produced at the top. To encourage compact growth, cut back tops in early spring and keep evenly moist. Avoid overheating or exposure to direct afternoon sun.

Opuntia sp.

Beaver Tail Cactus
Exposure: Full sun. Flowers: Yellow.
Zones: 1 to 7. Ornamental fruit: Red—edible.
Size: Small to very large.

These typically western cacti can be found growing wild in many parts of California, and some are quite capable of surviving very cold winters, even snow. In the early days they were planted as livestock enclosures by the Spanish in parts of California where timber was scarce. There are many species, but it takes an expert to tell them apart. Simple to propagate for the beginner. All that is needed is to place one fleshy leaf in a pot of sand, then water it occasionally. Opuntia rewards our patience with its sharp spines by flowering throughout the warm months with large, yellow blooms that draw bees and hummingbirds. These are followed by thick, juicy fruit called "tunas" by the Mexicans who find them are quite edible and taste similar to watermelon. **Be sure to remove *all* the thorns before peeling the skin.**

Phormium tenax

New Zealand Flax
Exposure: Full sun. Zones 3, 5, and 7. Size: 6 feet wide, 10 feet high. Flowers: Rusty maroon spikes. Foliage Plant. Blooms: Summer.

Although mature specimens of this flax do flower with 5-foot long spikes that rise far above the foliage, it is rare to find blooming specimens. Flax is really grown for its exotic yellow-green strap-leaved foliage which rises out of dense clumps. It is not particular about soil and even tolerates shade, but in over-dry conditions it develops dry or dead blades which accumulate around the base. Great when combined with cycads, palms and cannas to create an intense tropical effect. The variety 'Variegata' is more attractive, with beautiful striped leaves. Another variety, 'Atropurpureum' is smaller, with rusty red foliage which can be equally as striking as its larger cousins. Makes a good pot plant.

POTTED *PHORMIUM TENAX* 'ATROPURPUREUM'

STRELITZIA REGINAE

STRELITZIA REGINAE

IN THE DRY, ROCKY SOIL OF THE SUTTER BUTTES, THIS LANDMARK CALIFORNIA FAN PALM PERSISTS ON NATURAL RAINFALL LONG AFTER THE HOMESTEAD HAS BEEN ABANDONED. (*RANDY MEYER*)

Strelitzia reginae
Bird of Paradise
Exposure: Sun coastal. Zone: 7. Size: 3 feet wide, 3 feet tall. Colors: Single multicolored flower. Blooms: Summer.

Isolated specimens of bird of paradise can be found growing in very sheltered locations of gardens in the central and coastal valleys. But for the most part it should be limited to coastal areas where mild winters and moist air are more suited to this unique tropical plant. Bird of paradise takes well to container culture which allows plants to be moved into more protected areas for the winter months. Everyone can identify the exotic, oddly shaped flowers with waxy petals which are much in demand by florists. It requires little care but plants exposed to temperatures below 29°F will require a clean-up come spring to remove all the burned foliage. Feed older plants often and allow them to develop into large clumps for best flower production.

PALM TREES– A CALIFORNIA STAPLE

Palm trees are a unique group of plants that have become one of the most widely accepted symbols of California. There are stately specimens in parks, and many examples of street trees in San Francisco and Sacramento. One commonly planted species, the thick-trunked California fan palm, is native to the canyons around Palm Springs, and was essential to the material culture of the Native Americans of that dry, desert land.

Palms played a unique, but important role in the flat central valley of northern California by identifying the location of homesteads with a clump of foliage rising far above orchards and fields. Farmers found that drought-tolerant, long lived palms made excellent property-line or corner markers. In many cases these original plantings are still alive today.

USING PALMS IN THE LANDSCAPE

To the untrained eye, all palm trees look alike, but this is far from the truth. There are two major classifications based on the shape of their fronds. Fan palms have round, fan-shaped fronds with more compact foliage heads. Plume palms have long, thin fronds which resemble feathers, and these foliage heads are capable of offering considerable shade.

The uniformity of growth in some types of palms made them popular with designers. Uniformity means that if three fan palms are started from seed at exactly the same time, as adults they will be nearly identical in height.

A good example of this are the old plantings of California fan palms in the sidewalks that surround Sacramento's Capitol Park. This uniformity allows them to flank roadways, or in the case of the massive Canary Island date palm, they can be located on either side of gateways to act as living pillars.

In the desert Arab countries, plume palms are planted in orchard-like grids called "bosks" where the spacing allows their broad foliage heads to touch and shade large areas. Many palms grow naturally into groves. The taller trees drop seeds which germinate into smaller plants surrounding the base. As these grow up, they seed even more individuals and the size of the grove increases with each new generation.

The rediscovery of landscape palms over the past decade has driven the cost of large trees to an all time high. These trees are sold by the "trunk-foot," which means a dollar amount is applied to each vertical foot of trunk between the top of the rootball and the base of the foliage head. Buying large, commercially grown trees can be very expensive. But the high cost can be avoided by finding landowners wishing to remove the palm tree "eyesores" from their properties. It isn't uncommon to find rare and very valuable species growing abandoned that can be had free of charge. A professional tree mover should be hired to take care of moving the palm if it is one of the larger species.

NEWLY TRANSPLANTED MATURE *PHOENIX CANARIENSIS* SHOWING PROPER METHOD OF PRUNING LEAF STEMS OFF TRUNK. FRONDS ARE TIED INTO TIGHT BUNDLE AT TOP FOR TRANSPORT.

HOW TO GROW AND TRANSPLANT PALMS SUCCESSFULLY

Think of palm trees as giant grass plants with the water-storing capacity of a cactus. The palm tree trunk is a huge bundle of tubular water-moving structures. The reason palms will not blow over or break off in high winds is that the bundle is very flexible, with each water tube stretching independently. Bendable trunks reduce the need for a massive root system, thus making palms easy to transplant.

Because palms are grown for their foliage, lots of water and nitrogen make them grow faster, just as they do for lawns. But where frost is a problem, tapering off on watering during the late summer reduces the winter damage potential. Transplanting older palms should be done in the summer because soggy conditions of winter soils stimulates root-destroying diseases. Very little rootball is required, but taller trees should be transplanted by professionals as they are extremely heavy and difficult to move. Moreover, if newly transplanted large palms encounter winds before the small roots are able to take hold, they may blow over and cause serious damage and liability.

Many tree moving companies will transplant mature palms using a tool called the "tree spade." This device is mounted on the end of a large truck and it takes out the

FAN PALM MOUNTED ON "TREE SPADE" TRUCK READY FOR RELOCATION.

YOUNG *PHOENIX CANARIENSIS* BEING PLANTED IN NEW LOCATION WITH TREE SPADE.

palm, creating a cone-shaped rootball. This is in turn fitted into a cone-shaped hole dug previously at the new site and the tight fit, along with a greater depth of rootball are enough to hold it safely upright. Before allowing a tree-moving company to either remove or plant a new palm, make sure there are no underground utilities which may be damaged in the process. Also. make sure the tree company is properly licensed, bonded. and insured.

FROST TOLERANCE OF PALMS

Many species of palms are surprisingly frost tolerant. At nearly 2,000 feet elevation in the Sierra Nevada foothills, there are specimens of windmill palms which have withstood 4-foot snows and temperatures as low as 10°F. But the key to this longevity is the lack of supplemental watering, as they exist on natural rainfall. Irrigated palms are more susceptible to freezing because the water stored in their trunks expands and damages the nutrient transporting tubes. That windmill palm in the foothills goes without moisture from late spring and until late fall. By winter it is thoroughly dried out and ready to face the cold.

Palms become more frost tolerant as they age. Trees with thick trunks can survive damage to the outside layers of moisture-transporting tubes, which later act as an insulating blanket around the still-functioning interior tubes. This blanket of tubes remains in place to resist freezing in the winters to come. Young trees of the exact same species, with very small trunk diameters, cannot protect their moisture-transferring tubes and may be killed outright with the first frost. If very low night temperatures threaten your young palms, throw a bed sheet or plastic over the tops of them for added protection.

During the 1990 freeze, there was considerable damage to palms throughout northern California. Most lost all of their foliage, with the Mexican fan palms taking a far worse beating than their nearly identical cousins, the California fan palms. Canary Island date palms lost their foliage, but even those in the lower foothills survived. There will be other hard freezes for northern California in the future, and from this experience we know it is foolish to cut palms down right away, no matter how dead they appear. Wait until warm weather returns and watch for skinny new fronds poking out of the top of the trunk. If they have not done so by the middle of the following summer, then trees can be considered dead and should be removed.

PALM TREES FOR NORTHERN CALIFORNIA LANDSCAPES

Arecastrum romanzoffianum

Queen Palm, Cocos Plumosa, Pindo Palm
Exposure: Full sun. Solitary plume palm.
Size: To 30 feet tall. Frost tolerance to: 18°F, foliage damage to 24°F.

This is one of the most feminine palms, with a soft and lacy character. Its uniquely crinkled fronds can range from 6 to 8 feet long, and the foliage head resembles a cluster of ostrich feathers. The fronds of queen palms detach cleanly, without leaving behind the base of each stem like other palms. This species should not be considered very drought tolerant because it grows in deep, rich soil with regular watering. Insufficient moisture may kill it or reduce new frond development, which leaves the old leaves to become brittle and brown at the tips. Leaves turn yellow in saline soils. This palm has more variation than most and should not be used in situations where uniformity of growth is critical. Mature queen palms can be found in the central valley, but they took a terrible beating in the 1990 freeze and just barely survived.

NORTHERN CALIFORNIA TIP

As the fronds wither and die on many palms, they hang on the tree to develop a grass skirt very high above the ground. The thatch created by the fronds make a perfect home for bats and rats, a situation which should be discouraged. Keep your palms free of dead fronds; but if they are mature, cutting fronds can be very dangerous. Leave this high-wire job to a reputable tree trimming company experienced with palms. If the fronds are removed, the bases of the stems often remain on the trunk and can mar its beauty. Have them sheared off by the pros every few years so your palms always look their best.

ARECASTRUM ROMANZOFFIANUM

CHAMAEROPS HUMILIS

PHOENIX CANARIENSIS

Chamaerops humilis

Mediterranean Fan Palm

Exposure: Full sun, part shade. Clumping fan palm. Size: 6 feet to 12 feet tall. Frost tolerance: Varies, with low temperatures from 6 to 15°F.

These bushy little clustering palms are one of the most frost- and drought-tolerant species in use today. Old plants can be found growing as far north as Scotland, but are susceptible to persistent wind damage and require sheltering. *Chamaerops* are very slow growing and may put on less than 1 foot of growth each year. This makes them popular for small gardens or courtyards because they rarely outgrow their space, and the trunks will curve around one another into graceful forms. *Chamaerops* palms work well as a nighttime focal point where they come strangely alive under creative uplighting. Established clumps can be very expensive to buy and are in high demand for drought stricken gardens.

Phoenix canariensis

Canary Island Date Palm

Exposure: Full sun. Solitary Plume Palm.
Size: To 30 feet tall. Frost tolerance: To 12°F.

Here is the real top dog of northern California palms that has remained popular since Victorian times. With enormous feather-shaped fronds that can reach 15 feet, its umbrella-shaped head makes a reasonably good shade tree when planted at a high density. They can be found thriving in gardens from the coast to the lower foothills of the Sierra Nevada, wherever there is sufficient drainage to prevent pink rot. It is very slow growing;

PHOENIX DACTYLIFERA, DATE PALM

PHOENIX RECLINATA AT STATE CAPITOL, SACRAMENTO.

TRACHYCARPUS FORTUNEI

expect it to put on just 1 foot per year. Massive trunk, up to 4 feet in diameter, gives it stability but is heavy, weighing up to 650 pounds per trunk-foot. Keep this in mind when attempting to transplant or cut one down. Fruits with beautiful large sprays of inedible, but juicy orange dates which can be a problem staining pavement so trees are best planted in lawns. Trunks may require occasional cleanup by professionals as trees mature. Closely related to *Phoenix dactylifera,* the date palm of the southern California desert plantations.

Phoenix reclinata

Senegal Date Palm

Exposure: Sun, part shade. Clumping plume palm. Size: To 20 feet tall. Frost tolerance: Young trees killed at 23°F, mature trees to 20°F.

The name of this species, "reclinata," suggests its reclining growth habit and tendancy to sucker. Native to southern Africa, it grows in immense thickets in river beds. One of the best examples of these not so common palms is a large planting along the foundation of the state capitol building in Sacramento. Like *Chamerops, reclinata* is grown for its foliage, as a background plant enhanced by night lighting. It refuses to grow directly upwards and insists on producing new plants around the base. With its longer plume fronds, the thicket of beautiful, deep green foliage is hard to beat. Beware of unexpected cold pockets because they are marginal palms for this area.

Trachycarpus fortunei

Windmill Palm

Exposure: Full sun, part shade. Solitary fan palm. Size: To 20 feet tall. Frost tolerance: To 5°F.

Here is that sturdy fellow that takes Sierra Nevada winters in stride. Technically experiences foliage damage at 5°F, shows significant foliage burning at 0°F, and will be killed at the incredibly low -10°F. The windmill palm is a very rigid, upright grower, and its narrow trunk is wrapped in hairy fiber. Its neat, tight foliage head is made all the more beautiful by sprays of yellow flowers that mature into blue-gray fruit. The scale of these palms is very small and they do take to containers very well. If in doubt about a site sustaining palms during the winter, plant it with these cold- and drought-tolerant beauties and be guaranteed success.

Washingtonia filifera

California Fan Palm

Exposure: Full sun. Solitary fan palm. Size: To 60 feet tall. Frost tolerance: 20°F burn foliage, may die at 15°F.

Here is one of the first palms to be grown by early residents of California, with all the seed originating from just a few isolated stands. Today it has become a familiar site throughout the state, with its big fat trunk and hula skirt of dead, dry fronds. To see one of these huge trees fruit, with grayish-white arching sprays of flowers that extend many feet beyond the foliage, is inspiring. Unfortunately, most folks don't look up high enough to discover them. Plant these palms in well-drained soil where they remain on the dry side. When plants are young it is very difficult to tell the Mexican fan palm from this California native because the foliage is nearly identical. But the Mexican fan palm grows very tall, with a thin, rough trunk in the Hollywood style, while the California fan palm is more massive, with a smooth trunk surface. If in a frost-prone area, the California native is far more forgiving of unexpected dips of the mercury.

WASHINGTONIA FILIFERA IN ITS NATIVE HABITAT IN THE DESERT NEAR PALM SPRINGS, CALIFORNIA.

Washingtonia robusta

Mexican Fan Palm

Exposure: Full sun. Solitary fan palm. Size: To 100 feet tall. Frost tolerance: To 15°F (varies).

Mexican fan palms are both faster growing and far taller than their California cousins, which makes their species name "robusta" easier to remember. This fast grower can put on as much as 4 feet per year and is valuable for landscapes around tall buildings. Unfortunately, this feature also makes it grow "out of sight" very quickly, rendering it less valuable on a residential level. Old plants may have tall trunks, out of scale with their tiny foliage heads at the top. May suffer in poorly drained soils. Water generously for fastest growth.

WASHINGTONIA FILIFERA PLANTED ALONG THE EDGE OF CAPITOL PARK IN SACRAMENTO. ILLUSTRATES UNIFORMITY OF GROWTH AND THICKER TRUNK THAN THE MEXICAN FAN PALM.

WASHINGTONIA ROBUSTA

FERNS ARE GOOD PLANTS FOR LOW-LIGHT ATRIUMS.

NATIVE FERNS THRIVE IN THE COASTAL COOL CLIMATE OF MENDOCINO COUNTY. THE BLOOMING AZALEAS ATTEST TO THE SOIL'S ACIDITY CAUSED BY THE LITTER FROM PINES AND REDWOOD TREES.

THE FERNS

Some of the most beautiful ferns are California native plants. They thrive in the moist river canyons in both the Sierra and Coastal Ranges. Our native species range from the giant chain fern with enormous fronds to the fragile and rare maidenhair fern. In many cases the plant goes dormant during the hot, dry season of late summer and fall. As with the bracken fern, all aboveground portions of the plant wither and turn brown. But when the rains come, the crinkled fronds are miraculously replaced by succulent new leaves.

Ferns can play a strong role in gardens with sufficient shade, and a few very tough varieties are even considered low-maintenance plants. If a fern is planted in the correct location and provided with sufficient moisture, it will thrive on its own without special care. Ferns vary not only in size but in shape as well. The mature Australian tree fern can grow as tall as 15 feet with foliage nearly 10 feet wide. The sword fern can actually be treated as a groundcover because its short, upright fronds spread by underground stems. Ferns vary in their degree of frost hardiness. Maidenhair, woodwardia, and bracken ferns of California all tolerate both snow and very low winter temperatures.

BASIC FERN CULTURE

Ferns require moist, shady conditions to grow properly. When planted outdoors they should receive mostly north and sometimes eastern exposure. Plants should be sheltered from the dry north winds. Ferns are a good choice for very dark corners around buildings which receive too little light for most other plants. Plant ferns beneath arbors, lath structures, or under the canopy of shade trees, which is in keeping with their natural habitat. Oaks and pines have very acidic leaves, and ferns grow best in the organic soil beneath their branches.

It is essential that ferns receive plenty of water, especially during heat waves or windy conditions. Although ferns must remain damp, they cannot tolerate saturation, as poorly drained soil causes stems of some species to rot at the soil line. Mulch ferns in the spring with a thick layer of pine needles or oak leaves. This prevents the evaporation of surface moisture from the soil and regulates the temperature of the soil around roots.

FERNS FOR NORTHERN CALIFORNIA LANDSCAPES

Adiantum pedatum

Maidenhair Fern
California native 14 inches tall, 12 inches wide
Shade

This delicate, lacy fern hides in sheltered niches of

California's stream-fed rocky canyons. If you examine the stems of this little fern you'll find they are very strong, smooth, and straight, much like stiff plastic lanyard. The Maidu Indians of California used these ebony stems to weave dark patterns into their baskets. The fan-shaped leaves of maidenhair ferns are similar in shape to those of the ginkgo tree, thus its common name "maidenhair tree." Growing maidenhair ferns is not an easy task even for experts because its incredibly thin leaves can dry out in the blink of an eye. Location is everything, and success depends on just the right exposure, drainage, and soil acidity.

Cyrtomium falcatum

Holly Fern
Zones 2 to 7 30 inches tall, 24 inches wide
Shade, part sun

Holly ferns have long stiff fronds divided into many leathery leaflets. The plant is a low grower that tends to spread out on the soil, or, when planted in containers, the fronds droop gracefully down the sides. The foliage is similar to the shrub Oregon grape, and leaves bear rigid edges and sharp points much like true holly. This fern can tolerate winter freezes down to 25°F and is very easy to grow.

DICKSONIA ANTARCTICA

Dicksonia antarctica

Tasmanian Tree Fern
Zones 3 to 7 15 feet tall, 10 feet wide
Filtered shade, part sun

Tree ferns aren't fast growers, but they are rewarding plants when mature, with huge bright green fronds up to 7 feet long and 30 inches wide or more. Tree ferns look much like any other kind of fern when young, but gradually they grow taller, dropping lower fronds as new ones form. Eventually, the plant has a bare trunk and broad foliage at the top, making it resemble a palm tree. You will find excellent examples of these throughout Golden Gate Park in San Francisco. These ferns will survive temperatures as low as 20°F and there are many known cases of these ferns surviving even in snow. They grow well throughout the north state, but should be protected from the wind and provided with sufficient, but not dark, shade.

NEPHROLEPIS CORDIFOLIA

Nephrolepis cordifolia

Sword Fern
Zones 3 to 7 14 inches tall, 6 inches wide
Shade, part sun

Sword ferns are one of the most adaptable ferns for gardening because they grow differently from other species. The leaves are identical to the Boston fern houseplant, but swords stand straight up, hence the name. They can become invasive, spreading by underground stems that will rapidly fill a planter and crowd out less vigorous plants. Sword ferns are less frost hardy than some other ferns, but they are far more tolerant of overly dry conditions. They will do much better in sunnier locations

WOODWARDIA FIMBRIATA

because they are subtropical plants from warm regions. A sure bet plant for beginning gardeners.

Rumohra adiantiformis
(aka *Aspidium capense*)
Leatherleaf Fern
Zones 2 to 7 36 inches tall, 30 inches wide
Sun, part shade

Leatherleaf ferns appear similar to wild bracken ferns. Florists have long used their stiff triangular fronds, which hold their shape for a long time. These ferns also tolerate much more sun than most, and mix well with lilies, bird of paradise, and azaleas. Widely available, they are one of the best landscape ferns because they are low growing, tolerate some dryness, and are not burned by occasional direct sunlight.

Woodwardia fimbriata
Giant Chain Fern
Zones 1 to 7 California native
9 feet tall, 5 feet wide Shade, part shade

These huge ferns can reach 5 feet tall in the native environment of our coastal redwood forests. It doesn't grow nearly as large in the inland mountain ranges but survives very dry summers. In cultivated gardens the fronds still average about 4 feet long. Although difficult to find at nurseries, this is one of our most beautiful native plants and should be more widely available. It is a natural for the shaded areas beneath conifers where nothing else will grow. Plant woodwardia to create a wonderfully primeval character in the landscape. It is most attractive when planted in clusters of five or more. Definitely worth a special order at the nursery.

ORNAMENTAL GRASSES

Along the California coast, tall grasses take on a mystical appearance as their seed heads and foliage ripple with the persistent winds, almost as if they were dancing. These grasses make excellent plants for casual wild or meadow gardens, and along water courses, dry stream beds, and pools. Ornamental grasses are valued for their foliage, many species having variegated or unusually colored leaves and attractive seed heads.

These ornamental plants are different from those species used in turf. Many are not true grasses but technically rushes or sedges. There is concern that some ornamental grasses may become invasive in the garden or in native ecosystems.

Like all foliage plants, grasses require nitrogen fertilizer if they are to develop dense, well-colored foliage. But too much nitrogen weakens the stems and causes clumps to break apart and lie down. Most landscape species are hardy perennials, and, if well fed and cared for, they will persist for many years. The chief difficulty is obtaining them, because West Coast suppliers are only just now beginning to make them available to garden centers.

TALL ORNAMENTAL GRASSES IN A NORTH COAST GARDEN.

ORNAMENTAL GRASSES FOR NORTHERN CALIFORNIA GARDENS

Cortaderia selloana
Pampas Grass
Zones 2 to 7 15 feet tall, 10 feet wide
Full sun

This plant is easily recognized by the large fluffy seed heads on stalks which rise many feet above the plant. Pampas grass develops into immense mounds of thin, reedlike foliage with miniature teeth on the edges. This huge grass is nearly impossible to kill, and the foliage is often burned off before removal of the very dense root mass. The seeds from pampas grass travel a long way, and will contaminate natural ecosystems, especially along the coastal dunes. It has a strong ability to change the visual character of the natural environment. Plant this grass with considerable forethought because removing it after it matures is very difficult.

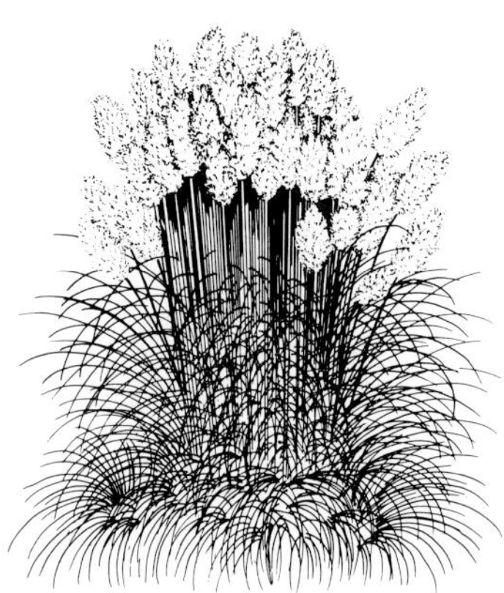

PAMPAS GRASS (*MONROVIA NURSERY CO.*)

FESTUCA OVINA GLAUCA

Festuca ovina glauca

Blue Fescue

Zones 2 to 7 8 inches tall, 12 inches wide

Sun, part shade

These little tufts of sharply pointed blue-gray grass become symmetrical domes of foliage. They can act as groundcovers, accent plants, and edging material because their size is naturally controlled. This fescue is perfect to fill in gaps between stepping stones or soften boulders near water features. Retains color better when shaded from hot afternoon sun. Blue fescue has insignificant flowers which appear in late spring and give the mounds a much softer look. It is an important plant for modern and Oriental inspired landscapes.

Miscanthus sinensis 'Gracillimus'

Maiden Grass

Zones 1 to 7 6 feet high, 30 inches wide

Full sun

The genus *Miscanthus* includes many different hybrids. Maiden grass is one of the more common varieties and is used as an accent when planted in isolated clumps in the landscape. This grass is grown primarily for its tall, wheat colored flower heads which curl in graceful shapes and makes them popular as dried material for florists.

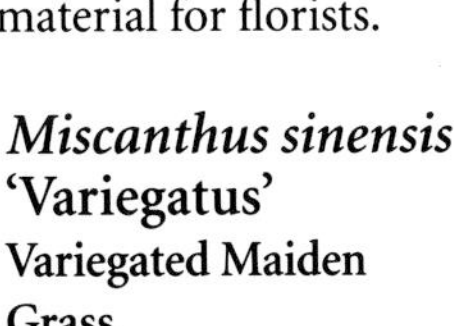

MISCANTHUS SINENSIS 'GRACILLIMUS' (MONROVIA NURSERY CO.)

Miscanthus sinensis 'Variegatus'

Variegated Maiden Grass

Perhaps more beautiful than Gracillimus, variegated maiden grass is nearly white with stripes of green in the leaves. It grows into tall, dense tufts which flower in the fall. Variegated maiden grass is planted for the value of its foliage, but the pale pink seed heads are also attractive.

Miscanthus sinensis 'Zebrinus'

Zebra Grass

Yet another variety of this versatile genus. Zebra grass is even more colorful with each blade banded in white, yellow, and green. When cold weather arrives it may turn to a straw color with rusty orange tips to each blade. Zebra grass has a more arching habit which makes it especially graceful.

Pennisetum setaceum

Fountain Grass

Zones 1 to 7 30 inches tall, 24 inches wide

Full sun

Fountain grass originates in southern Africa where it has developed a tolerance for heat and long, dry seasons. This makes it an important plant for dry California landscapes. It is grown for its tall, wandlike seed heads which rise and arch over the foliage. This grass blends well with native shrubs and is very attractive when used with Arizona flagstone paving. Note: Fountain grass is now considered highly flammable and should not be used near fire pits or barbecues, and is not a good choice where there is danger of wildfires.

Phyllostachys aurea

Golden Bamboo

Zones 2 to 7 27 feet high Full sun

There is no diameter indicated for this bamboo because it will literally continue to grow unchecked until some barrier prevents its spreading. This plant can be extremely noxious as are most of the bamboos because they are so invasive and nearly impossible to eradicate once established. If you want the exotic character of bamboo without the risk, plant it in containers where the root system is totally contained. If you must remove bamboo, beware of viable roots. Do not place any part of it in a compost pile or anywhere else except a landfill.

Phyllostachys nigra

Black Bamboo

Zones 2 to 7 30 feet tall Full sun

This is a more popular bamboo because the wood turns black about six months after each cane matures. In Asian gardens black bamboo has traditionally been planted adjacent to white gravel, which provides a contrasting background for the subtle dark coloring. Be cautious, because this plant spreads as well, and it's best grown in large containers. Consider planting it in urns, Persian style planters and terra cotta pots where it becomes less Oriental in character and more like a reed.

Chapter Eleven

Special Conditions

Each climate zone in Northern California has certain factors which influence how gardens are designed and planted. These are practical considerations relating to water availability, wildfire hazards, coastal influence, and erosion. Most of the plants discussed here are detailed in other chapters with more thorough descriptions and cultural requirements. But in the following sections they will be further classified according to their special abilities to solve problems.

Facing page: A collection of exotic, drought-tolerant, non-native plants in containers. Above: A garden of ornamental grasses with tall seed heads.

ON MORE EFFICIENT WATER USE

RULE OF GREEN THUMB

To make a drip or micro-spray system function better where the water supply may contain minerals or sediment, make sure to install a filter, which should be located between the water source and the first head or emitter. The filter screens are very fine because the orifices on the emitters are equally as tiny. Clean the filter often to prevent it from becoming filled with material. Restricted filters reduce the flow of water, and emitters furthest from the water source may be deprived.

Only a limited amount of water applied by standard sprinkler systems actually reaches the plant. Sprinkler heads deliver water in a fine spray, which is easily carried out of the planting area by winds, and the minute particles of water can evaporate before they ever touch the ground.

If the percolation rate of dense soils is slower than the rate your sprinklers deliver water, there will be runoff. Reducing watering times does eliminate runoff, but the plants will suffer from lack of moisture deeper down. Try changing the sprinkler heads to those which deliver water over the same area but at a slower rate. The need to water can also be reduced by mulching bare ground, which prevents evaporation of moisture from the surface of the soil. This has the added benefit of eliminating soil-surface crusting. which creates a barrier to water penetration.

And finally, the water absorbed into the soil is taken up by the roots at a rate which varies according to species. This is expressed as the evapotranspiration rate, which is a big word for how much water a plant needs to survive over a certain time period. Drought-tolerant plants have very low evapotranspiration rates, and this is the key factor in their success.

DRIP SYSTEMS

There are many new products designed to deliver water to landscape plants by the most efficient means. The goal is to concentrate water application at the immediate root zone rather than blanket an entire planter like spray systems do. Drip systems are the most widely used alternative form of irrigation, and operates at low static pressure. Despite the ease of installation and repair, they do have limitations.

The biggest problem with drip systems is that the emitters clog up and prevent water delivery. There is no way to know this is happening until the plant begins to wilt or die, and that may be too late. Emitters and fine spaghetti tubing can clog from algae, minerals, and organic matter in the water supply. Over time, if the tubing is exposed to sunlight, it can become brittle and crack under very little stress.

The drip system has evolved with new products that combine the best features of both drip and standard spray heads. Micro-spray irrigation systems run off similar supply tubing as a drip system. Instead of emitters they use little pencil-shaped heads just visible enough for easy spot checking. These heads have stakes at the bottom and the flexible supply line allows them to be moved around as plants grow larger, to adjust coverage. One head usually supplies three small shrubs, and it sprays low enough to be out of the wind and nearly invisible. A standard spray system can be adapted to micro-spray in the same way as a drip system.

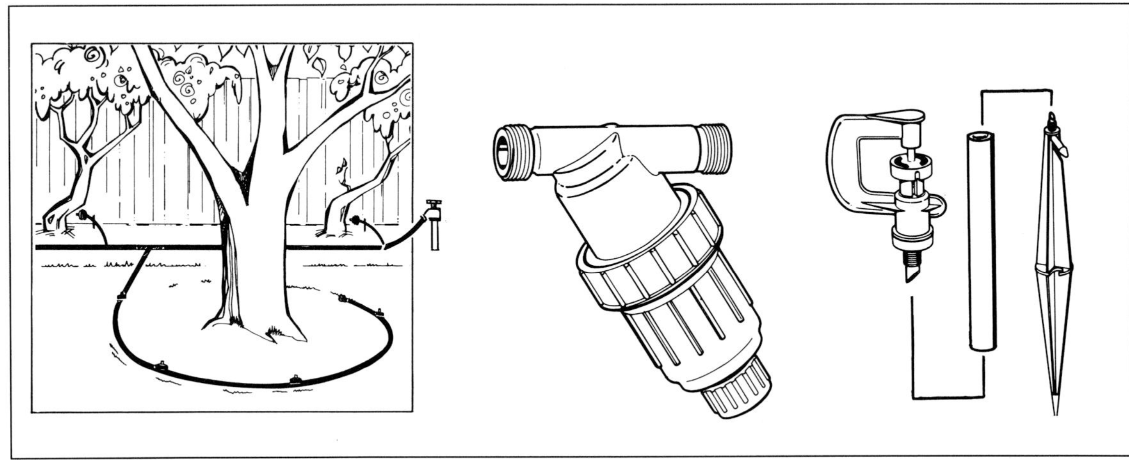

DRIP SYSTEM LAYOUT FOR TREES, DRIP SYSTEM Y FILTER, MICROSPRAY HEAD WITH SUPPORT STAKE. (*RAINDRIP CORP.*)

SMART WATERING

If new plants are watered by systems which moisten the surface of the soil down to just a few inches, root development will be concentrated there. When water is withheld, these shallow rooting plants are easily stressed, even though they may be drought tolerant species. The rule for irrigating plants during times of drought is to apply water directly into the root zone at a very slow rate which will saturate deeply. Then avoid watering again for a week or so, watching carefully for signs of temporary wilt that signals the depletion of deep soil moisture.

For existing landscapes that must bear a temporary reduction in water supply due to short-term drought conditions, the most valuable plants should be saved, and those more easily replaced may be sacrificed. Trees take a decade to approach maturity and they should be preserved at any cost. Large shrubs are next because they serve important purposes like covering foundations or screening unsightly areas from view. The plants that remain, including annuals, perennials, groundcovers, lawns, and vegetables may be sacrificed. Resourceful gardeners may be able to save some of these by using gray water from laundry and bath.

A DROUGHT-TOLERANT GARDEN CAN BE COLORFUL AND OFFER A WIDE DIVERSITY OF FORMS.

DROUGHT-TOLERANT NON-NATIVE LANDSCAPES

Xeriscape is a blanket term which refers to gardens designed with plants capable of surviving very dry periods. A large number of xeriscape plants are species that originate in Australia, South Africa, and arid Mediterranean climates.

To make the most of these unthirsty species, they should be irrigated so that their root systems reach deep into the soil or their drought tolerance will be compromised. How that plant is treated during its first two years will dictate its ability to survive drought for the rest of its life span.

The application of mulches is one of the most crucial factors in reducing water requirements of any landscape. An organic mulch is a layer of material which is spread evenly over the ground, beneath and around plants. It acts much the same way as fiberglass insulation does in a house. The thicker the mulch layer, the more effective it will be.

The mulch layer reduces water evaporation from the surface of the soil and helps water and fertilizer penetrate before it runs off. It also shades the soil above the roots, which helps to keep them cool and prevent erosion. As mulch gradually decomposes, the soil is enriched and

WOOD CHIPS MAKE AN ATTRACTIVE MULCH THAT DISCOURAGES WEEDS AND RETAINS SOIL MOISTURE.

DROUGHT-TOLERANT *OPUNTIA*, LANTANA, GREVILLEA, *AGAVE AMERICANA*, AND CALIFORNIA PEPPER TREE IN A SOUTHWESTERN SETTING.

biotic activity increases, making plants healthier overall. Mulch can be made of any kind of organic matter such as straw, compost, ground bark, rice hulls, and leaf mould. It should be renewed occasionally as it thins out from decomposition.

CALIFORNIA NATIVE PLANTS

California native plants are those species that are part of our state's natural plant communities. The environments where they grow wild vary, from moist river canyons of the north coast to hot, dry, rocky hillsides of the Sierra foothills. Just because a plant is a native doesn't mean it is drought tolerant, but those most frequently used in gardens are planted because they are highly suited to our dry climate.

Understanding our state's climate is the key to how native plants should be treated in gardens. Their active growing period is during winter when the seasonal rains come. They go dormant during the summer, slowing down growth to reduce the amount of water needed to survive. Some species will defoliate, either partially or entirely, depending on conditions. If water is applied during the wrong time of year, they are likely to die or become weakened. Insufficient drainage causes natives to suffer because their root systems rot very easily.

The most commonly used California native plants have been selected for their tolerance of garden condi-

REFERENCE LIST OF DROUGHT-TOLERANT NON-NATIVE PLANTS

The following list includes both individual species and groups under the same genus which exhibit the greatest drought tolerance.

Botanical Name	Common Name	Type
Achillea spp.	Yarrow	Perennial
Arbutus unedo	Strawberry Tree	Shrub
Callistemon citrinus	Bottlebrush	Shrub
Campsis radicans	Trumpet Vine	Vine
Cedrus deodora	Deodar Cedar	Tree
Centranthus ruber	Red Valerian	Perennial
Ceratonia siliqua	Carob Tree	Tree
Cistus spp.	Rockrose	Shrub
Coreopsis verticillata	Coreopsis	Perennial
Cortaderia selloana	Pampas Grass	Ornamental Grass
Cotoneaster spp.	Cotoneaster	Shrub
Cytisus spp.	Broom	Shrub
Dodonaea viscosa	Hopseed Bush	Shrub
Echium fastuosum	Pride of Madeira	Shrub
Eucalyptus spp.	Eucalyptus	Tree
Grevillea spp.	Grevillea	Shrub/Tree
Juniperus spp.	Juniper	Shrubs
Kniphofia uvaria	Red-Hot Poker	Perennial
Lantana spp.	Lantana	Perennial
Lavandula spp.	Lavender	Perennial
Limonium perezii	Sea Lavender	Perennial
Olea europaea	Olive	Tree
Palm Trees	Palms	Exotic Tree
Pennisetum setaceum	Fountain Grass	Ornamental Grass
Pinus spp.	Pine Trees	Tree
Pistacia chinensis	Chinese Pistache	Tree
Quercus spp.	Oak	Tree
Rhus lancea	African Sumac	Tree
Robinia spp.	Black Locust	Tree
Rosmarinus spp.	Rosemary	Herb
Santolina chamaecyparissus	Lavendercotton	Herb
Schinus molle	California Pepper	Tree
Senecio cineraria	Dusty Miller	Perennial
Wisteria	Wisteria	Vine
Xylosma congestum	Xylosma	Shrub
Yucca spp.	Yucca	Exotic

THE BEST CALIFORNIA NATIVE PLANTS FOR GARDENS

Botanical Name	Common Name	Type
Achillea	Yarrow	Perennial
Aesculus californica	California Buckeye	Tree
Arctostaphylos spp.	Manzanita	Shrubs
Baccharis pilularis	Dwarf Coyote Bush	Shrub
Ceanothus spp.	California Lilac	Shrubs
Cercis occidentalis	Western Redbud	Shrub
Convovulus cneorum	Bush Morning Glory	Shrub
Fremontodendron californicum	Fremontia	Shrub
Garrya elliptica	Silk Tassel Tree	Shrub
Heteromeles arbutifolia	California Toyon	Shrub
Juglans hindsii	California Walnut	Tree
Mahonia aquifolium	Oregon Grape	Shrub
Pinus spp.	Various Pine Species	Trees
Quercus agrifolia	Coast Live Oak	Tree
Ribes sanguineum	Flowering Currant	Shrub
Romneya coulteri	Matilija Poppy	Perennial
Sequoia sempervirens	Coast Redwood	Tree
Sequoiadendron giganteum	Big Tree	Tree
Umbellularia californica	California Laurel	Tree
Washingtonia robusta	California Fan Palm	Tree
Zauschneria californica	California Fuchsia	Perennial

CALIFORNIA NATIVE PERENNIALS ARE COMBINED WITH INTRODUCED SPECIES FOR A DRYLAND, FRONT YARD SCHEME.

FREMONTODENDRON CALIFORNICUM, COMMON FLANNEL BUSH, A CALIFORNIA NATIVE SHRUB THAT BLOOMS BEAUTIFULLY BUT QUICKLY DIES IF OVERWATERED.

tions. This means they may survive an untimely watering or two and heavier soils, but damage can still occur. Natives should only be coupled with others of their kind, or with non-native drought-tolerant plants with similar water requirements. Before adding natives to a garden, make sure there won't be any conflicts with sprinklers and the water needs of existing plants.

Most California native plants are nursery grown in containers. Many survive in the wild because they have the ability to root deeply into the soil to reach trapped water far below the surface. Container growing limits this rooting ability, and it takes about two years for a newly planted native to grow a root system large enough to survive drought. Natives should be planted in the fall, so that the active growth during winter months helps to develop a root system before the heat and stress of summer.

For best success, buy natives in 1-gallon container sizes or smaller, because younger plants adapt much more readily to new conditions. Plant on sloping ground or in raised planters filled with porous, gravelly soil that allows for perfect drainage. Under these conditions natives can be expected to grow rapidly and bloom the way they should. Be patient and allow time for each plant to become established and exhibit its best qualities.

Keep newly planted natives evenly moist during the first year, taper off during the second, and by the third year they should be strong enough to make it on their own. Where there are heavy clay soils, make sure to check moisture levels deeply because surface dryness can be deceiving.

Natives are pampered at the nursery, often spending their whole life under the protective shade cloth of the grower's yard. When these plants are thrust out into full sun after transplanting, there can be considerable stress and the plants may die quickly. It's better to provide shade for awhile at first and let them acclimate at a slower rate.

OAK ROOT FUNGUS

The technical name for oak root fungus is *Armilaria mellea*. The problem with this fungus is also covered in chapter 4 as it relates to native oaks. But this soil-borne killer also threatens landscape plants, as it spreads quickly under moist garden conditions. Oak root fungus is often present in soils which were once commercial orchards, although it can appear unexpectedly in other areas as well.

In many neighborhoods it is common knowledge that oak root fungus exists in the soil. The only chance of eradication is to fumigate the soil, which is toxic and expensive. Plus, there is no guarantee the fungus won't reappear because it tends to travel around wherever there is sufficient moisture to support growth. The only sure solution is to plant only those species that are resistant to the fungus. There are many resistant trees, but the selection is much narrower for shrubs and perennials. However, not all landscape plants have been tested yet, and there may be other resistant species discovered by gardeners through the costly process of trial and error.

NOXIOUS AND INVASIVE PLANTS

Many plants introduced to northern California gardens are valued for their ability to withstand drought. Often this means they are competitive species with invasive rooting, rank growth, and rapid seed germination, which can make them better adapted to our wild lands than some natives. When these species naturalize, they displace important habitat and visually disfigure pristine woodlands.

Plants can threaten forest ecosystems by crowding out young tree seedlings. As the large trees die, there are no saplings to take their places and gradually the altered

LANDSCAPE PLANTS RESISTANT TO OAK ROOT FUNGUS

The University of California extension service has made available an excellent booklet listing all plants known to be resistant to the fungus. Plants are separated into three groups, which are those considered highly resistant, moderately resistant, and susceptible. The following is a partial list of those plants which are designated highly resistant.

Botanical Name	Common Name	Type
Acacia longifolia	Sydney Wattle	Shrub
Acer ginnala	Amur Maple	Tree
Acer macrophyllum	Oregon Maple	Tree
Acer palmatum	Japanese Maple	Tree
Ailanthus altissima	Tree-of-Heaven	Tree
Arbutus menziesii	Madrone	Tree
Buxus sempervirens	English Boxwood	Shrub
Calycanthus occidentalis	Western Spice Bush	Shrub
Catalpa bignonioides	Common Catalpa	Tree
Celtis australis	Hackberry	Tree
Ceratonia siliqua	Carob	Tree
Cercis occidentalis	Western Redbud	Shrub/Tree
Chaenomeles lagenaria	Japanese Quince	Shrub
Cotinus coggygria	Smoke Tree	Shrub
Eucalyptus camaldulensis	Red Gum	Tree
Eucalyptus cinerea	Dollar Leaf Eucalyptus	Tree
Eucalyptus grandis	Rose Gum	Tree
Geijera parviflora	Australian Willow	Tree
Ginkgo biloba	Maidenhair Tree	Tree
Gleditsia 'Shademaster'	Locust	Tree
Hibiscus syriacus	Rose of Sharon	Shrub
Hypericum patulum	St. Johnswort	Shrub
Ilex aquifolium	English Holly	Shrub
Liquidambar styraciflua	American Sweet Gum	Tree
Liriodendron tulipifera	Tulip Tree	Tree
Lonicera nitida	Box Honeysuckle	Vine
Magnolia grandiflora	Southern Magnolia	Tree
Mahonia aquifolium	Oregon Grape	Shrub
Malus floribunda	Flowering Crabapple	Tree
Maytenus boaria	Mayten Tree	Tree
Nandina domestica	Heavenly Bamboo	Shrub
Pinus canariensis	Canary Island Pine	Tree
Pistacia chinensis	Chinese Pistache	Tree
Quercus ilex	Holly Oak	Tree
Quercus lobata	Valley Oak	Tree
Sapium sebiferum	Chinese Tallow Tree	Tree
Sequoia sempervirens	Coast Redwood	Tree
Sophora japonica	Japanese Pagoda Tree	Tree
Ulmus parvifolia	Chinese Elm	Tree
Wisteria sinensis	Wisteria	Vine

> **NORTHERN CALIFORNIA TIP**
>
> **Yellow star thistle is the biggest threat to California's ecosystems, and is spreading rapidly to displace native grasses and disrupt the food chain. This spiny weed introduced by animal feeds will poison livestock, and the sharp spikes on each seed head injure animals' mouths and faces. To gardeners it is a painful weed, noxious, fast growing, and difficult to eradicate once established. If you see even one yellow star thistle in your garden, remove it entirely before it has a chance to reproduce. Either burn plants or discard them in a landfill to avoid risking its spread outside your garden.**

ecosystem begins to decline. Likewise, those vital understory plants of the forest floor are also prevented from reproducing.

One of the most common examples is Scotch broom which was brought by gold miners to the Sierra foothills. Broom is so well suited to this environment that it invaded oak and pine forests and now blankets miles of woodlands. Eradication of a plant on this scale is impossible, and wildlife is forced to relocate to areas where native species are still dominant.

Think twice before planting the species in the following list if there is any chance they could be transported by birds, wind or livestock into adjacent wild lands. Prevention is always preferable to eradication.

INVASIVE PLANTS TO AVOID FOR RURAL GARDENERS

Botanical Name	Common Name	Type
Acacia baileyana	Bailey Acacia	Tree
Ailanthus altissima	Tree-of-Heaven	Tree
Brooms—all	Broom	Shrubs
Cortaderia selloana	Pampas Grass	Ornamental Grass
Hydrilla	Hydrilla	Water Weed
Ligustrum sinensis	Privet	Shrub
Lonicera japonica	Japanese Honeysuckle	Vine
Lythrum salicaria	Purple Loosestrife	Perennial
Pennisetum setaceum	Fountain Grass	Ornamental Grass
Phyllostachys/bambusa	All Bamboos	Ornamental Grass
Pueraria thunbergiana	Kudzu	Vine
Robinia pseudoacacia	Black Locust	Tree
Vinca major/minor	Periwinkle	Groundcover
Vitis	Wild Grapevine	Vine

BLOOMING YELLOW SCOTCH BROOM INTRODUCED BY GOLD MINERS IN THE NINTEENTH CENTURY HAS INVADED SIERRA PINE FORESTS TO DISPLACE IMPORTANT NATIVE UNDERSTORY PLANTS.

VINCA MAJOR, A COMMON GROUNDCOVER PLANT, HAS OVERWHELMED THIS ABANDONED HOMESITE WHERE IT THRIVES IN OUR CLIMATE AS WELL AS MANY NATIVE SPECIES.

PLANTING AROUND SWIMMING POOLS

Planting near swimming pools doesn't have to be a nightmare of junipers and colored gravel. If done properly, the landscape can enhance the character of your pool by offering colorful flowers, shade in desired areas, screens for unsightly views, and discouragement of wind-borne dust and leaves.

When selecting plants, keep these tips in mind. Deciduous trees and shrubs aren't necessarily a problem as

PLASTIC, TERRA-COTTA-LOOK CONTAINERS PLANTED WITH STRAP LEAFED PERENNIALS AND FLOWERING VINES (WHICH WILL SOMEDAY COVER THIS ARBOR) SHOW HOW POOL AREAS MAY BE ATTRACTIVELY LANDSCAPED WITHOUT CREATING LITTER PROBLEMS.

long as their leaves are large enough to be removed from the water with a skimmer net. Small compound leaves like those of locust and pistachio clog filters and are too small to easily get into the skimmer. Select varieties that shed their leaves all at once, like the ginkgo tree.

This also applies to evergreens. Although pines and their conifer relatives don't have an autumn leaf drop, they may shed year around and the needles, cones, and pollen are a real nuisance. Many broad-leafed evergreens like camphor trees shed leaves constantly. The best selections will be large, glossy-leafed varieties like southern magnolia.

Other plants to avoid are those with thorns, especially if children might slip and fall into them. Plants with flowers that draw bees are always undesirable. With so much pavement around the pool, plants with staining berries can disfigure patios directly beneath them, or birds will help to distribute the stains over a much larger area.

Beware of the heat reflected off pool decks. It can cause scorching of plants which are sensitive to very hot, dry conditions. Do not plant close to steps, ladders, or diving boards because the accumulation of chlorine and salt runoff will eventually alter the soil to such a high pH that the plants will die. Direct contact of pool water on plant foliage will cause burning. This often occurs around diving boards where water drips off bathing suits, or when a well-placed "cannonball" makes a much larger splash than usual.

Pools with rock coping or boulders set into the edge call for natural plantings. Plant strap-leaved perennials such as fortnight lily, daylily, agapanthus, and red-hot poker. Trailing plants such as verbena, lantana, petunia, rosemary, and star jasmine are colorful and tolerate reflected heat. Plants can also offer dramatic effects under night lighting. Good choices include coast live oak, New Zealand flax, dracaena, and yucca. Palms are always a good choice, and some are small enough to be potted up for movable accents. Palms are best used in the background as foliage plants.

THE SWAN HILL OLIVE HAS NO FLOWERS OR FRUIT, WHICH MAKES IT AN EXCELLENT CHOICE OF EVERGREEN TREE FOR SWIMMING POOL AREAS.

PLANTS FOR AROUND SWIMMING POOLS

Botanical Name	Common Name	Type	Botanical Name	Common Name	Type
Abelia 'Edward Goucher'	Abelia	Shrub	*Lantana* hybrids	Lantana	Shrubs
Agapanthus africanus	Lily of the Nile	Perennial	*Magnolia grandiflora*	Southern Magnolia	Tree
Agapanthus 'Peter Pan'	Dwarf Lily of the Nile	Perennial	*Nandina domestica*	Heavenly Bamboo	Shrub
			Palms—all	Palm Tree	Tree
Campsis radicans	Trumpet Vine	Vine	*Phormium tenax*	New Zealand Flax	Perennial
Canna	Canna lily	Perennial	*Pinus mugo*	Mugo Pine	Shrub
Cistus purpureus	Orchid Rockrose	Shrub	*Pittosporum* 'Wheeleri'	Dwarf Tobira	Shrub
Cordyline australis	Dracaena	Perennial	*Raphiolepis* spp.	Indian Hawthorne	Shrub
Fatsia japonica	Japanese Aralia	Shrub	*Rosmarinus prostratus*	Rosemary	Groundcover
Gazania hybrids	Gazania	Groundcover	*Santolina chamaecyparissus*	Lavendercotton	Perennial
Ginkgo biloba	Maidenhair Tree	Tree	*Sedum* spp.	Sedum	Succulent
Hedera spp.	English Ivy	Groundcover	*Trachelospermum jasminoides*	Star Jasmine	Vine/ Groundcover
Hemerocallis	Daylily	Perennial	*Verbena* hybrids	Verbena	Groundcover
Hypericum calycinum	Hypericum	Groundcover	*Vinca minor/major*	Periwinkle	Groundcover
			Wisteria	Wisteria	Vine
Juniperus spp.	Juniper	Shrubs	*Xylosma congestum*	Xylosma	Shrub
Kniphofia uvaria	Red-Hot Poker	Perennial	*Yucca* spp.	Century Plant	Perennial

PLANTING FOR EROSION CONTROL

A majority of the slope conditions facing homeowners in northern California are created by cut-and-fill subdivisions. Land prices and the value of view lots have forced developers to chop up hillsides with 2:1 slopes, the greatest degree allowable by local codes. This is very steep and is the maximum slope which can support plant life, but 3:1 is more realistic.

Most people have no control over how slopes are graded on their homesites, which are typically smooth-surfaced inclines. Natural slopes have little gullies, flat spots, and a few steep areas which all lend themselves to natural vegetation. This provides areas where slope-stabilizing planting can gain a foothold.

The chief problem with planting on any slope, especially the steep ones, is getting water into the ground. Applied water will run off so fast, very little is able to penetrate the soil. Plants frequently die for lack of moisture. Clay, rocks, shale, and even bedrock are not uncommon on the surface of cut slopes. Frequently, the topsoil removed from the cut side is deposited as fill material, which renders fill slopes more fertile but susceptible to erosion.

There are two main issues concerning the planting of slopes. The first is to beautify what is a very ugly garden condition, and the second, more important, goal is to stabilize the soil and prevent excessive runoff, surface erosion, and sluffing. Surface erosion is the gradual removal of soil particles from the top of the ground resulting in small gullies and unwanted silt at the bottom of the slope.

Sluffing is the invisible weakening of soil below the surface that results in dangerous mud slides when the ground becomes saturated. Overwatering slope planting, especially on fill material, can also cause sluffing even during dry months. This is because water penetrates more easily where soil compaction is incomplete, and this can result in very dangerous, invisible saturation.

The best way to approach slope stabilization is to incorporate trees, shrubs, and groundcovers into the planting program. Trees and shrubs work well to bind subsoil together, which discourages sluffing. Groundcovers, along with perennials, grasses, and wildflowers, act to hold the surface and prevent silty runoff. The combination of many different plants insures that if disease or insects attack one species, there are other species to make up for the loss and insure erosion control.

Rainfall in northern California is not sufficient to allow plants to become established on slopes where there is very little topsoil, if any at all. Some sort of irrigation

PLANTS SUITED FOR VEGETATING SLOPES AND REDUCING EROSION

Botanical Name	Common Name	Type
Acacia saligna	Acacia	Tree
Acacia longifolia	Acacia	Shrub/Tree
Arctostaphylos	Manzanita	Shrub/Woody Groundcover
Baccharis pilularis	Coyote Bush	Woody Groundcover
Ceanothus	California Lilac	Shrub/Woody Groundcover
Cercis occidentalis	Western Redbud	Shrub
Cistus spp.	Rockrose	Shrub/Woody Groundcover
Cotoneaster spp.	Cotoneaster	Shrub/Woody Groundcover
Echium fastuosum	Pride of Madeira	Shrub
Eucalyptus spp.	Eucalyptus	Tree
Euonymus fortunei	Wintercreeper	Groundcover
Gazania leucolaena	Trailing Gazania	Groundcover
Hedera helix	English Ivy Hybrids	Groundcover
Heteromeles arbutifolia	California Toyon	Shrub
Hypericum calycinum	Hypericum	Groundcover
Iceplant hybrids	Iceplant	Groundcover
Juniperus spp.	Juniper	Shrub/Woody Groundcover
Lonicera japonica	Japanese Honeysuckle	Vine
Parthenocissus cinquefolia	Virginia Creeper	Vine
Potentilla tabernaemontanii	Potentilla	Groundcover
Pyracantha spp.	Firethorn	Shrub
Rosa banksiae	Lady Banks' Rose	Vine
Rosa rugosa	Rugosa Rose	Shrub
Rosmarinus spp.	Rosemary	Shrub/Groundcover
Santolina chamaecyparissus	Lavendercotton	Shrub
Vinca major/minor	Periwinkle	Groundcover
Xylosma congestum	Xylosma	Shrub

will be needed to get the plants started. When planning an irrigation system, remember that the water does run downhill, and the driest part of a slope is always at the top. Don't underestimate how much water will be required to insure germination and a vigorous start for young plants. It can be very expensive to plant the slope a second time.

When slopes are hydroseeded, they need to be kept evenly moist for a time to insure the best germination rates. But as the little plants become established, taper off gradually because their root systems will begin to contact subsoil moisture. Just as deep and infrequent watering promotes strong rooting and better drought tolerance in other plantings, it will also do the same for slope plants. For areas with higher rainfall, irrigation may be eventually phased out completely except during the driest months or years of extreme drought.

PLANTING A SLOPE

The physical planting of a slope is best done in two phases. Plants grown in containers should be planted first, on small benches carved out of the slope or created by adding small retaining features. These can be made out of any material, such as rocks, reinforcing steel bars, and redwood 2x6s, or concrete block. These help to create enough level area to plant the rootball so that it won't be later exposed by surface runoff. When rootballs become exposed they dry out very quickly and getting them completely moistened again can be difficult.

The second phase involves either hand planting groundcovers or hydroseeding a mixture of seed designed for controlling surface erosion. A typical erosion-control seed mix contains a nurse crop and a second, long-term crop which is permanent. The nurse crop is usually made up of quick-to-germinate fast-growing grasses. The second crop includes the groundcovers, wildflowers, and soil-improving clovers. Once the container plants have been installed, the slope is hydroseeded over the tops of them.

Today, innovative growers have advanced these slope-stabilizing mixes to also contain seeds and even rootlets of trees and shrubs. Many companies will design seed mixes for a particular slope, taking into consideration irrigation, soil, local climate, and aesthetic preferences. This can be helpful where conditions are poor and the risk of slope failure is a serious concern.

The key to planting on slopes, be they massive cuts in hillsides or just slight inclines on a backyard planting mound, is to trap enough water to supply each plant. This can be done by artificial benching as described previously, or by creating a miniature cut-and-fill pad for each plant. Half of a planting pad should be dug out of the slope, and the excavated material used to create a berm on the downhill side. The plant goes into the ground at the center of the pad so that the outside top edge of the rootball is close to the actual, undisturbed soil line.

Sometimes this will be enough to trap water, but what usually happens is the berm on the downhill side quickly washes out and the ability to hold water is lost.

THIS NEWLY GRADED SLOPE HAS BEEN HYDROSEEDED WITH A WILDFLOWER MIX COUPLED WITH A NURSE CROP OF GRASSES. (*APPLEWOOD SEED CO.*)

The solution is to dig a banana-shaped trench at the back of the pad (the uphill side), which will place it right at the base of the newly carved miniature cut slope. It should be about 4 to 6 inches deep and reflect the curvature of the rootball but not contact the roots. When water is applied, it will run down the hill and become trapped in the banana trench. There it sits with no outlet, waiting to be absorbed directly into the rootball. The rate is slow enough to thoroughly saturate the roots and avoid waste. Use this technique when planting trees, shrubs, perennials, annuals, and groundcovers on slopes of any kind. It works.

COASTLINE GARDENING

Most gardeners who encounter the coastal environment live within two to five miles or more from the shoreline. This marine influence presents difficulties that include wind, fog, salt, and sandy soils. But the moist environment and filtered sunshine make perfect conditions for growing perennials, and some of northern California's most beautiful gardens are located here.

Sandy soils can be the most frustrating aspect of coastal gardening, despite the fact that they are well drained and easy to cultivate. Sand has the lowest fertility level of all soils and tremendous amounts of rich humus are needed to make it support many types of plant life. This humus is also important for absorbing water and keeping it within the root zone.

Salt can also create problems when it is present in soils. Large quantities of fresh water can be leached through the soil to carry away the salt. Leaching is less effective in dense soils because there is insufficient drainage for the water to move through fast enough. An alternative to leaching is to select plants with a high tolerance for saline soils. The blankets of colorful iceplant that naturalize on the cliffs above our north coast beaches are one of the best examples of this. Verbena is also very successful and some of our native species are so forgiving they grow directly in dune sand as a valuable part of that ecosystem. Even vegetables like potatoes and members of the cabbage family will put up with a good deal of salt. Globe artichoke is so tolerant it has gone wild in coastal hills.

Salts can be replaced in the soil by wind. Airborne salts can also be deposited on leaves and eventually build up if plants aren't washed off occasionally with fresh water. Sometimes salt air will leave behind a sprinkling of white minerals as a clue to its presence.

PERENNIAL GARDENS IN MENDOCINO, A SMALL TOWN ON THE CLIFFS ABOVE THE SEA.

PLANTS FOR WINDBREAKS, SALINE SOILS AND SALT AIR

Botanical Name	Common Name	Type
Acacia longifolia	Sydney Wattle	Shrub
Acacia melanoxylon	Blackwood Acacia	Windbreak Tree
Arbutus unedo	Strawberry Tree	Tree/Shrub
Arctostaphylos uva-ursi	Bear Berry	Woody Groundcover
Baccharis pilularis	Coyote Bush	Groundcover
Callistemon spp.	Bottlebrush	Tree/Shrub
Casuarina equisetifolia	She-oak	Windbreak Tree
Ceanothus griseus	California Lilac	Woody Groundcover
Cistus spp.	Rockrose	Shrub
Cordyline australis	Dracaena	Exotic Shrub
Cupressus macrocarpa	Monterey Cypress	Windbreak Tree
Cytisus spp.	Broom	Shrub
Dodonaea viscosa	Hopseed Bush	Shrub
Echium fastuosum	Pride of Madeira	Shrub
Escallonia spp.	Escallonia	Shrub
Eucalyptus camaldulensis	Eucalyptus	Windbreak Tree
Eucalyptus rudis	Eucalyptus	Windbreak Tree
Euonymus japonica	Euonymus	Shrub
Garrya elliptica	Silktassel	Tree/Shrub
Gazania spp.	Gazania	Groundcover
Hebe buxifolia	Boxleaf Hebe	Shrub
Iceplant spp.	Many Iceplant Species	Groundcover
Juniperus spp.	Juniper	Shrubs
Laurus nobilis	Sweet Bay	Tree
Nerium oleander	Oleander	Shrub
Pinus pinea	Italian Stone Pine	Tree
Pinus radiata	Monterey Pine	Tree
Pinus torreyana	Torrey Pine	Tree
Pittosporum sp.	Mock Orange	Shrub
Quercus ilex	Holly Oak	Tree
Raphiolepis sp.	Indian Hawthorne	Shrub
Rosa rugosa	Rugosa Rose	Shrub
Rosmarinus officinalis	Rosemary	Shrub

Most coastal gardeners here in the north state have to contend with persistent offshore winds. Not only do these constant breezes dry out the soil and scour its surface, they also draw moisture directly out of plant leaves. With the wind comes particles of sand and salt which pit the surface of tender foliage. The contorted shapes of plants along the coast is a result of wind drying out tender growing tips on the windward side while the lee side grows normally. In many cases plants will survive this punishment but they may not bloom.

All these factors illustrate why wind-tolerant plants have thick, leathery leaves, deep roots, and a very low profile. Along the Mendocino coast nothing except cypress trees, pasture grass, and ground-hugging natives survive unless gardens are enclosed by a windbreak. Unfortunately, windbreak trees can take decades to grow large enough to have an impact. Often buildings and low walls or solid fences are strategically designed into landscapes in order to reduce direct exposure to the wind.

Coastal trees must be able to withstand gale-force winds without becoming uprooted or breaking the trunk and limbs. Palms have always survived coastal conditions with their flexible grasslike trunks which bend with the wind rather than fight it. Old cypress and eucalyptus windbreaks in northern California attest to those species which most successfully reduce wind while surviving on natural rainfall. Another highly drought-, wind-, and salt-tolerant tree is *Casuarina equisetifolia*, also called the she-oak. It is a relative newcomer to the north state but has great promise.

The many varieties of eucalyptus are northern California's most common windbreak trees. They are inexpensive, fast growing and very drought tolerant. The most successful way to plant a eucalyptus windbreak is with seedlings about a foot tall. Not only are they less expensive, they are also better able to anchor their roots deeply into the soil than older container-grown eucalyptus. Before planting in fall or winter, wash the soil from the roots and spread them out in the planting hole as you would a bare-root. Water heavily, but infrequently the first year to encourage deeper rooting, which will increase the tree's drought tolerance and improve stability as an adult.

Eucalyptus grows so rapidly their roots do not develop in proportion to the above-ground mass of the tree. The result is a dangerous, weak limbed, top-heavy plant. Discourage this by topping the tree during its early years. Topping trees forces more growth energy into the root system, and reduces the overall mass of leaves and branches. Professionals like to remove 30 percent or more of the new growth each year for the first three to five years, depending on growth rate. This forces stronger branching and greater foliage density for blocking wind.

PROTECTED BY FENCES AND SMALL RAVINES, GARDENS ALONG THE NORTH COAST GROW WITH UNUSUAL LUSHNESS FOR CALIFORNIA'S ARID CLIMATE.

(*RANDY MEYER*)

LANDSCAPING FOR FIRE PROTECTION

The specter of wildfires haunts everyone who lives in rural parts of northern California. Before early settlers came to this area, seasonal fires ripped through the forests and grasslands. Native American tribes regularly burned off foothill chaparral to clear the countryside and make it easier to hunt. Wildfires even assisted in the germination of seed and renewal of native vegetation.

Since these regular fires have stopped, native chaparral plants have grown so dense that foothill areas are now impenetrable. The litter of dead twigs and leaves which covers the forest floor has become so thick, fires burn far longer and at much hotter temperatures. Homes located near these overgrown areas, and those surrounded by ungrazed dry grass are at greatest risk. This situation is compounded by dead branches and trees broken by heavy snows, which lie dry and ready to be touched off by a single spark.

The '49er fire in Nevada County is a good example of how homes could have been saved by sound, fire-preventative landscaping practices. In a planned community where the greatest loss of homes occurred, residents were restricted by local codes, which demanded trees and natural vegetation be preserved to promote a more natural character. When high winds touched off a brush fire that summer, it raged through the community burning homes that had the most dry grass, shrubs and trees close to the house. Sadly, these homes were in strict compliance with the ordinances. A similar situation occurred in the Berkeley Hills fire in 1992. The homes were surrounded by dry, drought stricken landscapes which were so volatile that when coupled with high winds there was no hope for controlling the blaze.

Another important factor is the nature of chaparral plant communities in general. In many areas, manzanita and sage are the dominant species, and both contain a large amount of volatile oil in their wood. Manzanita is so oily that the foliage becomes iridescent at night when moonlight or artificial light is reflected off leaf surfaces. Even while green and fully alive, manzanita has been known to explode into flame as the oils are touched off. In light of this, it's surprising to find manzanita is frequently listed as a low-fuel-volume plant, and perhaps this reference only applies to the ground hugging species.

Some experts suggest that a 30-foot-wide band around the house be cleared of all dead vegetation. This means pruning dead wood out of trees, mowing or hoeing off dry grass, and the disposal of any accumulations of leaf litter. For homes in chaparral areas, a 100-foot-wide band around the house should be cleared of all native brush. Trees which overhang rooftops make saving a structure more difficult because the house cannot be isolated from burning vegetation. The tree need not be removed, just the overhanging branches.

This band of cleared ground becomes the single barrier between the fire and your house. Year-around care and management are important to its effectiveness should an unexpected fire occur. These areas can be very attractive when planted with seas of blooming groundcovers or low mats of foliage. Other landscape plants can be used around the house as long as they aren't allowed to dry out, which is what occurred in the Berkeley fire.

There is no such thing as a plant that will not burn.

PLANTS FOR FIRE PROTECTION BANDS

Botanical Name	Common Name	Type
FIRE ZONE 1—HOUSE		
Acceptable:		
Agapanthus africanus	Lily of the Nile	Perennial
Arbutus unedo	Strawberry Tree	Tree
Buxus microphylla japonica	Japanese Boxwood	Shrub
Ceratonia siliqua	Carob Tree	Tree
Cercis occidentalis	Western Redbud	Shrub
Citrus Varieties	Lemon, Orange	Trees
Convolvulus cneorum	Bush Morning Glory	Shrub
Ligustrum texanum	Texas Privet	Shrub
Magnolia spp.	Magnolia	Tree
Nerium oleander	Oleander	Shrub
Olea europea	Olive	Tree
Pittosporum spp.	Mock Orange	Shrubs
Punica granatum	Pomegranate	Shrub
Pyracantha spp.	Firethorn	Shrub
Rhamnus alaternus	Italian Buckthorn	Shrub
Schinus molle	California Pepper	Tree
Tecomaria capensis	Cape Honeysuckle	Vine
Trachelospermum jasminoides	Star Jasmine	Vine
Xylosma congestum	Xylosma	Shrub
Not Acceptable:		
Acacia spp.	Acacia	Trees
Cedrus spp.	Cedar	Trees
Cortaderia species	Pampas Grass	Ornamental Grass
Cupressus spp.	Cypress	Trees
Dodonaea viscosa	Hopseed Bush	Shrub
Eucalyptus spp.	Eucalyptus	Trees
Gelsemium sempervirens	Carolina Jessamine	Vine
Juniperus spp.	Junipers	Shrubs/Trees
Pennisetum spp.	Fountain Grass	Ornamental Grass
Phormium tenax	New Zealand Flax	Perennial
Pinus spp.	Pines	Trees
Sapium Sebiferum	Chinese Tallow Tree	Tree
FIRE ZONE 2—INTERMEDIATE		
Baccharis pilularis	Coyote Bush	Groundcover
Cistus salviifolius	Sageleaf Rockrose	Groundcover
Dietes vegeta	Fortnight Lily	Perennial
Eschscholzia californica	California Poppy	Perennial
Gazania rigens leucolaena	Trailing Gazania	Groundcover
Iceplant spp.	Iceplant	Groundcover
Lupinus spp.	Lupine	Annual/ Perennial
Mimulus spp.	Monkey Flower	Perennial
Penstemon spp.	Penstemon	Perennial
Salvia sonomensis	Creeping Sage	Perennial
Santolina chamaecyparissus	Lavendercotton	Perennial
Sedum spp.	Sedum	Perennials
Trifolium fragiferum	O'Connors Legume	Groundcover
Vinca major/minor	Periwinkle	Groundcover
Zauschneria californica	California Fuchsia	Perennial

Firestorms caused by dry winds can reach much higher temperatures than in calm air. Under these conditions, even succulents will ignite. The key is to reduce the amount of fuel available to the fire in order to slow it down before it threatens a house. The ideal solution is to surround the dwelling with perennial grasses kept lush by frequent irrigation and occasional mowing.

Unfortunately, drought-stricken neighborhoods can't afford this luxury, but less thirsty groundcovers make a good substitute. Planting low-growing species offers less fuel volume than upright species but if dry, even they will ignite. If water supply is limited, household gray water becomes a vital resource to retain a plant's fire-resistant qualities. If no water is available, a close mowing early in the season cuts down grasses and weeds to their lowest fuel volumes.

TRIPLE-BAND PROTECTION SYSTEM

Fire-protective landscapes can be planned by establishing three bands which extend outward from the house. **Band #1** includes plantings around the house, which should consist of landscape plants most resistant to fire. Avoid those with more flammable qualities.

Band #2 is intermediate, and should be limited to low-fuel-volume plants. Ideally this band should be lawn, irrigated pasture, or groundcover which can be accented with succulent perennials. Where water availability is limited, drought-tolerant groundcover plants which grow no taller than 18 inches high are the best choice. However, these groundcovers will be far more fire resistant if given supplemental irrigation.

Band #3 consists of native vegetation. In areas of forest or chaparral, the management of this transition zone is very important. Thin and clean out the trees and shrubs by removing all dead or dry branches. Selectively remove plants where the vegetation is particularly dense. This not only reduces fuel volume but also makes it accessible to fire fighters who may be able to stop the fire at that point. If you are surrounded by grassland, make sure this outside band is mowed close to the ground to reduce fuel volume and slow fire movement.

ABOUT THE PLANTS

Not all landscape plants have been tested for their degree of fire resistance. In general, annuals and perennials are the best because they contain lots of moisture and lack woody twigs and branches. Succulents are also excellent choices as long as are well watered, because when stems shrivel and dry out they become flammable.

The key factor is low fuel volume, and the majority of plants used in fire-sensitive landscapes are selected for their prostrate growth habits. There are other, more uncommon plants which also have these same characteristics. Consult with a local fire station or the California Department of Forestry for more information and assistance in setting up an effective fire-protection landscape zone around your home.

IMPORTANT DEFINITIONS:

Low fuel volume. Larger upright plants have more branches and leaves to feed a fire. Low, ground-hugging plants have less mass and offer only a small amount of fuel to feed an approaching fire.

Fire retardant (resistant) plants. Studies show that certain plants require higher temperatures before they ignite. There are no fireproof plants. All will eventually burn, but fire-retardant plants have special characteristics relating to the nature of their leaf surfaces and overall moisture content.

CHAPTER TWELVE

KITCHEN GARDENING

You don't have to be a gourmet cook to know that fruits and vegetables from your own garden always taste better than produce from the supermarket. At the end of a busy day it's easier to step into the garden and gather your evening meal than fight crowds at the store. Better yet is the fun of growing unusual varieties and testing their unique tastes. Even with limited space, a small 10-foot-square plot can support a surprising number of plants and trees. New hybrids offer smaller plants that yield full-sized fruits and vegetables, making high-density gardens possible for nearly everyone.

FACING PAGE: A CASUAL, COUNTRY-STYLE HERB GARDEN ORNAMENTED WITH COSMOS AND OLD ROSES. ABOVE: 20TH-CENTURY ASIAN PEAR (*STARK BROS. NURSERY*)

A WELL-PLANNED AND TENDED KITCHEN GARDEN WITH ORCHARD.

HOW CLIMATE AFFECTS YOUR KITCHEN GARDEN

The seven climate zones of northern California can be divided into three main areas. Cool summer coastal areas include zones 6 and 7. Foothill and mountain areas consist of zones 1, 2, and 4. The warm valleys are in zones 3 and 5. In each of these three areas, there will be some vegetable crops that grow well and others which do not.

• **Coastal** Northern coastal areas may not receive enough summer heat to ripen vegetables like corn, melons, and peppers. But this weather is perfect for salad greens, root crops, and potatoes. Winter gardens grow exceptionally well here, in areas of light frosts. Fruit trees with greater chilling requirements may not produce well due to lack of winter frost.

• **Foothills and mountains** Your exact climatic conditions will vary with elevation. In the high country the growing season is only a couple of months long, so vegetables that mature rapidly are your best bet. Lower in the foothills, summers may be long and hot, making lettuce and other leaf crops bolt in late spring. Nights are cooler than in the valley and melons may not ripen. Hard frosts make winter gardens difficult, but in mild years plants may be set out in February. Late frosts can delay summer garden planting until May. Most fruit and nut trees grow well here as long as the soil doesn't freeze in winter.

• **Warm valleys** These are the very best areas for vegetable gardens because soils are fertile and the growing season is very long. Valley nights also remain quite warm, which allows all crops to thrive. Winter gardens can be planted in the fall, and if frost is not too severe they will bear right through to spring. Most nut and orchard fruit trees thrive and produce heavily here.

Warm-Season and Cool-Season Vegetables

Vegetable garden plants can be divided into two groups, those which grow in warm weather, and those which prefer cooler temperatures. In general, leaf- and root-crop plants can be grown in late fall, winter, and early spring. The remaining vegetables are frost tender and may only be grown during late spring, summer and early fall. There are a few exceptions with the versatility to become both warm- and cool-season crops.

• **Warm-season plants** These plants require warm soil to germinate. They mature during late spring, and crops ripen in the heat of summer. In the valleys, warm-season crops may be planted in March as long as there are no unseasonably late frosts. Along the coast, planting time may be slightly earlier. The higher foothills are subjected to late frosts which force planting to be delayed until early May. Starting vegetable plants indoors or in a cold frame helps to compensate for these late frosts.

• **Cool-season plants** This second group of plants require cooler air and soil temperatures to germinate and mature properly. Leaf crops such as lettuce become bitter and bolt into flower stalks at higher temperatures. Once a plant has bolted, it is of little use as a food crop. Brussels sprouts, broccoli, and cauliflower are common cool season plants which actually improve in flavor with exposure to frost. Cool season crops may be grown year around along the coast where frost is less common. In foothill regions, the ability to grow in late winter depends on local air movement and solar exposure. Warmer inland valleys not subjected to deep frost pockets will support many cool season crops during the winter.

WARM AND COOL SEASON VEGETABLES

Warm Season	Cool Season
Beans	Beets
Beets	Broccoli
Carrots	Brussels Sprouts
Chard	Cabbage
Corn	Cauliflower
Cucumber	Chard
Eggplant	Kale
Melons	Lettuce
Okra	Peas
Garlic	Potatoes
Onion	Radishes
Peppers	Spinach
Potatoes	
Radishes	
Squash	
Tomatoes	

FRUIT TREE SIZES AND TIPS FOR PROPER SELECTION

Proper selection of fruit trees depends on many factors, which include size, method of planting and the unique cultural requirements of each species. The following criteria should be thoroughly considered before choosing any fruit tree variety.

Size

Common varieties of fruit trees are grafted and growers can adjust the size of the mature tree without changing the fruit at all.

• **Standards** Standard fruit trees grow from 18 to 25 feet tall. Orchard ladders may be needed for pruning and picking from the highest limbs. Tall standard trees are more deer resistant when mature as their branches are high enough to remain out of reach. Plant standard fruit trees at least 20 feet apart.

• **Semi-dwarf** Perhaps the most ideal size, semi-dwarf trees grow to 12 or 15 feet tall. Proportionally they produce more fruit for their size than a standard tree. Fruit is within reach, and pruning is easier. Plant semi-dwarf trees 15 feet apart.

• **Dwarf** Even smaller yet are the dwarf trees which mature at about 10 feet tall. These are the very best choice for urban gardens and make attractive small landscape trees. Dwarf trees bear at an earlier date than larger trees of the same variety. Plant dwarf trees 10 feet apart.

Bloom time

Each fruit tree variety blooms at a certain time each spring, although weather patterns will influence the exact dates. The earlier the bloom date, the more vulnerable the pollination becomes to weather. Rain, wind, late frosts, and even snow can disturb this delicate process and prevent fruit development. At higher elevations of northern California foothills and mountain regions, earlier-blooming varieties may never produce fruit due to weather problems.

Chilling requirements

Fruit trees such as apples and cherries require exposure to a minimum number of hours per year below 45°F. This insures they become fully dormant in winter. If denied their chilling requirement, the trees may never bloom or produce fruit. If you live in warm coastal communities south of San Francisco, make sure you select fruit trees with very short chilling requirements.

Pollination

Most fruit trees are self-fertile, which means the pollen from its own flowers will be sufficient to produce fruit. But some trees will not set fruit at all unless cross pollinated with another variety. A second pollinator tree must bloom at the same time as the fruiting tree so pollen and flowers are ready simultaneously. In smaller urban gardens constraints on space should limit your choices to only self-fertile varieties.

PLANTING FRUIT AND NUT TREES

Refer to chapter 4 for detailed instructions on planting trees. As a reminder, make sure to plant the trees at the proper depth to discourage crown rot. The soil level should line up with the slight change in bark color on the trunk which marks the level of the growing field. Place the tree so the bulk of the graft union faces north or east. This keeps this vulnerable area out of the hot afternoon sun and protected from sunscald. After planting remove any thin, spindly branches and head back the others to about 12 inches long.

Nut trees have a single tap root with smaller lateral roots on its sides. Your planting hole should be at least as long as the tap root, and wide enough to fit the laterals without bending them. Make the sides of the hole rough so the lateral roots can penetrate better. Fill the hole in layers and tamp them down as you go. Arrange the lateral roots so they are in a horizontal position. There is no need to add any fertilizer to the planting holes of nut trees.

After planting fruit or nut trees, paint the trunk and unshaded branches with white paint to prevent sunscald until the canopy becomes larger. Mulching is helpful to maintain even moisture in the root zone. Create watering basins and water generously to encourage deep rooting.

SOIL PREPARATION FOR KITCHEN GARDEN PLOTS

Kitchen gardens depend on well prepared, fertile soil to produce a good crop. Since few homesites have perfect soil to begin with, the garden must be continually improved or the nutrients will be exhausted. Drainage

FRESHLY TILLED AND PLANTED VEGETABLE PLOT.

NORTHERN CALIFORNIA TIP

If you have access to manure or other dry organic fertilizers, they can be made into a liquid "tea" that is poured around plants like fish emulsion. Some gardeners keep an open-top 50-gallon drum in the garden filled with water. They add whatever type of manure is available and let it steep for a few days with occasional stirring. This water is later drawn out in buckets as needed to fertilize plants. You'll find this very useful for young seedlings that will not stand much soil disturbance.

can be a problem for winter gardens when soils tend to be saturated. But if drainage is poor in summer, you must install a drainage feature or construct raised beds.

The soil improvement cycle for vegetable gardens is very simple. In spring, incorporate manure and compost into the soil before you plant. During summer, maintain a thick layer of mulch around the plants to discourage weeds and reduce surface evaporation. By fall, the mulches should have begun decomposing and can be tilled back into the soil. If you plant a winter garden, new mulches can be added to keep the roots warmer. If the garden lies fallow during winter, use this time to stockpile humus and mulching materials for spring and summer use.

NUTRIENT CONTENT OF ORGANIC FERTILIZERS

Nutrient contents expressed in percent of weight.

Material	Nitrogen	Phosphorus	Potassium
Wood ashes	-	2.0	5.0
Bloodmeal	13.0	2.0	1.0
Bonemeal	4.0	22.5	-
Cottonseed meal	7.0	3.0	2.0
Fish emulsion	9.5	7.0	-
Bat guano	13.0	12.0	2.5
Steer manure	2.0	1.5	2.0
Poultry manure	5.0	3.0	1.5

PLANTING YOUR KITCHEN GARDEN

Organization is essential when planning the vegetable garden. Plants which climb or sprawl over the ground should be given supports or be placed where they have plenty of room to spread out without overwhelming smaller plants. Tall plants are best located on the north end of the garden where they won't cast shade on shorter plants nearby. Root crops can be planted in blocks to avoid disturbance. Fast-growing salad plants may be placed where they are accessible and easily reseeded throughout the season.

Use the rainy days of winter to draw up your proposed garden and locate each plant or row. Seed catalogs are very helpful in this process. Try to estimate the area needed for each plant and drawn it on the plan. This helps you know how many different varieties of seed you must buy.

VEGETABLE GROWTH HABITS FOR GARDEN PLANNING

Name	Growth habit/ height	Support required
Bush beans	Low	no
Pole beans	Vine/tall	Trellis or Tepee
Beets	Low root	no
Broccoli	Medium	no
Brussels sprouts	Medium	Staking
Cabbage	Low	no
Carrots	Low root	no
Cauliflower	Medium	no
Chard	Low leaf	no
Corn	Tall	no
Cucumbers	Vine/tall	Trellis or Tepee
Eggplant	Medium	Staking
Kale	Low leaf	no
Lettuce	Low leaf	no
Melons	Sprawling vines	no
Okra	Tall	Staking
Onion	Low	no
Peas	Vine/tall	Trellis or Tepee
Peppers	Medium	Staking
Potatoes	Medium	no
Radishes	Low root	no
Summer squash	Medium	no
Winter squash	Sprawling vines	no
Tomatoes	Vines/tall	Trellis or wire cage

KEY TO SUPPORT TYPES:

Staking As plants age they tend to lie down because of crop weight or heavy leaves. Stake and tie as needed to keep them upright.

Trellis These plants climb by tendrils. Construct a trellis by anchoring posts in the soil with a network of wire, twine, or netting between them to keep fruit off the ground.

Tepee Use wood poles or sticks to create a tepee tied together at the top. Plant at the base of each pole so plants may begin to climb as soon as possible.

Wire cage Either use special tomato support cages or construct your own with wire field fencing. Place cages over young plants to support runners as they grow to keep fruit off the ground.

FIVE GOLDEN STATE STEPS TO PLANTING YOUR VEGETABLE GARDEN

1. **Prepare the soil.**
   Thoroughly till the garden area and remove any roots, sticks, rocks or dirt clods. Work in humus and organic matter. Rake the surface smooth and even.

2. **Make hills and/or rows.**
   Fashion hills of good soil or lay out rows with a string and stakes at each end. Make these stakes tall and strong so they can be left at the ends of the rows to protect plants from the garden hose.

3. **Plant seed or seedlings.**
   Plant the seeds at the depth indicated for that variety on its package. Gently plant seedlings, taking care not to pinch their tender stems with your fingers.

4. **Apply mulch layer.**
   The seed beds must remain evenly moist, and mulching the surface with fine organic materials encourages more even germination and reduces washout. Carefully spread mulches around the base of transplanted seedlings to trap moisture and reduce the need to water more frequently.

5. **Water all seeds and seedlings in thoroughly.**
   Seeds and seedlings must be watered in with the garden hose after planting. Use a fine-misting nozzle

PERMANENT RUSTIC SUPPORTS FOR VINE CROPS CAN BE ATTRACTIVE ENOUGH TO REMAIN IN PLACE YEAR AROUND.

NORTHERN CALIFORNIA TIP

One good way to construct a climbing trellis for peas and other vine crops is to use untreated twine. This is twine that is fully biodegradable and contains no chemicals or synthetic fibers. Plant a stout pole long enough to be 4 feet above ground on either end of your row. Weave the twine back and forth into a network that is strong enough to support the weight of the vines. When the season is over, simply cut the ends of the twine off the poles, roll the whole thing up, vines and all, and dispose of it in your compost pile. Untreated twine has no chemicals to contaminate the compost or damage the microorganisms which activate the decomposition process.

A POLE TEEPEE FOR VINE CROPS HAS A PLASTIC OWL ATTACHED TO THE TOP TO SCARE BIRDS AWAY FROM THE NEARBY FRUIT TREES. WELL-MULCHED SOIL HELPS REDUCE THE AMOUNT OF WATER NEEDED BY THE GARDEN.

NORTHERN CALIFORNIA TIP

Most people prune their fruit trees and discard the prunings. But straight fruit tree suckers and water sprouts make an excellent source of free staking materials for perennials and bedding plants. Extra long, thick whips make perfect poles for tepee structures to support climbing beans and peas. Separate out the straightest whips from your prunings, cut off side branches or curving parts, and pile them flat on a well-drained concrete slap or gravel surface in the sun. By summer they should be stiff and dry, just in time for the vegetable garden.

for seed beds to avoid washing away seed or the thin soil covering.

PRUNING FRUIT AND NUT TREES

Deciduous fruit and nut trees in northern California are pruned during January or February while they are dormant. Late pruning, after the insect population has become more active, leaves moist wounds which become an entryway for parasites. Borers, one of the worst enemies of fruit trees, enter most frequently from late pruning wounds and sunscald blisters.

Pruning can be simplified by using a process of elimination to remove obviously unwanted growth *before* going into specifics of pruning each species. As discussed in the chapter on trees, always remove branches which may be diseased, damaged, or broken, and those not in keeping with the tree's shape. Any twigs or branches that touch or grow into the center of the tree are also undesirable. Two additional types of unwanted growth in fruit trees are called suckers and water sprouts.

• **Suckers** A sucker is rank growth that originates at the base of the trunk. If it originates below the graft union, from the rootstock, the leaves may be slightly different from those on the rest of the tree. Suckers siphon growth energy before it can reach the productive branches. They should be removed both during the growing season and when winter pruning. While very small, suckers can be rubbed off with your finger which leaves a neat, dry scar.

• **Water sprouts** Water sprouts are thin, whiplike limbs which grow out of much thicker framework branches on the inside of the tree. They grow very quickly, usually in a single season. You must keep these pruned out, as they distort the shape of the tree, block light from more productive interior branches, and consume valuable growth energy.

Pruning Apples, Pears and Cherries

Apples, pears, and cherries are best grown with a single, central trunk called a leader. You want the side branches to be evenly dispersed throughout the tree with each one located from 4 to 8 inches above the next. These trees flower on stubby growths with big fat buds called fruiting spurs, and if they are cut off during pruning there will be no fruit. The goal is to head back the longer growing tips of the side branches in order to force growth energy into the development of spurs. Cut back thin, lanky growth which is too weak to bear fruit, especially while trees are young.

Pruning Peach, Nectarine, Apricot, and Plum Trees

These trees develop fruit on the branches which grew the year before. If you prune off all the growth of the previous summer, the remaining wood will be too old to bear fruit. If this growth remains untouched, the fruit crop will be heavy but small, and branches may break under the load. Winter pruning reduces the length of these year-old branches by half or two-thirds to make them stronger and produce larger fruit.

The Five Most Common Fruit Tree Pests

Refer to the least-toxic process of pest control in the appendix for more details.

1. Leaves and flowers on new growth are distorted and discolored. Black sticky substance and/or large numbers of ants on the tree. *Possible cause: aphids. Damage potential: moderate.*

2. Leaves appear to have silver sheen on the front, and on the back you'll see tiny black or red spots and

NORTHERN CALIFORNIA TIP

Soils in mountains, foothill regions, and redwood country are acidic because of the buildup of leaves from native conifers and oak trees. Orchard trees in these rural regions should be supplemented with phosphorus to unlock the nutrients tied up in the soil by the low pH. Super phosphate is an excellent granular source of phosphorus. Bone meal is a good organic alternative which rarely burns, but is not as potent as super phosphate and heavier applications are needed. You can apply phosphorus supplements in the very early spring to help trees get off to a good start.

even very fine webbing. *Possible cause: spider mites. Damage potential: low.*

3. Pieces of bark seem to be loose and may be completely detached. Beneath the bark is a mealy wood residue and signs of tunneling. May be associated with sunscald blisters. *Possible cause: borers. Damage potential: very high.*

4. Leaves of peach and nectarine trees are very distorted and may have a reddish tinge. Leaves drop off tree. *Possible cause: peach leaf curl. Damage potential: high.*

5. Presence of concentrated thick spiderlike webs. May or may not contain populations of small caterpillars. *Possible cause: tent caterpillars. Damage potential: moderate.*

COMMON GARDEN QUESTION

"Why do the plants beneath my black walnut trees grow poorly or die soon after I plant them?"

Native California black walnut trees growing wild must often survive strictly on natural rainfall. They have a built-in mechanism for reducing the competition for moisture from other plants growing nearby. The roots, leaves, and husks of black walnut trees exude a chemical called juglone. It restricts the growth of other plants which can consume moisture and nutrients required by the walnut. Eucalyptus do much the same thing and there is no way to correct the condition except to remove the black walnuts. However, even after the tree is removed, there may be a residual amount of juglone remaining in the soil which may take some time to leach away.

FRUIT AND NUT VARIETIES FOR NORTHERN CALIFORNIA GARDENS

For each type of fruit, nut, or berry there are dozens of hybrids which display a wide variety of special characteristics. Many fruit tree varieties can be purchased in standard, semi-dwarf, and dwarf sizes. Rather than listing every possibility, a few of the most widely available varieties are described here.

P–Requires a pollinator

L–Extra late blooming for frost-prone foothill and mountain zones.

Almond
Suggested varieties:
All-in-One, Ne Plus Ultra-P, Nonpareil-P.

Apples
Suggested varieties:
Fuji, Gala, Golden Delicious, Red Delicious-P, Granny Smith, Gravenstein-P, Jonathan, Liberty, Yellow Newton Pippin.

Apricot
Suggested varieties:
Blenheim Royal, Chinese-L, Harcot, Puget Gold-L, Tilton.

DANGERS OF FRUIT AND NUT TREES AND DOGS

Accidental poisoning in dogs is not a common condition, but it has occurred when the fruits and nuts from orchard trees have been ingested. Boredom in dogs who are kept chained or fenced in a run leads them to chew on just about anything within reach. Puppies, whether confined or not, are chewing machines always in danger of consuming poisonous substances.

The nuts inside the pits of stone fruits can be extremely toxic, and so are the husks of walnuts. The husks of other types of nuts are not toxic, but if left on the ground in damp weather they develop fungus growth which is dangerous. A bored dog may have the opportunity to ingest a considerable amount of toxin before it has an effect. To be safe, avoid planting any fruit or nut tree where it may drop a portion of its crop into your pet's area. If your fruit trees are existing, locate the dog's run outside the dripline of the tree canopy.

RED FUJI APPLE (*STARK BROS. NURSERY*)

GRANNY SMITH APPLE (*STARK BROS. NURSERY*)

HOSUI ASIAN PEAR (*STARK BROS. NURSERY*)

SWEET CHERRY (*STARK BROS. NURSERY*)

FIGS (*STARK BROS. NURSERY*)

REDHAVEN PEACH (*STARK BROS. NURSERY*)

BARTLETT PEAR (*STARK BROS. NURSERY*)

Asian Pear, Apple Pear
Suggested varieties:
20th Century, Sinseiki, Hosui.

Cherry
Suggested varieties:
Bing-P, Black Tartanian-P, Craig's Crimson Dwarf, Stella.

Fig
Suggested varieties:
Black Mission, Kadota, Improved Brown Turkey, Coronaria White Mission.

Nectarine
Suggested varieties:
Double Delight, Fantasia, Goldmine, Independence

Peach
Suggested varieties:
Babcock, Elberta, Fantastic Elberta, Frost-L, July, O'Henry, Redhaven, Rio Oso Gem, Strawberry Free. Indian Free (Immune to peach leaf curl.)

Pear
Suggested varieties:
Bartlett, Red Bartlett, Bosk, d'Anjou, Seckel, Comice.

Plum, Prune
Suggested varieties:
Catalina, Elephant Heart-P, Santa Rosa, Satsuma-P. Italian Prune, Stanley Prune.

Persimmon
Suggested varieties:
Giant Fuyu, Apple Persimmon. Hachiya, Acorn Persimmon.

BOSK PEAR (*STARK BROS. NURSERY*)

PLUM (*STARK BROS. NURSERY*)

PRUNE (*STARK BROS. NURSERY*)

BLUEBERRY (*STARK BROS. NURSERY*)

Pomegranate
Suggested varieties:
Wonderful

Walnut
Suggested varieties:
Hartley, English Walnut. Mesa, Carpathian Walnut. Pedro, English Walnut.

BERRIES FOR NORTHERN CALIFORNIA

Blackberry
Blackberry vines are invasive plants that have naturalized throughout the north state. Once established they are difficult to control and gardeners should think twice before introducing them to the cultivated landscape. It's better to plant raspberries in the garden and gather blackberries from wild plants.

Blueberry
Blueberries are woody shrubs and commercial cultivation is limited to Sonoma, Mendocino, and Humboldt counties. Blueberry plants prefer very acid soil (3.5 to 4.5) and moist conditions, with low summer temperatures. Each plant must receive at least an inch of water per week for the first three years. Avoid highbush, and stick with rabbiteye varieties. Blueray is the most heat tolerant and requires no pollinator.

Raspberry
Growing this crop is best in foothill and mountain areas where plants are exposed to sufficiently low winter temperatures. One of the few perennial crops tolerant of winters in the Lake Tahoe area. Raspberries bear fruit on year-old canes which grew the previous summer. To prune, cut back the canes to 4 or 5 feet long and remove the weaker ones entirely. Canes which fruited the previous summer may die back naturally, but if not, they should be removed to make room for new growth. Strive for eight or nine canes per bush. Heritage and Latham are suggested varieties.

Strawberry
You can expect your strawberry plants to bear well for about three years, with the crop growing a bit smaller each season. Many gardeners suggest picking the flowers off your *new* strawberry plants the first year to encourage better stem and leaf growth. Many gardeners cycle their patches adding a few new or "daughter" plants every

spring or fall. Strawberries spread by sending out special stems that take root and become daughter plants. Once rooted they can be detached from the mother plant and transplanted. Garden centers stock the most suitable varieties for the immediate area. Set out new plants from 12 to 14 inches apart in well-drained, humus-rich soil. Mulching with straw or compost is advised. If birds attack the fruit, cover with plastic tree netting for protection.

RUBY RED STRAWBERRY (*STARK BROS. NURSERY*)

GROWING CITRUS IN NORTHERN CALIFORNIA

Citrus trees make great landscape plants, with rich foliage, sweetly fragrant flowers, and colorful fruit. The chief enemy of citrus trees is frost, although many varieties will survive considerably cold winters if planted in a sheltered location. Some of the most cold-tolerant citrus types include Meyer lemon, mandarine orange, naval oranges, and tangelos.

Although evergreen, citrus have a period of rest when temperatures drop below 54°F. During this time the existing leaves and twigs begin to harden off and become more frost tolerant. Do not stimulate plants with fertilizer in late fall or early spring because active growth during this rest period may result in frost damage.

Citrus trees flower on new growth put on during late fall or early spring. Water heavily during the summer for large, juicy fruit. Some citrus varieties bear only every other year. Buy only small, young trees which become established more quickly. Water heavily after planting to prevent leaf drop. Step up watering in hot and/or windy weather by soaking the entire root zone, especially in the first year after planting. Citrus trees are susceptible to bark diseases and mulches should be kept a few inches away from the trunk.

Fertilizers designed for citrus are worth the investment because they contain important magnesium, zinc, and iron along with the usual N-P-K. If starved for nutrients the leaves will clue you in by turning yellow or developing light or dark patterns around the veins. You can fertilize three or four times a year with light dosages according to the instructions on the container label. Scatter the fertilizer evenly beneath the dripline of the tree, but no closer than 6 inches from the trunk. Citrus have shallow roots and the fertilizer must be watered very well to prevent burning. Pruning of citrus is limited to shaping and removal of conflicting, broken, diseased, or dead branches. The bark and trunk are subjected to sunscald if not shaded by low foliage or painted white.

Suggested varieties:
The following varieties are suitable for zones 3 to 7 except in low frost pockets. Some may survive at lower elevations of zone 2 if conditions are right.

Bearss Seedless Lime
Minneola Tangelo
Nagami Kumquat
Eureka Lemon
Meyer Improved Lemon
Dancy Tangerine
Dancy Seedless Tangerine
Kara Mandarin Orange
Satsuma Mandarin Orange
Valencia Orange
Washington Navel Orange

GRAPES IN NORTHERN CALIFORNIA

The art of pruning grapes is a skill that takes time to learn. Since we have so many commercial vineyards in northern California, it helps to visit one and inspect the vines firsthand. Look at vines of different ages to become familiar with how a grape vine should develop over time. If you're lucky there will be a guide eager to describe in detail how the grapes are trained, trellised, and pruned. This is also a great opportunity for a crash course in grape care and feeding. In general, grape vines require only generous watering during the growing season to produce a crop.

WHITE WINE GRAPE (*STARK BROS. NURSERY*)

CONCORD GRAPE (*STARK BROS. NURSERY*)

PLANTING BY THE MOON

Each year the *Farmer's Almanac* lists the dates best for planting crops from seed. These dates are based on phases of the moon, and for a long time was considered an old wives' tale. The rule is to sow seed and transplant only when the moon is waxing, and never under a waning moon.

But new scientific evidence indicates lunar rhythms affect the earth's magnetic field and do influence plant growth. This is because just as the moon turns tides, it also moves the water within plant cells. Another theory is that it is more likely to rain after a full or new moon, and early farmers found germination to be more successful because of the increased moisture at that time. Whatever the reason, you may choose to follow the lead of both ancient and modern day farmers by considering the moon to determine just when to plant your seeds.

Nearly all varieties of grapes grow well in northern California, and the following chart contains just a few of the most popular ones.

GRAPE VARIETIES AND THEIR USES

Name	Color	Use	Seeds
Cabernet Sauvignon	Red	Wine	Yes
Chenin Blanc	Green	Wine	Yes
Concord	Purple	Table/Juice	Yes
Flame Seedless	Red	Table	No
Interlaken Seedless	Green	Table	No
Perlette Seedless	Green	Table	No
Thompson Seedless	Green	Table	No
Zinfandel	Red	Wine	Yes

VEGETABLES SUITABLE FOR NORTHERN CALIFORNIA GARDENS

AAS–All American Selection Winner—Superior Hybrids

Note: Almost all varieties of vegetable plants grow well in California. These are just a few of the many you can grow.

Bush Beans	**Pole Beans**
Bush Kentucky Wonder	Kentucky Blue AAS

Blue Lake
Derby AAS
Topcrop AAS
Romano
Purple Pod
Kentucky Wonder Wax

Beets
Ruby Queen AAS
Detroit Supreme

Brassicas
Hybrid Green Comet Broccoli AAS
Hybrid Premium Crop AAS
Hybrid Jade Cross Brussels Sprouts
Super Snowball Cauliflower AAS
Snowball Self-Blanching Cauliflower

Carrots
Gold-Pack AAS
Thumbelina AAS (miniature)
Tendersweet

Corn
How Sweet It Is Hybrid - White AAS
Silver Queen—White
Early Sunglow—Yellow
Golden Cross Bantam—Yellow
Miracle—Yellow

DERBY POLE BEAN (*ALL AMERICA SELECTIONS*)

KENTUCKY BLUE BUSH BEAN (*ALL AMERICA SELECTIONS*)

THE IMPORTANCE OF MULCHING

Much of the water applied to gardens is wasted as it evaporates off the surface of the soil, or runs off. The best way to make the most of each drop of this precious resource is to mulch kitchen gardens heavily. Mulch layers also discourage weeds, and insulate the ground to help keep plant roots cool and make them less thirsty in the heat.

For a mulch layer to be successful it must be from 3 to 5 inches thick, not just a scattering of material on the surface of the soil. It takes a lot more material than you may think to sufficiently cover the surface of the average garden. Use anything at hand, such as the stems of last year's plants, shredded newspapers, straw, wood chips, and leaves. Keep in mind that at the end of the season these materials can be cultivated into the soil to help lighten its texture for the next season's garden. Avoid using materials that have thorns and those that show signs of fungus mold which may spread to living plants. Also be aware of what kind of seeds the mulch may contain in order to avoid contaminating your garden.

THUMBELINA CARROT (*ALL AMERICA SELECTIONS*)

NORTHERN CALIFORNIA TIP

Broccoli, Brussels sprouts, cabbage, and cauliflower are all members of the genus *Brassica*. These hardy plants are best grown as winter crops here in California because they are sensitive to heat. For gardeners in San Francisco and other places along our foggy north coast, the *Brassicas* are one of the most reliable, year-around crops. Inland, seed is best planted in late summer and will tolerate autumn frosts for harvesting around Christmas. If planted in spring, *Brassicas* will probably bolt and flower much too fast to mature into a good crop. Kohlrabi and turnips are other, less popular *Brassicas* grown as root crops. Those grown for greens include kale, bok-choi, mustard, collards, and a wide variety of Oriental greens.

GOLDEN CROWN HYBRID WATERMELON (*ALL AMERICA SELECTIONS*)

Cucumber
Hybrid Sweet Success Seedless AAS
Straight Eight AAS
Bush Pickle—pickling
Armenian Cucumber
Lemon Cucumber

Eggplant
Hybrid Dusky—Oriental
Millionaire—Oriental
Black Beauty—Bell-Shaped

Greens
Fordhook Giant Swiss Chard
Lucullus Swiss Chard
Burpee's Rhubarb Chard
Dwarf Blue Curled Kale
Green Curled Scotch Kale

Lettuce
Grand Rapids—Looseleaf
Ruby—Bronze looseleaf
Black-Seeded Simpson—Looseleaf
Buttercrunch—Butterhead
Burpee Bibb—Butterhead
Little Gem—Romaine
Parris Island Cos—Romaine
Iceburg—Crisphead
Great Lakes—Crisphead
Ithaca—Crisphead

Melons
Redball Seedless Watermelon
Sugar Baby Watermelon
Crimson Sweet Watermelon
Burpee Hybrid Cantaloupe
Quick Sweet Cantaloupe
Earlidew Honeydew

Onions
Walla Walla Sweet
Yellow Sweet Spanish
Red Torpedo

Peas, Edible Pods
Oregon Sugar Pod II
Sugar Snap AAS
Sugar Ann AAS

Peppers
Hybrid Bell Boy—Sweet Pepper AAS
Hybrid Big Bertha—Sweet Pepper
Hybrid Gypsy Yellow—Bell Sweet Pepper AAS
Super Chili Hybrid—Hot Pepper AAS
Super Cayenne—Hot Pepper AAS
Jalapeño—Hot Pepper

Potatoes
Yukon Gold—Yellow
Red Pontiac—Red
Russet Burbank—Russet

Radishes
Cherry Belle AAS

SUPER CAYENNE HOT PEPPER (*ALL AMERICA SELECTIONS*)

WINTER SQUASH, CREAM OF THE CROP (*ALL AMERICA SELECTIONS*)

A FEW WORDS ABOUT MESCLUN

Mesclun may sound like some kind of psychedelic mushroom but it is really a technique from Italy for using a mixture of salad greens harvested while still very young. In today's terms, it is a great way to utilize the seedlings we pull from rows of lettuce, leaf *Brassicas*, annual herbs, and various exotic greens. You can buy special seed mixes of mesclun which are designated for certain seasons, and each mix offers new and exciting taste combinations. Mesclun seedlings are snipped off at the soil with scissors, washed, and served as a salad. For a regular supply of seedlings, plant new seed each week. Experts say to allow 1 foot of row per salad.

A MANICURED HERB GARDEN.

Champion AAS
White Icicle

Squash, Summer
Black Jack Zucchini
Early Prolific Straightneck AAS—yellow
Scallop Peter Pan Hybrid AAS

Squash, Winter
Waltham Butternut AAS
Tivolia Bush Spaghetti Squash AAS
Bush Acorn Table King AAS
Cream of the Crop AAS

Tomatoes
Hybrid Celebrity AAS
Hybrid Beefmaster
Better Boy
Hybrid Early Girl
Sweetie Cherry Tomato
Roma
Many variety names are followed by the abbreviations V, F, N, or T, which indicates improved resistance to these common diseases that plague tomatoes:

V–Verticillium wilt resistant
F–Fusarium wilt resistant
N–Nematode resistant
T–Tobacco mosaic virus resistant

OREGANO, BASIL, AND OTHER HERBS.

TIPS ON HARVESTING HERBS

Herbs are best harvested when their aromatic oils are at peak levels. Some folks say perennial herbs a bit stressed for water contain less moisture and more concentrated oils. The best time of day to harvest herbs is early in the morning, but after the dew has fully evaporated from the leaves. If done later in the day the leaves may wilt too quickly in the heat. You need not pull the entire annual herb up roots and all. Instead, cut it back severely and continue watering. You may be able to coax a second, but smaller, crop very late in the season if the weather cooperates.

After harvesting, get the herbs indoors as soon as possible, then rinse each kind separately in cool water to clean them off. Shake off the water and spread the plants out on newspaper and work through every stem, removing shriveled leaves, insects, or discolored flowers. Gather the herbs into bunches, tie the stems together, and hang them upside down in a well ventilated, dry place.

GROWING AN HERB GARDEN

There are no great secrets to growing herbs, which are simply annuals and perennials with foliage containing aromatic oils. The leaves can be used strictly for their fragrance, for crafts, or as seasonings. Perennial herbs grow for many years and are permanent plants in the landscape, with attractive foliage and flowers. Annual herbs must be reseeded each year like other flowers and should be treated as a vegetable crop. They are grown and harvested in larger quantities to be dried at the end of the season for winter storage.

An herb garden disguised as landscaping. Plants include thyme, rosemary, and lavender.

THE MOST COMMON HERBS AND HOW THEY GROW

Annuals	Perennials	Biennial
Anise	Aloe vera	Parsley
Basil	Catnip	
Borage	Chives	
Camomile	Garlic	
Cervil	Lavender	
Cilantro	Lemon Balm	
Dill	Lovage	
Fennel	Peppermint	
Marjoram	Spearmint	
Summer Savory	Oregano	
	Rosemary	
	Sages	
	Winter Savory	
	Thymes	

EDIBLE FLOWERS TO GROW IN THE VEGETABLE GARDEN

You may be surprised to discover the flowers of many common annuals and perennials are completely edible. Cooks have used them to add color and unique garnishes to their dishes since medieval times.

Flowers suitable for eating:

Calendula	Nasturtium
Chrysanthemum	Pinks
Scented geraniums	Roses
Lavender	Squash
Viola	

Chapter Thirteen

Appendix

PEST CONTROL

The philosophy of organic gardening is that pesticides kill all insects, both good and bad, and that if predators are killed off, new pests can move in, reproduce unhindered, and pose a greater threat to plants than before pesticides were used.

WHAT MAKES PLANTS VULNERABLE TO INSECTS?

Plants have a natural ability to resist pests and diseases. In fact, some tropical plants contain chemicals so strong they are commercially extracted and used as pesticides. Plants weakened by improper exposure, drought, soggy roots,

FACING PAGE: *STRELITZIA REGINAE*. ABOVE: DAYLILY 'LITTLE MAGGIE' (*DAYLILY DISCOUNTERS*)

overcrowding, lack of fertilizer, and many other factors lose much of their natural resistance. Healthy plants make a more pest free garden.

ASSESSING THE PROBLEM

Inexperienced gardeners overreact to the presence of a few bugs by drenching plants in insecticide. This approach is not only toxic and time consuming, it may not be effective in the long run. You must thoroughly understand what kind of pest you're dealing with, and determine the potential threat *before* taking action.

1. Seeing is preventing.

Knowing how a plant looks when it's healthy helps you distinguish the early signs of invaders, which may be tiny and well camouflaged. Successful gardeners spend a lot of time with their plants and view each as an individual. Like good friends, they gaze at one another closely and wonder if all is well. Prevention by inspection is the best excuse I know for abandoning housework to go out and smell my flowers.

2. Know your enemy.

Identification of the insects you encounter in the garden is the first and most essential step toward pest control. You must be able to distinguish good insects from bad ones, and then decide how to control undesirable species.

3. Assessing the degree of damage.

Once a pest has been identified, the speed and degree of potential damage can be evaluated. For example, a caterpillar can do far more damage in one night than a few aphids. And, a few aphids on growing tips is far less of a problem than an infested plant. Each of these scenarios presents a different degree of damage. The control measure should be selected by how rapidly it becomes effective, how well it controls that specific pest, and the relative toxicity of the material.

CONTROLLING INSECT PESTS USING THE LEAST-TOXIC PROCESS

When a pest problem has been found, identified and the degree of damage considered, the next step is to select a method of control. The least-toxic selection process begins with the most benign methods, but if these do not solve the problem, you can step up to a more potent material. The following list of pest control measures begins with the most benign and increases in toxicity with each number.

1. Manual controls.

Larger insects can be simply picked off the plant and discarded, if there are not to many in the colony. This unpleasant job can be very effective with roving grasshoppers and big caterpillars. Old-time gardeners syringe their plants with a strong jet of water on a regular basis. It literally knocks the bugs off the plant while cleaning the leaf surfaces. Syringe only in the early morning so water can evaporate before the sun hits the foliage.

2. Traps.

Traps are available for a wide variety of insects, as well as for snails and slugs. Some use colors, lights, dark recesses, and even sexual hormone scents (pheromones) to attract the pests. Once inside, the bugs are trapped or stick to a flypaperlike surface. But many feel that traps may lure pests in from places well outside the garden and may actually increase insect populations. Traps must be cleaned or replaced on a regular basis, as the attractant loses its potency over time. Some of the pests may not respond at all to the attractant.

3. Barriers.

The life cycles of some insects require they crawl either up or down a trunk or stem to reproduce. If this migration can be stopped, the insect populations will become smaller. Old-time farmers used molasses, and sometimes added Sevin pesticide to create a sticky substance that was smeared around the trunk. If insects tried to cross, they became stuck. A simple, but ingenious idea that has been commercially marketed under various trade names and has proven very effective for selected insects.

4. Insecticidal soaps.

Detergent diluted and sprayed on plants is an old-time pest-control method that works. Demand for least-toxic controls has promoted sales of commercially prepared insecticidal soap concentrates. They are easy to use, safe, and very effective. Many find these soaps the only pest-control material needed.

5. Horticultural oils.

Oil sprays are mixed with water and applied to plants in a thin film. The film is capable of smothering hard-to-kill scale insects, eggs of many species and even pupae. Oils are used on fruit trees as dormant sprays to kill eggs and small insects overwintering in bark crevices. Oil sprays are either heavy, for winter dormant spraying, or lighter, for use during the growing season. **Caution:** Never use an oil spray on plant leaves when in direct sunlight or when the temperature is over 90°F. Spray in the evening. Read the entire label of your oil spray container before usage, as some plants cannot tolerate them.

6. Biological controls.

This is the area of pest management that the entomologists are so excited about. It is the introduction of predator insects and other organisms to control undesirable insects in the garden. These natural predators are the bugs you don't want to kill with chemical pesticides.

To control destructive caterpillars entomologists came up with nontoxic *Bacillus thuringiensis*, called BT for short. If BT is ingested by caterpillars it causes stomach atrophy followed by a quick death. The material comes in either a wettable powder or a dust that is applied to plants. Renew on a regular basis because it loses potency in just a few days.

7. Botanical controls.

Botanical insecticides are natural, but very potent chemicals extracted from certain tropical plants. Botanicals kill insects on contact and also act as repellants. Most botanicals sold today are broad-spectrum killers, and do away with both undesirable and beneficial insects. Handle these toxic products with care, especially in their concentrated form. Wear protective clothing, eye shields, and a respirator when handling botanicals. The following are the most common botanical insecticides which are packaged in formulas under a variety of trade names.

BOTANICAL INSECTICIDES

Trade name	Comments
Pyrethrum	Fast acting; kills bees and ladybugs.
Rotenone	Highest toxicity to humans and wildlife.
Sabadilla	Broad spectrum; effective only 2 days.
Neem	Repellant and insecticide, okay for beneficials.

8. Baits.

Baits work by attracting pests to the pesticide and are effective on elusive night feeders. Although they contain chemical as well as botanical insecticides, baits concentrate the toxic material in a single location instead of spreading it in a blanket application throughout the garden. If you use baits of any kind, make sure children and pets are unable to access the material.

9. Chemical pesticides.

Chemical pesticides are the "big guns" of the pest control world. Unfortunately, organic aficionados and environmentalists have given these products a bad rap, despite clearances from the EPA. Unusual infestations of pests caused by environmental or manmade factors can do a tremendous amount of damage in a very short time. Unless populations are controlled right away, the garden will decline.

Let's face it, sometimes it's okay to use chemical pesticides. They have been developed over many years of testing, and if used properly, many are no more toxic than some botanical controls. Chemical pesticides are sold in different forms, such as premixed liquids, liquid concentrate, dust and dry granules. **Always read the entire label before using any chemical pesticide, and wear protective clothing when handling these products. Use only as directed.**

RULE OF GREEN THUMB

There is a special relationship between ants and two garden pests: aphids and scale. Both aphids and scale secrete a sticky, sweet substance called honeydew, which is preferred cuisine of ants. Ants will actually farm scale and aphids on your plants to encourage production of honeydew. Whenever ants are present, chances are they've gone into the livestock business. Look much more closely for aphids or scale in order to stop production as soon as possible.

GETTING TO KNOW YOU—COMMON GARDEN PESTS AND BENEFICIALS

Most of the wildlife you find in the garden can be classified either as pests, beneficials, or neutrals, which have no influence on plants one way or another. It's just as important to be able to identify the beneficials as it is the problem bugs.

Beneficials–The Good Guys

These insects serve important roles in the garden scheme, feeding off undesirable species to keep them under control. If you experience repeated bug problems, importing populations of these beneficials can often restore the proper balance of insect life.

• **Green Lacewing** Lacewings are lovely light green insects with large transparent wings. It is the larvae of the lacewing that is the true beneficial, and in that state old-timers often call them aphid lions or aphid wolves because they consume those insects at such an incredible rate.

• **Ladybugs** The family of over three hundred species of ladybugs are notorious for feeding on aphids, but they also eat thrips, leafhoppers, and even scale insects. Ladybug larvae are voracious eaters of aphids and are just as important to have around as the adults. The black larvae are very small, but easily identified by their spiny skin and large orange spots.

• **Praying Mantids** Terrifying to look at, praying mantids are aggressive insects which will attack pests nearly as big as themselves! Omnivorous mantids will also consume beneficial bugs, as well as small reptiles and amphibians.

The Bad Boys of Northern California Gardens

When inspecting plants for signs of trouble, watch closely for these ten most common pests. Fortunately, California has a relatively small number of species capable of significant damage.

ARMYWORM. MAY BE FOUND IN LARGE POPULATIONS THAT FEED OFF LEAVES OF TREES AND SHRUBS. (*DOWELANCO*)

SOD WEBWORM. COMMONLY FOUND IN LAWNS, COMES OUT AT NIGHT TO FEED. CONSUMES ROOTS AND LEAVES OF GRASS PLANTS. (*DOWELANCO*)

CUTWORM. USUALLY ATTACKS ANNUALS AND PERENNIALS, EATS STEMS, LEAVES AND FLOWERS. (*DOWELANCO*)

EARWIG (*DOWELANCO*)

SOW BUG (*DOWELANCO*)

GRASSHOPPER (*DOWELANCO*)

• **Aphids** These fat little insects are the scourge of rose growers, but they can do considerable damage to other types of plants as well. There are many different types of aphids, but most either suck juices out of the backs of leaves, or attack the soft, juicy new growth. A shot of water from the garden hose should discourage them, but if not, try insecticidal soap and then botanicals.

• **Caterpillars** A huge assortment of moths and other insects begin life in the larval stage where they are easily identified as caterpillars. Rather than going into the subtle distinctions between them, it's safe to say they can all disfigure plants and should be controlled just as soon as they appear. Tomato horn worms, armyworms, and cutworms are just a few of the many species. Since the advent of BT, they can be controlled with this single, nontoxic product.

• **Tree borers** Borers are the larvae of beetles, who lay their eggs in damaged bark. The eggs hatch into burrowing grubs that are difficult to control once in the tree, which makes prevention very important. Signs are blistered or loose, peeling bark with a mealy residue underneath. Like cleaning a human wound, you must remove the dead bark and residue. You may find the borer grub, or it may have already exited as an adult beetle. Clean and seal the wound with latex paint and make sure the tree bark is protected from sunscald to prevent further blistering.

• **Spider mites** Spider mites prefer our hot, dry weather and first appear on dusty leaves or those lower on the plant. They suck from the backs of the leaves, resulting in a silvering of the front side. Look for tiny black or red speckles as well as very fine, weblike filaments. Wash leaves frequently to control them.

• **Scale** Scale is an insect that lives beneath its own protective half-shell (like an abalone), which is attached to the leaves or twigs of a plant. Their favorite meal is citrus, holly, and olive trees, but they will appear on other species as well. Oil sprays have been the most successful in eradicating these pests, but you can also try insecticidal soaps timed at regular intervals to disrupt the reproductive cycle.

• **Slugs and snails** Northern California is big-league banana slug country. These monsters can reach nearly 5 inches long and will consume enough vegetation each day to equal 35 percent of their body weight. Big slugs require big solutions.

There are volumes of information on controlling garden snails because they do so much damage, yet there is still no single surefire trick. Bait laced with chemicals is the traditional control material, but the danger to children, pets, and wildlife is a problem. Organic gardeners have cooked up a whole slew of unique ideas:

Barriers prevent these soft-bodied pests from crossing without wounding themselves. Use them around individual plants or planting areas, and replace frequently in rainy weather. Good materials are dry, sharp, or caustic, such as lime, marble dust, crushed oyster shells, diatomaceous earth, fireplace ashes, egg shells, and sawdust.

Traps are simply containers filled with a liquid bait that also drowns the snail. A pie tin, the bottoms of a gallon milk jug or anything else that holds the water can be used for the trap. Bury it up to the rim in the soil then fill with potent malt liquor. You must check the trap each day to renew the bait and clean out the dead bodies.

Hides take advantage of the slug's or snail's need to retreat to a cool, dark, moist place during the daytime. Suitable hides are simply boards raised above the ground about 1/2 inch with twigs or pebbles. You can use two boards on top of one another but slightly separated for a high density duplex. Make them more attractive by moistening between layers and smashing a few snail bodies for a grotesque, but effective bait.

• **Earwigs (aka pincher-bugs)** Earwigs have slender, flat bodies with noticeable pinchers on the tail. They can be a serious problem some years, when populations explode for no particular reason. These bugs slide into heads of greens and also slip into flower buds to wreak havoc, eating leaves, petals, and even stems. The best control is with poisoned baits, which work quickly and efficiently. Old-timers set out wet rags around the garden in the evening so the earwigs will hide in them. During the day they dip the rags in a pail of warm, soapy water to release the earwigs hiding there.

• **Sow bugs, aka pill bugs** Sow bugs are those little armadillo-like bugs that roll up into pea-sized balls when disturbed. Like earwigs, sow bugs feed on decaying organic matter, but also attack seedlings and other plants with fine surface-root systems.

• **Whiteflies** Whiteflies are a big problem for commercial growers because they tend to infest greenhouse environments, and also are a problem for houseplants in general. When purchasing any new plant, shake it to see if tiny white flies come out from under the leaves. If so, put it back and seek out a healthier plant. Since whiteflies reproduce so prodigiously, controls such as insecticidal soap or botanicals require repeated applications to become fully effective.

• **Grasshoppers** In our northern California grasslands and foothill chaparral belts, grasshoppers can create damage in gardens. They are totally mobile and will feed heavily for a day and then move on. Grasshoppers are most vulnerable early in the morning, before they warm up and get active. There is a biological parasite called *Nosema locustae* that works like a BT for grasshoppers. Or if you know an avid fisherman, perhaps he or she will come by and liberate you from whatever grasshoppers are still around.

ANIMAL AND WILDLIFE PESTS

Insects aren't the only ones that plague northern California gardeners. Pesky rodents and wildlife can be far more difficult to control than bad bugs.

Know Your Garden Wildlife

Many kinds of animals, reptiles and amphibians are beneficial to gardens and should be treated with care. Your goal should be to encourage their residence despite your feelings toward organisms that aren't soft and fuzzy.

Battling the Big Three: Deer, Rabbits, and Gophers

Northern California gardeners are bothered most by three major offenders: deer, rabbits, and gophers. All are very difficult to get rid of, and there are endless old wives' tales concerning control measures.

• **Deer** The wild deer herds in many parts of our state have been growing larger because hunting is forbidden in developing areas. Deer easily adapt to life in rural subdivisions like Lake Wildwood in the Sierra foothills, where herds are enormous. Hungry deer think nothing of invading a garden to ruin it overnight. Bucks can seriously damage tree bark as they rub the felt off their antlers. Few problems are as discouraging to gardeners because there is little that can be done except to plant only deer-resistant species, build expensive fencing, and experiment with repellants.

Deer are fickle creatures and their dietary habits will vary in different parts of the north state. A plant considered deer-proof inland may be immediately eaten in coastal areas. Lists of deer resistant plants aren't foolproof and investments in "resistant" species may be futile. As a general rule, California native plants can be less

GARDEN TREES AND SHRUBS TEMPORARILY PROTECTED BY INDIVIDUAL CAGES CONSTRUCTED OF WIRE FIELD FENCING.

ATTRACTIVE, DEER-PROOF FENCE USES A CANTILEVERED DESIGN TO WIDEN THE AREA OF THE FENCE. THE ARBOR OVER THE GATEWAY, AND THE WIRE ARCH ON TOP OF THE GATE DISCOURAGES DEER FROM LEAPING OVER THE GATE, WHICH IS NOT CANTILEVERED.

THE GOODS AND BADS OF GARDEN WILDLIFE

Animal	Good Qualities	Bad Qualities
Lizards	Eat bugs	
California King Snake	Eats rodents Eats bugs Colorful	
Gopher Snake	Eats rodents Eats bugs	Looks like rattler
Toad, Tree Frog	Eat bugs	
Mole	Eats bugs in soil	Damages plants
Skunk	Eats bugs in soil	Stinks! Digs up lawns
Squirrels	Lots of fun	Eats seed from bird feeders
Birds	Eats bugs	Eat fruit from orchard trees Stain pavement.
Deer	Beautiful	Eats almost everything. Difficult to deter. Damage tree bark as bucks rub felt from horns.

desirable than the juicy ornamental plants used in landscaping today.

The theory behind deer repellent materials is often misunderstood. Deer are nervous animals and rely on their sense of smell to warn them of danger. Potent odors overwhelm this olfactory warning system and the deer will not hang around to feed. As the odor of the deterrent loses its kick, the deer will return.

Deer repellents are sold commercially, but there are a whole slew of common materials that can be used, although their effectiveness will vary. Common materials include: moth balls, house cat fur, cougar scent, bloodmeal, and bonemeal. Rags soaked in creosote and attached to the ends of stakes at "nose" height can be placed at various points throughout the garden. If they lose their smell, simply dip the end of each stick into a bucket of creosote and replace it in the ground.

Far more expensive, the ultimate solution is deer fencing. Fortunately the "concentration camp" look is out in favor of shorter, but even more effective fence designs.

Individual trees and shrubs can be protected with tubes of small-mesh, stiff-wire fencing. Although not attractive, this is sufficient to get trees established until they grow tall enough to survive a mild browsing of the lower leaves.

Experts have determined deer can leap very high, but not wide. As a result, two less drastic designs have proven effective: the double fence and the cantilevered fence. Double fencing is simply the construction of two parallel fences 4 feet high, separated by 4 feet. This space is too wide for deer to jump over and the fences are too close together to allow a double jump. They don't have to be very strong, just sturdy to enough present a barrier. Most people use wire field fencing and metal 'T' posts.

Cantilevered fencing is more difficult to build.It consists of a 4-foot-tall fence shaped like an upside down 'L'. The arms must project out 4 feet and require bracing at the posts.

• **Rabbits** Jackrabbits and cottontails can become real problems because they eat almost anything green and rapidly overpopulate. When very hungry they kill trees and shrubs by gnawing the bark. This kind of damage is easily mistaken for gouges from string trimmers and mowers.

Farmers solve the problem by arranging rabbit hunts when populations become too large and begin damaging crops. Early morning and late evening are the best time to catch rabbits in the act. Individual trees and shrubs can be protected with 12-inch to 24-inch-tall collars of plastic pipe around the trunk. Be sure to replace the collars as trees grow larger to prevent girdling. Vegetable gardens must be fenced with small mesh chicken wire to a height of about 2 feet above ground, with the bottom edge buried a few inches under the soil. The chicken wire can be attached to an existing fence to make it more rabbit proof.

• **Gophers** Next to deer, gophers are the worst problem facing any gardener. Gophers literally tunnel under a plant, grab it by the roots and yank it down into the hole, leaving nothing behind. Mounds of earth excavated by gophers as well as depressions from collapsed tunnels can seriously disfigure lawns. The shallow tunnels of moles are often mistaken for those of gophers, which burrow through the soil at a much deeper level.

Garden areas can be protected by barriers of buried sheet metal or fine metal mesh buried around the perimeter. Gophers will not tunnel through the poison roots of narcissus bulbs and they will form a barrier when planted close together. Some folks make baskets of aviary wire and install them around and beneath each new plant. If the basket is made too shallow or planted too deeply, gophers will go over the top to reach plant roots.

Gophers already in the garden and threatening plants must be caught or killed. Don't bother trying to flood them out because gophers design their dens well above the water level in their tunnels. Trapping gophers is

A CLOSE-UP OF THE DEER-PROOF FENCE SHOWING HOW WIRE FIELD FENCING HAS BEEN SECURED ON TOP OF THE CANTILEVERED PORTION.

A UNIQUE PICKET FENCE WITH DEER AND RABBIT CONTROL IN MIND. THE TALL PICKETS ARE CONNECTED WITH WIRE TO DISCOURAGE DEER FROM JUMPING OVER THE TOP. THE TIGHTLY SPACED PICKETS AT THE BASE PREVENT RABBITS FROM ENTERING THE GARDEN.

EARLY AMERICAN PIONEERS PROTECTED THEIR VEGETABLE GARDENS WITH RUSTIC PALING FENCES OF HAND-SPLIT WOOD. THE FORERUNNER OF OUR COUNTRY PICKET FENCES, IT WAS EFFECTIVE IN KEEPING LIVESTOCK AS WELL AS RABBITS AND OTHER PESTS OUT OF THE GARDEN.

STILL RUSTIC, BUT USING MILLED LUMBER, THIS FENCE HAS TIGHTLY SPACED PICKETS EFFECTIVE FOR KEEPING RABBITS OUT OF THE GARDEN.

a fine art, and pronged gopher traps are the most effective, although box traps work well too. Don't be surprised if you aren't successful with traps because they need to be set in the freshest tunnel in just the right way and then carefully camouflaged.

There are even more old wives' tales about gophers than there are for deer. If trapping doesn't work, try commercial gopher bombs, which can be set off in the runners to gas gophers in their lairs. Poison bait is also a possibility, but it can be dangerous to children and pets as well as other wildlife. Other unusual options are to insert granules of calcium carbide into the hole and seal it up. The carbide reacts with the soil moisture to create toxic gasses. If you are at your wits' end over gopher problems, don't feel bad, there are many other people who also struggle with the problem. For help, contact your nearest University of California Agricultural Extension office, farm advisor or county agricultural commissioner.

MONTH BY MONTH GARDENING GUIDE

The difference between a so-so gardener and one who is considered a green thumb is the amount of attention and nurturing given to each plant. Gardens are not static, but gradually mature to change the character of the surrounding spaces. Trees grow larger to increase shade, shrubs fill out, perennials thicken into clumps, and soil beneath the lawn becomes compacted. Dealing with this constantly evolving environment is what gardening is all about.

Like any other challenge, the first step towards orderly gardening is to break all activities down into individual tasks. These tasks can be organized by the season or month during which they occur most frequently. Tasks such as pulling weeds or raking leaves are strictly clean-up, which must be done promptly or the job becomes more difficult.

It is important that this guide not be taken as absolute gardening law. Our northern California climate can be fickle, with false springs in February and late snows in May. Use common sense, and watch the weather patterns in order to adjust for regional differences or climate variations.

SEASONAL OVERVIEW

In order to help gardeners see the big picture of the entire gardening year, the following overview covers the most general tasks according to season. This also acts as a quick reference to aid in purchasing materials and equipment before they are needed.

Winter
-Bare-root season
-Prune deciduous trees, shrubs, and vines
-Repair and service hand and power tools
-Select and order seed for vegetables and annuals
-Dormant spray fruit trees
-Improve soil
-Construction projects, weather permitting
-Renovate turf
-Transplant trees and shrubs
-Winter prune roses
-Sow hardy annuals
-Turn compost pile

Spring
-Start seed of tender annuals indoors
-Plant all container stock
-Plant hardy perennials
-Plant vegetables and annual color
-Repair winter damage
-Prune old roses after flowering
-Plant lawns
-Begin fertilizer applications
-Plant summer bulbs
-Cut flowering wood on roses
-Turn compost pile

Summer
-Fertilize plants and lawn
-Water heavily in hot weather
-Order spring bulbs
-Prune dead wood from evergreen trees and shrubs
-Cut flowering wood on roses
-Turn compost pile

Fall
-Plant California natives
-Plant all container stock
-Leaf clean-up
-Plant winter vegetable garden
-Plant hardy perennials
-Dig summer bulbs and divide
-Plant spring bulbs
-Divide perennials
-Turn compost pile

MONTHLY GARDEN GUIDE

January

January in northern California is time for bare-root planting, sowing of hardy annuals, pruning, soil improvement, and sprinkler repair. In drier years, landscapers will be planting gardens right through the winter, pausing only when the soil is too wet and unworkable. Plants under eaves of buildings may be denied rainwater because of their sheltered location and should be watered. Wet, rainy days soften the soil and make weed pulling much easier.

LAWNS Lawns grow slowly and require only an occasional mowing to remain tidy. Beware of foot traffic or vehicles which compact wet soil beneath lawns, especially heavy clay.
TREES Prune deciduous trees while fully dormant. Buy and plant bare-root trees. Apply dormant sprays to fruit trees. Transplant young trees now, while sap is low.
SHRUBS Prune only late-flowering deciduous shrubs, which include: rose of Sharon, hydrangea, and spiraea. Keep the flowers of camellias picked up to control petal blight. Transplant evergreen or deciduous shrubs. Plant new bare-root or container-grown shrubs, including camellias, azaleas and rhododendrons.
VINES Cut back deciduous vines while bare. Remove accumulations of dead wood beneath the foliage of evergreen vines. Prune grapes and berries.
GROUNDCOVER Keep all weeds pulled or hoed off to reduce the number of seedlings in spring. Pull weeds in wet weather while ground is soft.
PERENNIALS If soil isn't too wet, divide larger clumps of perennials while they are dormant, then replant. Plant hardy perennials. Cultivate, add fertilizer and amendments to soil around perennial plants. Kill grubs found in newly turned soil. Inspect and remove all dead leaves and stems. Plant lilies, primroses, ranunculus, bleeding heart, and peony.
ANNUALS Sow seed of hardy annual flowers such as poppies and wildflowers which require low soil temperatures to germinate. Plant hardy winter garden vegetables. Plant pansies, violas, snapdragons, and other winter annuals in sheltered planters with sufficient sunlight.
ROSES Plant bare-root roses. Transplant dormant roses. Winter-prune all tea roses. Turn soil with a spading fork to expose and kill eggs of garden pests. Apply dormant sprays.
IRRIGATION SYSTEMS Make repairs while not in use. Clean, repair, or replace filters on drip systems. Adjust automatic watering times and frequency; turn off entirely in rainy weather.
TOOLS Take power tools in for annual servicing. Replace and repair hand tools, oil all moving parts. Sharpen or replace pruning tools *before* winter pruning.
GENERAL TASKS Protect marginal, frost-tender plants from nights of deeper frost. Turn the compost pile. Order seeds from catalogs for spring vegetable garden. Cultivate and improve all garden soil.

February

During this month we gain an hour and ten minutes of daylight. The last day of February ends bare-root season, and all plants should be in the ground, or planting should be delayed another year. Beware of false spring and avoid the temptation to planting tender bedding plants too early.

LAWNS In drier areas, lawns can be renovated while conditions are still cool and moist. Thatch and aerate lawns. Overseed and top-dress with sand or humus.
TREES Complete all pruning of deciduous trees. Apply slow-release fertilizer, and mulch young saplings.
SHRUBS Prune early flowering shrubs back 1/2 or 1/3 of overall size after blooming. Bring the cuttings with flower buds indoors and they will bloom.
VINES Plant sweet pea vines from seed.
GROUNDCOVERS Weed bare areas and apply a thick mulch to discourage more seedlings.
PERENNIALS Complete divisions and replant. Plant hardy perennials: coreopsis, candytuft, sweet William, chrysanthemum, and dianthus. Plant summer bulbs in well-drained soil: canna, lilies, sparaxis, watsonia, gladiola, dahlia, ranunculus, and allium. Provide stakes when planting taller varieties. Spring bulbs should be in full bloom by now.
ANNUALS Sow seed of hardy annuals and veggies. In warmer areas plant seedlings of viola, pansy, snapdragon, English daisy, and fairy primrose. Start seed of tender annuals indoors. Construct trellises for vegetable vines. Begin cultivation and improvement of soil in annual beds.
ROSES Complete dormant winter pruning. Apply dormant sprays for insects and fungus. Turn soil deeply with tiller or spading fork and improve with manure or humus if not too wet.
IRRIGATION SYSTEMS Make final repairs and adjustments before weather begins to warm up. Readjust watering times on automatic timer as temperatures rise. Don't forget to turn the system off in rainy weather.
TOOLS Sharpen mower blades. Complete winter service and repair. Restock string trimmer line, motor oil, two cycle engine oil, and buy fresh gasoline. Clean, repair, and repaint power equipment.
GENERAL Work all winter mulches into soil. Stockpile spring and summer mulching materials.

March

This is the month of the spring equinox, when both night and day are of equal length. Spring officially begins in March with the first warm days. Coastal gardens and those subject to inland tule fog may have difficulties with mildew, which is stimulated by cool nights and warmer days.

LAWN Complete all winter damage repair caused by soil compaction, overly wet conditions, and erosion. Renovate, overseed, and top-dress. Begin fertilizing with a mild application while growth is slow. Good time to use herbicide treated fertilizer to stop broadleaf weeds early.
TREES AND SHRUBS Plant container stock. Inspect for early signs of fungus diseases. Fertilize and begin shearing hedges. Make sure all newly planted bare-root trees are well staked. Trim off faded flowers of azaleas, camellias, and rhododendrons to prevent seed formation and encourage a tighter branching structure.
VINES As new growth occurs, train vines to get foliage and flowers where you want them by summer. Repair or replace trellises that may have been damaged during winter. Continue to plant early spring vegetable vines and sweet peas.
GROUNDCOVERS Ideal conditions for filling gaps in existing plantings with rooted cuttings from flats.
PERENNIALS Plant perennials grown indoors from seed or nursery-grown seedlings. Mulch to keep soil moist. Provide stakes for taller varieties when planting to avoid damaging roots. Divide chrysanthemums and take cuttings to root into new plants. Divide old clumps of hardy perennials like phlox, delphinium, asters, Shasta daisy, and rudbeckia after they bloom. Pinch back perennials to encourage compact branching. If no late frosts are expected, bring fuchsias out of storage and begin watering. As spring-flowering bulbs fade, don't cut back the foliage, but fertilize instead.
ANNUALS In warmer zones, tender annual flowers and vegetables may be planted out but beware of unexpected late frosts. Mulch plantings for weed control. Continue to plant winter crops while weather is still cool.
ROSES Spray every 7 to 10 days with insecticide and fungicide to reduce blackspot and mildew. Avoid watering foliage late in the day. Apply mild dose of fertilizer. Remove suckers or damaged, diseased, and unruly canes.
IRRIGATION Step up watering times as needed, depending on weather. Make sure newly planted bare-root trees and shrubs receive sufficient water in well-drained soils, especially during the first hot days. Beware of root rot in clay, where poor drainage may be hidden beneath the dry surface. Check drip system filters.
TOOLS Oil and repair fertilizer spreader *before* filling with material.
GENERAL Clean all organic debris out of water gardens and repot aquatic species. Put out bait or create traps for snails, slugs, and earwigs before populations increase. Continue to watch for cold nights, and supply protection for tender plants which will be pushing new growth.

April

If we are lucky, there will be plenty of mild weather and April showers to get the garden off to a vigorous start. A perfect month to plant just about everything except at higher mountain elevations. Beware of fungus diseases if rains and fog are plentiful. Weed on rainy days, and cultivate soil to reduce compaction and cracking when it dries out later. Keep up with weeding; this is the point of no return. Either get rid of them or fight 'em the rest of the season.

LAWNS Turf will begin to feed heavily as the days grow longer. The best time to aerate or renovate. Keep up the fertilizer applications at full strength and mow frequently. Watch for lawn fungus diseases or moss growth in shade.
TREES AND SHRUBS Replace weed barrier fabric that has rotted or torn. Renew mulches while soil is damp, and water deeply. Prune all early-flowering shrubs when they're through blooming: forsythia, quince, and lilac. Plant container-grown trees and shrubs. Mulch acid-loving plants with conifer or oak leaves, and pinch back azaleas.
VINES Grapevines will need some guidance depending on the type of trellis system. Direct growth of all vines and prune off runners which cannot be properly trained.
PERENNIALS Watch for insects and make sure soil is cultivated or mulched. Plant summer bulbs in higher elevations. Tie the remaining foliage of spring bulbs in knots or bundle with rubber bands. Plant all types of perennials. Stake and tie plants loosely before they fall over and break the stems.
ANNUALS Begin planting tender annuals from nursery stock or those started indoors. Cut back violas. Fertilize winter annuals for renewed vigor. Begin regular inspection and picking of spent flowers to keep plants blooming. Nip back the growing tips of zinnias, African marigolds, and other cutting flowers for stronger branching and more blooms. Keep up with weeding the vegetable garden; cultivate and mulch heavily. Seed annuals directly into garden soil which should be warming by now.
ROSES Old rose varieties and species with a single bloom season should be cut back after they quit flowering. Prune flowering wood on repeat blooming roses. April begins the season of heavy feeding and all roses will need plenty of fertilizer and deep watering. Watch for aphids and fungus diseases. Cultivate often and mulch to keep in moisture.
IRRIGATION Continue to adjust watering times with changes in weather. Check coverage to minimize runoff. Clean drip system filters and check emitters for clogs. Provide extra water to new trees planted in lawns. Repair catch basins of plants on slopes.
TOOLS Give the underside of the lawn mower a good cleaning and sharpen the blade. Check oil levels on all power equipment. Sharpen hoe to make weeding easier.
GENERAL Repair or replace weed barrier fabric as needed. Keep up with applying mulches so they are in place by the time summer arrives. Renew insect and snail baits.

May

Summer is just around the corner and it's time to get all the planting completed to beat the heat. This month marks the last of the frost-prone days at higher elevations. All vegetables and flowers should be in the ground. If a vacation is planned, make sure the garden will be well cared for while you're away. Don't discover a sprinkler malfunction after you return to dead plants. Coastal gardens are subject to mildew with the lingering fogs of early summer.

LAWNS Keep lawns evenly watered and mow frequently. Fertilize every 4 to 6 weeks. Watch for signs of lawn moth.
TREES AND SHRUBS Construct watering basins for trees and shrubs less than 2 years old, and water deeply with the garden hose to promote deep rooting. Apply sticky rings around American elms and other species subject to elm leaf beetle. Inspect shrubs for signs of mildew, aphids, or scale.
VINES Keep up on training vines because they will be growing rapidly by now. Thin branches where growth is too dense to expose leaves to even lighting.
PERENNIALS Many perennials will bloom a second time in the fall if they are trimmed and fertilized after the first flowering. Make a second planting of gladioli bulbs for late-summer cutting flowers.
ANNUALS Continue to pick off dead flowers and fertilize often with liquid based products. Sow short-term vegetables at regular intervals to insure a continual crop. Stake cutting flowers.
ROSES As the last of the seasonal roses finishes blooming, make sure to cut back canes and encourage new growth for next year's flowers. Use spading fork to turn over the soil and reduce crusting if plants aren't mulched. Don't underestimate how much fertilizer a large, established plant needs. Stay on top of mildew and blackspot. Train new canes of climbing roses while they are young and still flexible.
IRRIGATION Check all drip emitters. Warm weather promotes algae growth around emitter orifices and will clog them up. Remove end plug from drip and micro-spray systems; flush the main lines. Clean out filters. Fine-tune watering times, especially on sloping turf with increased runoff. Double check fixed risers and micro-spray heads to make sure plant growth hasn't blocked coverage.
GENERAL Watch for insects this time of year and have some insecticidal soap on hand for quick applications. Beware of roving grasshoppers; save them for the chickens. Hot days mean potted plants dry out much quicker and may require water every day.

June

The twenty-first of June marks the summer solstice and the longest day of the year. These are the heydays of destructive larvae that consume whole flowers overnight. California gardens are starting to bake, and unmulched soil will turn hard as concrete when it dries out. If you are planning a short vacation, water all plants deeply with the garden hose as extra insurance.

LAWNS Continue to fertilize on a regular schedule. Make sure the edges and corners of lawns which contact hot paving are receiving enough water. Watch closely for excessive runoff and aerate if necessary. Thoroughly clean mower after cutting lawns which contain bermuda.

TREES AND SHRUBS Mulch acid-loving plants with pine needles or oak leaves. Add iron chelate or bloodmeal if chlorosis is a problem. Cut off remainders of spent blossoms on lilacs and other late-flowering shrubs. Wash down plants very early in the morning to reduce dust buildup and brighten leaf color. Cut off suckers and water sprouts on trees and shrubs to keep growth energy where you want it. Make sure young trees planted in lawns are receiving enough water.

VINES Remove seed pods from flowering vines to send growth energy into the foliage. Overhead watering in bright sunlight can cause leaf burn on ivy and similar foliage vines. Give vines growing in paving pockets a deep soaking.

GROUNDCOVERS Heat reflected off dry soil can burn tender new groundcover seedlings and discourages established plants from spreading out. Mulch bare soil and water frequently to entice groundcovers into new territory.

PERENNIALS As lily-of-the-nile, daylilies, and red-hot poker flowers fade, remove the long stems by cutting them off close to the foliage clump. Transplant succulents and cacti now while soil is dry, to prevent rotting. Cut back gamolepis and euryops daisies to encourage more foliage. Plant new perennials in shade gardens. Take care to stake tall dahlias, and for more massive blooms cut off lateral stems and their buds.

ANNUALS Annuals may still be planted, but very hot days makes it difficult get them off to a strong start. Take cutting flowers from annual plants to encourage more horizontal branching and new blooms and apply fertilizer on a regular basis. Watch for bugs and caterpillars, or ants, which indicate there may be aphids or scale insects nearby. Thin seedlings of annuals sown directly into garden soil.

ROSES Feed roses at 6-week intervals and water frequently to encourage repeated blooming. Prune back the last seasonal bloomers when the flowers fade. Keep flowering wood on both shrubs and climbers cut back, and reward yourself for the effort with fresh bouquets. Continue watching for fungus diseases and aphids. Cut off suckers from rootstocks. If strong new canes appear, make room for them by thinning older branches, which they will replace. Train new canes on climbing varieties to the proper angle while they are still new and supple.

IRRIGATION In very hot weather, use the garden hose to deeply soak new plants or those which show signs of weakening from the heat. Double-check drip-system emitters and filters. Be attentive to outdoor potted plants, as they require lots more water in the heat.

TOOLS Keep the compressed-air sprayer clean. If gasoline for power tools has been sitting for a few months, dispose of it and refill the gas can with fresh, high octane fuel. This also applies to two cycle oil-gasoline mixture.

GENERAL Do away with weeds this month before they go to seed. Do not place weeds with seed heads into the compost pile. Make weeding easier by soaking the soil thoroughly a day or two before, so that the roots come out intact and are less likely to remain behind to sprout again. Attack shrubby weeds with herbicide now while they are actively growing.

July

This month marks the middle of the summer, and with it comes the hot north winds that dry plants out very quickly. If there is insufficient water in the soil, plants may defoliate and even die. Water, water, water. It can be tough to tell whether California natives are stressed or just resting. When in doubt, dig a little hole to assess soil moisture. Also watch rock garden plants where stones and masonry can absorb so much heat they burn tender plants nearby.

LAWNS Allow the lawn to grow a bit longer than normal to reduce surface evaporation. If your gardening time is limited by vacations and family outings, make sure to water well and continue feeding.

TREES AND SHRUBS Transplant palms while conditions are dry enough to discourage root rot. To speed up growth, deep water all trees with a trickle from the hose. Watch for signs of insects: black residue of honeydew, unusual leaf drop, skeletonized or spotted leaves. Plane trees may be showing signs of mildew and anthracnose; call a professional to spray large specimens. Prune summer-flowering deciduous shrubs after they stop blooming, then water and feed. Keep fruit cleaned up beneath trees to discourage fruit flies. Inspect trunks for signs of sunscald, and protect with white trunk paint or wrap susceptible areas.

VINES Arrange vine runners while they are still short enough to work with. Nip back longer runners to stop end growth and encourage side shoots which will bear more leaves and flowers. Pick off seed pods.

GROUNDCOVERS Keep weed mulches renewed and soil moist enough to promote spreading. Shade or provide extra water for new seedlings. Pull weeds before they set seed and become a problem.

PERENNIALS As late-flowering varieties come into bloom, tie stalks securely to support stakes and do not water from overhead. Continue to pinch back side shoots on dahlias for larger flowers. As bearded iris finish blooming, the thick rhizomes may be dug, divided, and replanted. Feed peonies and gladiolus well. Lift all early spring bulbs as foliage finally dies back. Divide new bulblets and store in a cool dry place.

ANNUALS Midsummer apathy strikes with high temperatures, but don't let all your efforts go to waste. Now is when serious gardeners go to work on their annuals.

Make a point of spending some time in the cool of the evening or morning picking off dead flowers, pulling weeds, cultivating crusty soil, fertilizing and watering generously. Caterpillars can be especially devastating if uncontrolled. Remove the remains of winter and early spring annuals killed off by the hot weather.

ROSES Continue to feed roses, water deeply and thoroughly. Dig a basin around the base of each plant in order to concentrate watering directly above the root zone. Cut flowering wood on a regular basis and remove stems thinner than a pencil. Watch for insects and signs of fungus. Cultivate, then mulch well to cool roots and retain soil moisture.

IRRIGATION In hot or windy weather, set sprinklers to go on in the early morning or late evening to reduce evaporation. High winds may leave some parts of the lawn dry and will need additional hand watering to prevent brown spots. Add new drip emitters to shrubs that have grown larger in the last six months. Check heads, emitters, filters, and watering times often. During extreme hot spells, use the garden hose for spot applications. Double check for unnecessary lawn water runoff. Take advantage of household gray water which contains phosphorus and nitrogen in small enough quantities to act as a light fertilizer.

TOOLS Resharpen mower blade. Check pulley belts and hoses for cracking. Check oil consumption in all power tools. Sharpen hoe to make weeding easier.

GENERAL Add or renew mulches in all planting areas. It's best to apply mulches after cultivating and watering to seal in moisture.

August

These dog days of late summer are the time for county fairs and bountiful harvests. Inspect the exhibits on flowers, fruit, and vegetables for inspiration. Demonstration gardens at the California State Fair in Sacramento are very instructive, showing how to properly grow a variety of crops and flowers. While most seasonal gardeners are burned out by the heat, the true believers are actively seeking out sources of materials for next year's mulches and soil improvement. Serious planters of bulbs are ordering their large quantities through mail order catalogs.

LAWNS Make sure all parts of the lawn are watered thoroughly, especially those next to very hot paving. Aerate and renovate entire lawn if soil is compacted and shedding water faster than it can be absorbed. As solar orientation changes, new areas will receive more or less sun, and watering should reflect these changes. Apply weed control fertilizers to discourage bermuda grass while it is still actively growing. If a new fall lawn is planned, begin to gather up the tools and supplies needed to do the work. For fall overseeding of existing lawns, a late summer aeration or thatching is advised before planting.

TREES AND SHRUBS Trim and shape woody shrubs. Native oaks are beginning to show some leaf change. In cold winter areas of zone 1, avoid encouraging new growth at this time which may be subject to winter frost damage. Continue to cut off spent flower stems from crape myrtle. Keep rotted fruit cleaned up beneath trees. Wildlife drawn to the fermented fruit may become intoxicated.

PERENNIALS Cut back all perennials after they are finished blooming. Stake late gladiolus, and after blooming, feed and water well to nutrify the corm for next year. Continue to feed peonies. Stake chrysanthemums if they want to lie down. Begin new perennials from seed for late fall planting.

ANNUALS To renew annuals that are fading, cut off the weaker branches and flowers, then feed, water, and mulch. Many vegetable plants can be coaxed to bear well into winter if not neglected in late summer. Don't fall prey to late summer malaise, but apply your efforts toward fall and winter planting.

ROSES In zone 1 it's best to begin slowing down roses so they don't put on growth prone to frost damage. In warmer areas, roses will bloom through the early frosts and need plenty of food and water until then. Remove weak growth so the main framework wood hardens off before winter. Place orders for bare-root roses now.

IRRIGATION Continue with summer maintenance and checking of all drip system emitters. Inspect all standard heads adjacent to paved areas, as vehicles may have crushed heads, risers, or underground fittings. Watch for the telltale signs of breaks such as over-wet areas or silty buildup.

GENERAL Toward the end of the season plants have less resistance to insect pests. Keep a sharp eye out and dispose of infested plants quickly so others nearby are not invaded. Spray for insects wherever possible while populations are still small and controllable.

September

This is the month of the fall equinox and harvest moon. Trees are showing a few autumn highlights as the night temperatures begin to cool. Vegetable gardens are still bearing heavily in most areas and the latest flowers are beginning to bloom. Now is the time to begin preparing for winter by ordering bare-root plants, and planting early spring bulbs. Clean up the garden to reduce the amount of rubbish where insects can hide to overwinter. Do not allow weeds to go to seed now or they will be a nuisance next spring.

LAWNS The last chance to attack invasions of bermuda grass with herbicide while it is actively growing. Reseed or sod bare spots and plant new lawns. Stop using the mulching mower now. If any discolored patches show up, consult with the garden center expert on diagnosis and treatment.

TREES AND SHRUBS Trees and shrubs are slowing down for their winter rest period. Inspect deciduous plants and remove dead wood. This month begins the best season for planting California native trees and shrubs. Don't forget they need deep watering the first two years to encourage deep rooting. Prepare for winter bare-root planting by digging holes and amending soil ahead of time. Rake leaves as they fall and add to a leaf-mould corral or compost pile along with nitrogen fertilizer. Leaves left on lawns in damp weather not only shelter unwanted pests but can also rot the grass plants beneath them.

GROUNDCOVER Plant slopes so the winter rains will help plants become established before summer. Hydroseed mixes of slope-stabilizing plants may be applied now if there is an irrigation system to hold them over until the rains come. If no system is in place, hydroseed later in winter.

PERENNIALS Dig up the last of the summer bulbs and store them for the winter. Last chance to divide and replant iris. Order tender bulbs so they are delivered in time for late spring planting. Plant early-spring-flowering bulbs such as daffodils and crocus. Protect tulip bulbs from moles and gophers with baskets made of woven wire. Cut down hollyhock stalks and save the seed to broadcast for naturalized spring planting. Cut back perennials which have bloomed for a second time. Plant hardy perennials for spring bloom.

ANNUALS If the summer annuals are looking tired, replace them with pansies, primroses, calendula, and snapdragons. Clean up all dead or weak plants and amend soil if beds are to remain fallow for a few months. Collect seed from most vigorous annuals with the best colors for broadcasting in early spring. Continue to sow hardy annuals from now until early spring.

ROSES Since roses in warmer areas sometimes remain evergreen throughout the winter, we must force them to become at least partially dormant by reducing fertilizer applications during the fall. Plants still need water and attention to diseases or insect pests. If you haven't made your bare-root rose orders, do so now to insure availability. Dig holes for the new plants and backfill with amended soil to allow biotic activity to increase before roses are planted.

IRRIGATION In the very coldest areas the first frosts may hit at the end of the month. Make sure all hoses are gathered up and stored. Flush and drain all sprinkler pipes, and pull freeze plugs on aboveground pumps. In milder areas, readjust sprinkler timer to reduce watering times as temperatures become more moderate. Don't forget to turn the system off when it rains. All plants appreciate deep watering from the garden hose at this time, and evergreens tolerate the dry winds of winter better when fully hydrated.

TOOLS Have the rotory tiller serviced before fall tilling. Regular tilling also kills soil-borne pests as well as seedlings, and reduces the amount of viable seed in the soil. Beware of spreading bermuda grass with the tiller.

October

Gardening activities are beginning to slow down as the early frosts arrive. The maples and liquidambars should be in full color. Avoid burning as this fouls October skies and is an unhealthy practice. Rather than burn leaves, put them to good use in a leaf-mould corral or compost pile.

LAWNS Stay on top of leaf cleanup on lawns. Lawns can still be planted during this month but it's chancy, especially in mountain and foothill areas.

TREES AND SHRUBS Make sure leaves are raked out of corners along buildings, fence lines, and around the bases of trees and shrubs where they become overwintering havens for insects Continue to plant California native trees and shrubs. Lightly shape the earliest deciduous flowering shrubs like forsythia for better spring form. Remove suckers, damaged and old woody branches from last year's growth so that the remaining branches bear more flowers. Water evergreens heavily because fall winds can dry them out as they begin their winter growth period.

PERENNIALS During this in-between time, soil in all planting beds can be deeply cultivated and improved with manure or humus. Hardy perennials may still be planted in all but the coldest zones. If soil has frozen in the high country, apply a thick layer of winter mulch to reduce damage from freeze-thaw heaving. With the first frosts, potted fuchsias and tuberous begonias should be brought to a more protected area and prepared for winter storage. Continue to plant early spring bulbs.

ANNUALS Switch beds from summer annuals to those which will bloom through the winter and give the soil a good working-over in the process. Deep cultivation with a tiller or spading fork exposes grubs, which should be destroyed.

ROSES Continue to withhold fertilizer but water regularly. Tie up and stabilize new canes on climbers with fabric strips to protect from snow and winter winds. In the high country, apply winter protection mulches after soil has frozen.

IRRIGATION The dry winds of fall not only dehydrate plants but also the soil. As the rains come during late fall and winter, dismantle old drip systems and replace damaged or mineral-encrusted emitters, as well as any plastic tubing which has become brittle from age or exposure to UV light.

TOOLS Begin to get winter pruning equipment in good working order with razor-sharp blades. Be sure to let Santa Claus know about special tools or equipment he might bring, if you promise to be a diligent gardener next year.

GENERAL October is the month for soil conditioning.

Humus and manures added during the fall have the best effect on soil fertility. Where soils are acid, the sprinkling of fireplace ashes around trees, shrubs and into cultivated ground helps to neutralize pH, and the charcoal is useful for lightening the structure of heavy soils.

November

Get all the outdoor tasks wrapped up this month so you're not out in the mud and wet with last-minute duties. Stay out of flower beds when soils are saturated because your weight compacts clay soil. Finish all the cleanup tasks so your garden will be neat come spring. Send off ahead of time for garden catalogs which offer hours of armchair shopping pleasure during these dark days. Read back issues of garden magazines which may have been overlooked during busier months. Make plans for improvements and design new plantings for beds or garden expansion. Spend time in the workshop repainting garden furniture, or if you're more creative, make birdhouses, feeders, and garden sculptures.

LAWNS When soil is saturated, subtle low spots in lawns become visible as they collect water. Bring up the grade with sandy topsoil, then compact it to prevent washing out. During snowfall, make sure driveway edges are visible so adjacent lawns and sprinkler heads aren't crushed by vehicles. Continue to keep leaves and other debris off lawns to maintain health and prevent rotting.

TREES AND SHRUBS Trees and shrubs from containers can still be planted in November except where soil freezes. Have bed sheets, towels, and gunny sacks on hand for protecting marginal exotic shrubs and young palms in case there is an unexpected deep freeze. If temperatures below 32°F are predicted, cover plants in early evening. Remove protection in the morning just before sun reaches the garden. Double check ties and guy wires on newly planted trees. Add more ties or longer stakes if the tops threaten to break off in the wind.

VINES Deciduous vines should be fully dormant before pruning. This is a good time to untangle overgrown vines and thin the runners so they are manageable. Boston ivy should be leafless and can be easily controlled. Prune flowering vines like clematis and wisteria through December. Complete pruning grape vines if weather has been cool enough.

PERENNIALS As chrysanthemums finish blooming, cut them back to a few inches above the soil so that they get a stronger start in the spring. Time is running out to plant early spring bulbs, especially tulips.

ANNUALS Only the most rugged winter flowering annuals will be growing now, and in very cold areas they will die back entirely. Protect beds by laying a lightweight cloth over the plants if unexpected drops in temperature are forecast.

ROSES Prepare dormant sprays and sharpen equipment for winter pruning during December and January. If soil around roses has standing water, create small ditches to drain it off. Use this time to work organic matter into rose beds, but be careful not to cultivate too deeply because feeder roots may be damaged.

IRRIGATION All sprinkler systems, hoses, pumps, and valves should be insulated to prevent damage by winter freezing. If rains are late, continue irrigating in warmer areas. Avoid overwatering because there is very little evapotranspiration during the winter and soils become saturated very quickly.

TOOLS Take power equipment in for winter service while mechanics are free. Replace weak or damaged tools now, rather than waiting until one breaks in the middle of spring planting.

GENERAL Continue to use restraint when burning garden refuse. If poison oak is a problem, eradicate it by digging out roots or cutting back stems while it is dormant. Do not put prunings from these plants in burn piles because the toxic oils travel in the smoke to severely damage lungs. Even the barren sticks and roots will cause serious rashes. Beware of bark damage from hungry deer, rabbits, and field mice.

December

This is the month of the winter solstice, the shortest day of the year. This is when gardeners regret not planting enough berry-bearing plants to spice up the dull winter landscape. Providing seed and other goodies invites winter birds into the garden. Many landscape services are slow this month and offer a much better deal for large pruning or cleanup jobs. Consider building a cold frame to start tender seeds outdoors.

LAWNS Continue to remedy low spots or washouts in lawns. Bermuda grass will be visibly dormant and can be dug out and replaced with sod, or left until spring and be killed to the roots with herbicide before removal. Continue to keep organic matter off the lawn. During wet weather, keep toys, bikes, vehicles, and foot traffic off the lawn so the soil will not become compacted.

TREES AND SHRUBS Thin branches of berry-bearing shrubs and trees, use prunings as indoor decorations. Begin pruning all fruit trees. Prune out all touching, broken, or diseased branches from evergreen trees and shrubs. Plant bare-root trees and shrubs now through the end of February. While leafless, large shade trees can be shaped with the least amount of cleanup.

VINES Continue to prune and thin out vines.

ROSES Winter-prune all roses except old varieties which bloom but once in the spring. Apply a light dose of phosphorus to the soil and continue to incorporate amendments after pruning is completed.

ANNUALS Store seed packages in a cool, dry place safe from mice and other rodents. Refrigerate poppy seed.

Seed heads of sunflower, zinnia, cosmos, and marigold can be set out to attract birds. Order summer annual flower and vegetable seed from mail order catalogs.
IRRIGATION Rain gutter downspouts may discharge directly into planters or lawns. Avoid this by adding an extra length of pipe to carry water away from garden areas. Either turn off automatic sprinklers or reduce watering frequency, depending on rainfall. Provide extra water to foundation plantings sheltered by overhanging eaves.
GENERAL Stockpile manure or humus for spring activities. Use the ashes from fall burn piles or fireplace as soil conditioner, which is a valuable source of potash. Keep up with the weeds.

GARDEN PLANTS KNOWN TO BE POISONOUS

All garden plants should be considered poison unless you know otherwise. Avoid planting these species where they are accessible to children or pets.

TOXIC PLANTS

Note: spp. indicates multiple species.

Botanical name	Common Name	Type of plant
Convallaria majalis	Lily of the Valley	Bulb
Crocus spp.	Crocus	Bulb
Cycas revoluta	Sago Palm	Perennial
Daphne mezereum	Daphne	Shrub
Delphinium	Perennial Larkspur	Perennial
Digitalis	Foxglove	Perennial
Euphorbia spp.	Many	Succulent
Gelsemium sempervirens	Carolina Jessamine	Vine
Hedera helix	English Ivy	Groundcover
Hyacinthus orientalis	Hyacinth	Bulb
Hydrangea macrophylla	Hydrangea	Shrub
Ilex spp.	Holly	Shrub
Ipomoea spp.	Morning Glory	Vine
Iris spp.	Iris	Bulb
Laburnum anagyroides	Golden Chain Tree	Tree
Lantana	Lantana	Perennial
Larkspur	Larkspur	Annual
Lathyrus odoratus	Sweet Pea	Annual
Laurus nobilis	Laurel	Tree
Ligustrum spp.	Privet	Shrub
Narcissus spp.	Daffodil	Bulb
Nerium oleander	Oleander	Shrub
Nicotiana	Flowering Tobacco	Annual
Paeonia lactivlora	Peony	Perennial
Parthenocissus spp.	Boston Ivy	Vine
Rhododendron/azalea	Rhododendron	Shrub
Robinia pseudoacacia	Black Locust	Tree
Solanum pseudocapsicum	Jerusalem Cherry	Shrub
Taxus spp.	Yew	Shrub/Tree
Tulipa gesnerana	Tulip	Bulb
Wisteria	Wisteria	Vine

SOURCE LIST

(C)–California company.

Antique Rose Emporium
Route 5, Box 143
Brenham, TX 77833
(409) 836-9051
Color catalog $5.00
• Beautifully prepared catalog of old-rose varieties. Many have been propagated from plants found at old Texas homesteads. Plenty of how-to information. Well worth the price.

Breck's
U.S. Reservation Center
6523 North Galena Road
Peoria, IL 61632
(309) 691-4616
Free color catalog
• Supplier of Holland bulbs.

W. Altee Burpee & Co
300 Park Avenue
Warminster, PA 18991-0001
(215) 674-9633
Free color catalog
• America's most popular supplier of seed and plants for a wide selection of vegetables, annual and perennial flowers, and other garden products.

Carmel Valley Seed Co. (C)
P.O. Box 582
Carmel Valley, CA 93924
(408) 626-8200

Clyde Robin Seed Company (C)
P.O. Box 2366
Hayward, CA 94546
(415) 785-0425
Free color catalog
• Well-illustrated catalog of wildflowers and specialized mixes for slopes, drought, and erosion control.

Daylily Discounters
One Daylily Plaza
Alachua, FL 32615
(904) 462-1539
Full-color catalog $3.00
• The very best source for daylilies. Excellent catalog with large color photos and generous descriptions of hundreds of varieties. Includes detailed growing tips.

DeGiorgi Seed Company
6011 'N' Street
Omaha, NE 68117
(402) 731-3901
Black-and-white catalog $2.00
• Seed for vegetables, annual and perennial flowers, ornamental grasses, wildflowers, as well as other garden products.

Ed Hume Seeds, Inc.
P.O. Box 1450
Kent, WA 98035
(206) 859-0694
Catalog $1.00
• Specializes in seed for short season climate of zones at higher elevations.

Foothill Cottage Gardens (C)
13925 Sontag Road
Grass Valley, CA 95945
(916) 272-4362
Catalog $3.00
• Perennials for rock gardens and herbaceous borders. Important information about deer- and drought-resistant plants for rural California gardens.

Gardener's Eden (C)
P.O. Box 7307
San Francisco, CA 94120-7307
(800) 822-9600
Free color catalog
• Great source of gardening gifts, tools, books, materials, plants, garden furniture, and other accessories.

Gardens Alive!
5100 Schenley Place
Lawrenceburg, IN 47025
(812) 537-8650
Free color catalog
• Great source for all types of least-toxic pest-control materials, including beneficial insects.

Guerney's Seed and Nursery Co.
110 Capital Street
Yankton, SD 57079
(605) 665-1671
Free color catalog
• Source for everything from seed to trees and shrubs. Valuable for zone 1 mountain gardeners.

Henrietta's Nursery (C)
1345 North Brawley
Fresno, CA 93722-5899
(209) 275-2166
Black-and-white catalog $1.00
• This is a little cactus and succulent nursery with a very big sense of humor! Fun-to-read catalog has a wide assortment of rare and unusual varieties grown right here in California.

Henry Field's
415 North Burnett Street
Shenandoah, IA 51602
(605) 665-4491
Free catalog
• Diverse catalog includes seed for both ornamental and vegetable crops, nursery stock, fruit trees.

Jackson & Perkins
1 Rose Lane
Medford, OR 97501
(800) 292-4769
Free color catalog
• The largest and most respected U.S. supplier of retail hybrid tea roses. Catalog is inspiring and includes some old varieties. Also sells a wide selection of perennial plants and other garden products.

Lilypons Water Gardens
P.O. Box 10
Buckeystown, MD 21717
(800) 723-7667
Large, full color-catalog $5.00 (refundable with first order)
• Offers aquatic plants and fish, as well as all the necessary equipment to build and maintain a water garden.

Moon Mountain Wildflowers (C)
P.O. Box 725
Caprnteria, CA 93013
(805) 684-2565
Catalog $2.00
• Catalog includes over 60 North American wildflowers and their growing requirements. Good source of bulk wildflower seed.

Park Seed
P.O. Box 31, Highway 254
Greenwood, SC 29648-0031
(803) 223-8555
Free color catalog
• Broad selection of seeds, bulbs, and plants, all shown in full color.

Peaceful Valley Farm Supply (C)
P.O. Box 2209
Grass Valley, CA 95945
(916) 272-4769
Black-and-white catalog $2.00
• Extensive 100-page catalog of supplies for organic gardening, including fertilizers, least-toxic products, and hard-to-find tools.

Pecoff Bros. Nursery & Seed, Inc. (C)
Route 5, Box 215R
Escondido, CA 92025
(619) 744-3120
No Catalog
• Specialty grower of seed mixtures for erosion control under poor conditions. Plants tolerant of drought, heat, and salt. Large-scale projects only; will design seed mixes for individual sites.

Ronniger's Seed Potatoes
Star Route
Moyie Springs, ID 83845
No telephone.
Free black-and-white catalog
• As close to heaven as you can get for potato lovers! This small but mighty catalog includes dozens of varieties from purple Peruvian to white, red and russets. A must for the creative kitchen gardener.

Roris Gardens (C)
8195 Bradshaw Road
Sacramento, CA 95829
(916) 689-7460
Color catalog $3.00 (refundable)
• Offers over 300 varieties of tall bearded iris with gorgeous full-color photos.

Roses of Yesterday and Today (C)
802 Brown's Valley Road
Watsonville, CA 95076
(408) 724-3537
Black-and-white catalog $3.00
• Northern California's best source of quality old-rose varieties best suited to California. Lengthy descriptions and tips from satisfied customers to help with selection.

Shady Hill Gardens
Geranium Specialists
821 Walnut Street
Batavia, Illinois 60510
(708) 879-5665
Color catalog $2.00
• Offers nearly 800 different geranium varieties including zonals, ivy, scented, and novelty hybrids, with much more. Good descriptions and color photos.

Shepherd's Garden Seeds (C)
6116 Highway 9
Felton, CA 95081
(408) 335-6910
Black-and-white catalog $1.00
• A unique selection of vegetable, herb, and flower seeds. Includes heritage and gourmet varieties with lengthy descriptions.

Smith & Hawken (C)
25 Corte Madera
Mill Valley, CA 94941
(415) 383-2000
Free color catalog
• California's most beautiful catalog of gardening accessories, high quality tools, clothing, books, plants, gifts, and much, much more. A must for novice and experienced gardeners alike.

Spring Hill
Reservation Center
6523 North Galena Road
Peoria, IL 61632
(309) 689-3811
Color catalog $2.00
• Supplier of trees, shrubs, perennials, and bulbs. Useful catalogs provide extensive information on perennial garden making and other important subjects.

Stark Bros.
P.O. Box 10, Dept B216AM
Louisiana, MO 63353-0010
(800) 325-4180
Free color catalog
• Excellent supplier of fruit and nut trees, berries, and ornamentals. Many exclusive varieties of high quality fruit trees with details on bloom dates and pollinators.

Stokes Seeds Inc.
P.O. Box 548
Buffalo, NY 14240-0548
(416) 688-4300
Free color catalog
• A Canadian company supplying seed varieties for both

flowers and vegetables. Caters to farmers and large-scale growers, but sells seed in packets as well. May be one of the most well-written, informative catalogs on large-scale kitchen gardening.

The Cook's Garden
P.O. Box 535
Londonderry, VT 05148
(802) 824-3400
Black-and-white catalog $1.00
• Good source for kitchen-garden seed, with unusual varieties and valuable information on growing. Mesclun seed mixtures and other salad leaf crops.

The Country Garden (C)
P.O. Box 3539
Oakland, CA 94609
(415) 658-8777
Black-and-white catalog $2.00
• A local source of seed for fresh-cut flower varieties and everlastings. May be the only supplier of many unusual and old-fashioned flowers.

Thompson & Morgan
P.O. Box 1308, Dept 133-3
Jackson, NJ 08527-0308
(908) 363-2225
Free color catalog
• Informative seed catalog with color photos of a wide variety of plants, including unusual and unique varietes.

University of California Agricultural Publications Catalog
Publications
University of California
Agriculture and Natural Resources
6701 San Pablo Avenue
Oakland, CA 94608-1239
(415) 642-2431
• Send or call for free catalog of valuable booklets on gardening in California.

Van Bourgondien Bros.
P.O. Box 1000
Babylon, NY 11702-0598
(800) 622-9997
Free color catalog
• Premier supplier of quality Holland bulbs and perennials.

Van Ness Water Gardens (C)
2460 North Euclid Avenue
Upland, CA 91786-1199
(909) 982-2425
Color Catalog $6.00
• This pricey, but excellent, catalog is a crash course on how to build and care for water gardens. Local California supplier of plants, equipment, fish, and many other specialized products, with generous descriptions and details.

Wayside Gardens
1 Garden Lane
Hodges, SC 29695-0001
(803) 223-7333
Free color catalog
• Generously sized catalog with many color photos on each page. Useful as a plant identification guide as well as a source of plants.

White Flower Farm
Litchfield, CT 06759-0050
(203) 496-9600
Free color catalog
• Catalog in itself is packed with detailed, and very useful, information on plants they sell. Specialty perennials, shrubs and bulbs.

Index